ELECTION CAMPAIGNING
JAPANESE STYLE

STUDIES OF THE
EAST ASIAN INSTITUTE
COLUMBIA UNIVERSITY

GERALD L. CURTIS

ELECTION CAMPAIGNING JAPANESE STYLE

1971
COLUMBIA UNIVERSITY PRESS
NEW YORK & LONDON

Copyright © 1971 Columbia University Press
Library of Congress Catalog Card Number: 70-154343
ISBN: 0-231-03512-8
Printed in the United States of America

The East Asian Institute
of Columbia University

The East Asian Institute of Columbia University was established in 1949 to prepare graduate students for careers dealing with East Asia, and to aid research and publication on East Asia during the modern period. The faculty of the Institute are grateful to the Ford Foundation and the Rockefeller Foundation for their financial assistance.

The Studies of the East Asian Institute were inaugurated in 1962 to bring to a wider public the results of significant new research on modern and contemporary East Asia.

For My Parents

Preface

THE STORY OF how men are elected to public office in systems
of representative government is one of the most exciting and
important of contemporary politics. For the electoral process
is the heart of modern democracies, and the way in which it
beats says a great deal about the health of the larger political
system. Whether there is real competition for office, whether
party organization is strong or personal organization predomi-
nates, whether large numbers of voters become involved in the
campaign or only a small number of bosses gather the vote—
all these issues and many more involved in the electoral
process have an important bearing on a nation's politics.

Japan has been experiencing elections for nearly one hundred years. Its parliament, the Diet, is the oldest elective legis-
lative body in Asia. Though it took post-World War II constitutional reforms to make the Diet the "supreme organ of
state power," politicians since 1890 have been campaigning for
elective office. Thus elections are not new to Japan and the art
of campaigning is a highly sophisticated one derived from a
long and rich tradition. But in the relatively short period
since the end of World War II Japan has experienced economic, social, and political change of extraordinary scope.
A soaring economic growth rate has transformed a predominantly rural country into an urban one, new technologies and
new ideologies have changed life styles, and new, fervently
embraced ideals of democracy and popular sovereignty have
transformed the political system.

Amidst momentous changes but within a long and sophisticated tradition, the Japanese politician has had to develop
campaign strategies to mobilize voter support. The following
pages tell the story of how one politician did this.

[ix]

One can examine politics from a number of perspectives. One may opt for macroanalysis, seeking a comprehensive overview of the entire system, or one may choose to use the political science equivalent of the microscope, focusing on one part of the system to discover characteristics that will aid in understanding the greater whole. For nearly a year and a half I was privileged to examine in microscopic detail the campaign of a candidate for the Japanese Diet. Living in the candidate's home, participating in campaign strategy meetings, visiting innumerable farms and mountain villages, talking for long and enjoyable hours with local politicians, newspaper reporters, and voters, I gradually saw emerge the pattern of campaign strategy and organization documented here.

The Japanese politician is confronted with a dynamic dialectic between old patterns and new. Reliance on local traditional elites and creation of *kōenkai* to reach beyond elites to mass mobilization, perception of the idealized "hard vote" farmer, sensitive of hierarchy and committed to community consensus, and the reality of the apartment-dwelling "floating" voter, constraints of an overly restrictive election law and development in spite of it of new campaign techniques—are just some of the contrasts that came to surface in the efforts of one Satō Bunsei to win election to the Lower House of the Japanese Diet.

Satō ran for election in 1967 as a nonincumbent candidate of the ruling Liberal Democratic Party (L D P). His district, in the northeastern corner of Kyūshū, the southernmost of Japan's four main islands, included a busy and crowded resort city and miles of rice paddies and mountain villages. It is one of the country's semirural districts and, as such, representative of a large number of constituencies. Of the country's 123 districts, sixty fall into this category and elect 235 of the Diet's 486 members.[1]

---

[1] Semirural districts are defined as those having between 20 and 40 per cent of the working population over fifteen engaged in the primary sector of the economy. The failure of district reapportionment to keep pace with demographic change has made these districts heavily over-represented in

No candidate, whether in Japan, the United States, or else-where, can be regarded as "typical," but the study of individual candidates does provide insights into campaign practices and political processes. All candidates, regardless of their own idiosyncrasies, must operate within a structure determined by institutions, laws concerning the electoral system and campaign practices, historical tradition, cultural norms, economic characteristics of the constituency, and so on. All these variables create a certain opportunity structure that limits the range of alternative strategies available. By examining one politician's campaign we can gain insights into the characteristics of this structure and thereby achieve a better understanding of the dynamics of political processes.

In May 1966 I went to Japan with little idea whose campaign I would observe. I had set few considerations in my own mind. I wanted the candidate to be of the Liberal Democratic Party, since this is the majority party in the Diet and has with its predecessors been such, with one brief exception, throughout the postwar period. While an examination of an opposition party candidate's campaign would also be of value I was interested in examining how a candidate of the winning party won. I also was looking for a candidate who had not previously been elected to the Diet, hoping to be able to capture more of the process of building organization and formulating strategies than could be seen in the campaign of a candidate already successful in a number of elections. I also wanted the candidate to be from a district that had both urban and rural components and a local dialect comprehensible to one with a modest command of standard Japanese.

With these thoughts in mind I met Mr. Nakasone Yasuhiro, a man whose name reappears in this study as that of cabinet

---

the Diet. Metropolitan districts (less than 10 per cent in agriculture) number only 28 and elect 113 members. Urban districts (10 to 20 per cent) elect 74 members from 18 districts and rural districts (over 40 per cent) number 17 and elect 62 members.

minster and faction leader of the LDP. Mr Nakasone introduced me to Mr. Satō, and in June 1966 I descended upon a somewhat bemused but ever gracious and generous Satō household. At that time an election was expected in early autumn and my stay accordingly was to be about three months. Events proved otherwise. The election was held at the end of January 1967 and my stay was extended to the following July.

Satō Bunsei the politician is examined in the chapters that follow, and each reader will assign his own marks for political skill and sagacity. But a few words must be said about Satō Bunsei the man, for if it were not for the extraordinary qualities of this gentleman neither this book nor one of the most memorable years in the author's life would have been realized. It was only because of Satō's willingness to provide all data, no matter how confidential, and to discuss for hours on end points with which I was particularly concerned, that this study has any value. He, his wife, children, and staff accepted me as a member of the family, providing a unique and extremely valuable experience for one interested in Japanese society and politics. No attempt was made to restrict my access to data or people, and after an initial period of a month or so everyone accepted my presence and settled down to business "as usual." I feel certain that neither Satō's campaign nor the outcome of the election would have been significantly different had I not been present.

All Japanese names used in the text are given in the Japanese style: that is, family name first. For purposes of consistency, the given ages of people are, unless otherwise noted, their ages as of January 1967. References to national and regional newspapers (the *Asahi, Mainichi, Yomiuri,* and *Nishi Nihon Shinbun*) refer to the edition distributed in Ōita Prefecture. The back pages of these newspapers are devoted to local news from the area in which they are distributed. Unless otherwise noted, references to newspapers that have both morning and evening editions are to the morning edition.

PREFACE

It is inevitable that any attempt to acknowledge the help of people who have made this study possible would both omit names of people whose help was crucial and would fail to give satisfactory expression to my indebtedness to those people cited. Scores of politicians, campaign workers, newspaper reporters, and voters in Ōita Prefecture gave me their time, their wisdom, and their encouragement. To all I express my sincere gratitude. A few people must be singled out for special thanks. Most of all, I wish to thank Satō Bunsei for allowing me to observe his campaign and live in his home. To Mrs. Satō and Mr. and Mrs. Satō's three sons, Kazuo, Masami, and Haruo, I also acknowledge my deepest gratitude and affection. Also my thanks go to Saita Matato, Mr. Satō's campaign manager and, more than anyone else, my *sensei* on campaign techniques, and to Mr. Satō's office manager, Mr. Shuto Talcashi. Finally, I wish to thank my professors at Columbia University for encouraging me to undertake this study and for giving me support and advice during the period of its writing. Particular thanks go to Professor James Morley, who first interested me in the study of Japan and provided encouragement and advice through my years of graduate study and after; and to Professor Herbert Passin for commenting on early drafts of this study and sharing with me his extraordinary knowledge of Japanese society. All these people share the credit for what is useful in this study.

GERALD L. CURTIS

Contents

ELECTION CAMPAIGNING
JAPANESE STYLE

I

The Politics of Party Endorsement

🀄 BECOMING A CANDIDATE for public office in Japan is tech-
nically a rather simple matter. Any citizen can run for
the Lower House if he submits a letter of intent to do so and
a government bond in the sum of 150,000 yen (about 415 dollars) at least four days prior to the election.[1] Politically, however, becoming a Diet candidate takes more than 400 dollars
and a lot of ambition. It requires organized support and, in
postwar Japan, a critical element in this support has been the
endorsement of one of the country's political parties.

Over the past twenty years candidates running without party
endorsement have been increasingly unsuccessful in getting
elected to the Lower House. Independents were successful in
large numbers only in the immediate postwar election of 1946.
Since 1952, as Table 1 indicates, they have won less than 5 per
cent, and in 1967 only 1.8 per cent, of the seats.[2] The story of
Satō Bunsei's campaign for election to the Diet rightly begins
with the story of how he obtained the endorsement of the Liberal Democratic Party.

Within the L D P the majority of those elected to the Diet
come from two distinct occupational backgrounds. The largest
single group (see Table 2) is composed of men who made their
careers in the bureaucracy and first entered elective politics
after reaching a fairly high level within the bureaucratic hierarchy. Among the 283 members of the LDP elected in the 1967
general elections, 87 (31 per cent) were of such bureaucratic
background. The second largest group is that of men who had

1 Articles 86–92, *Public Offices Election Law.*
2 In the election held on December 28, 1969, Independents fared somewhat better, getting 3.29 per cent of the seats.

[1]

Table 1

Percentage of Seats Won by Independents and Candidates of Minor Parties

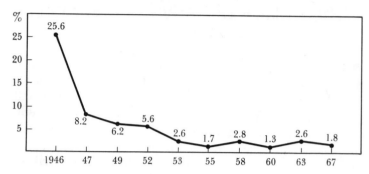

Adapted from: Taguchi Fukuji, *Gendai Seiji to Ideorogii* (Tokyo, 1967), p. 212.

Table 2

Occupational Backgrounds of LDP Members Elected to the Diet in the 1967 Election

	Number	Per cent
Bureaucrat	87	30.7
Local Politician	69	24.3
Businessman; Representative of economic organization	43	15.1
Journalist	32	11.4
Lawyer, Doctor	15	5.3
Other (e.g. secretary to former Diet member, son of former Diet member)	37	13.2
Total	283	100.0

Adapted from: Sugimori Yasuji, "Jimintō Zengiin No Keireki Bunseki," *Jiyū,* x (May, 1968), p. 38.

[2]

careers in local politics; men who worked their way up through City and Prefectural Assemblies and finally achieved success in being elected to the Diet. In the same 1967 election, sixty-nine (24 per cent) of LDP candidates elected came from this group. The rest of the elected members came from a variety of occupational backgrounds, as indicated in the table.

These differences in occupational background have a direct bearing on the ways in which aspirants for public office seek party endorsement. To better understand this relationship it is convenient to divide all the occupations represented into two groups, the nationally oriented and the locality-oriented.[3] The ex-bureaucrat is the dominant element in the nationally oriented group. Also included within this group are journalists for national newspapers, owners of large enterprises, and representatives of national interest groups. All are nationally oriented in that their careers were made in Tokyo and their political ties and influence are concentrated in the nation's capital. "Men in this group," writes one author, "use their influence on the national level as the base for becoming politicians."[4]

The local politician is the dominant element in the locality-oriented group. Also included in this category are owners of small and medium-size businesses, representatives of local interest groups, and owners of local newspapers. All have been engaged in occupations on a local level and their political connections and influence are concentrated within their respective localities. Ties with the political world at the national level tend to be minimal and indirect and members of this group "advance to becoming Diet members on the basis of the influence they command within their localities."[5]

Within the LDP, endorsement of Diet candidates is determined by the national party organization after it receives rec-

[3] This classification scheme is adapted from Sugimori Yasuji, "Jimintō Zengiin No Keireki Bunseki," *Jiyū*, x, (May, 1968), p. 40.
[4] *Ibid.*
[5] *Ibid.*, pp. 40–41.

[3]

ommendations from its Prefectural Chapters. Prefectural Chapters do not have the power over endorsements that are commanded, for instance, by the Conservative or Labour Party constituency associations in Britain.[6] Neither does the national organization determine endorsements with the degree of control exercised, for example, by the national organs of political parties in Israel.[7] Both national and prefectural party organs play important roles in the nomination process, and the extent to which a candidate concentrates his efforts for endorsement at the different levels of party organization is directly related to his placing within this two-group division.

The general pattern for those who have made their careers at the national level is to seek party endorsement by exploiting ties with national party leaders and relying on this leadership to secure the support of the relevant Prefectural Party Chapter. For the locality-oriented type the pattern is reversed. Major emphasis is placed on obtaining the support of the leadership of the local Party Chapter and, through this leadership, pressing one's case for endorsement by the national organization. The nature of a Diet hopeful's political orientation, whether national or local, is a major determinant of the strategies he will employ to obtain party endorsement.

Satō Bunsei belongs to the group I have designated the locality-oriented type. He was elected in 1951 to the Ōita Prefectural Assembly, and his adult life has been spent in local politics. The strategies he employed to obtain LDP endorsement and, indeed, the strategies he employed in his campaign to be elected to the Diet are intimately related to his background as a professional politician.

Satō was born in 1918, the eldest son of the owner of a small inn in a hot springs resort area on the western fringe of the city of Beppu, Ōita Prefecture. After attending local public

6 See R. T. McKenzie, *British Political Parties* (New York, 1966), pp. 241 ff.; Richard Rose, *Politics in England* (Boston, 1964), p. 148.

7 See Leon D. Epstein, *Political Parties in Western Democracies* (New York, 1967), p. 226.

schools he entered the Politics Department at Meiji University, a large private university in Tokyo. Graduation was followed by World War II, during which Satō served as captain in the Imperial Army. He returned to Beppu at the end of the war, twenty-seven years old and married, and took a job as a car salesman for a firm located in neighboring Ōita city.

In Beppu and Ōita Prefecture, as in the country generally, the immediate postwar years witnessed a highly unstable political situation. The Occupation-sponsored purge of people who had held elective office during the wartime years was so thorough that it practically wiped the slate clean of politicians throughout most of Japan.[8] Political parties formed and dissolved with maddening rapidity. New politicians fought for office, some on their own initiative, others at the behest of purged politicians. In Ōita Prefecture the situation was no less confused than in other parts of the country. In the 1946 Diet elections, forty-nine candidates ran for the seven seats. Thirteen ran as Independents and the remaining thirty-six as members of eighteen different political parties.[9] Throughout the country traditional voting patterns were being upset, and in 1947 the Socialist Party won a plurality of seats in the Diet and formed the first Socialist-led government in the history of parliamentary government in Japan.

It was at this time that Satō Bunsei became active in politics. In Satō's view these years were characterized by an appalling growth of leftist and particularly communist influence. He believed that the wide-reaching reforms undertaken by the Occupation in pursuit of its objective of democratization had, in effect, created a dangerous political vacuum into which the communists would step unless young men, reaffirming their belief in conservatism ("maintaining the good in Japanese tradition" in Satō's definition), became politically active and

8 For an analysis of the Occupation-sponsored purge, see Hans Baerwald, *The Purge of Japanese Leaders Under the Occupation* (Berkeley, 1959).

9 Figures taken from Ōita Ken Senkyo Kanri Iinkai, *Senkyo No Kiroku 1946–1961*, II (Ōita, 1962), 3.

revitalized the parties of the right. Satō began to involve himself in the politics of the city, campaigning for conservative candidates in various elections and looking for the opportunity to enter the political world himself.

Satō's family had no history of direct involvement in politics, and his lack of close connections with the leading politicians of Beppu was a major obstacle to his entering a career that he hoped would someday see him elected to the Diet. But three years after the war and his return to Ōita Prefecture, Satō's entree into the local political world was given a considerable boost when his younger sister married the son of the then Speaker of the Ōita Prefectural Assembly, Aragane Keiji.

In the first postwar Prefectural Assembly election in April, 1947, Aragane was one of the three candidates elected from the Beppu constituency. Because of the purge's application to most wartime prefectural assemblymen, almost all those elected to the Assembly in the 1947 election were freshmen. Aragane, though himself a first-term member of the Assembly, was made Speaker, as he was the only member to have served as Speaker of a city (Beppu) Assembly. As his term of office drew to a close Aragane decided he would not stand again for election to the Assembly but would contest the mayoral race in Beppu. An associate who was to run for the Assembly seat fell ill shortly before the campaign and Aragane was forced to look elsewhere for a successor. He found him in the energetic and ambitious brother of his daughter-in-law. And Satō, at age thirty-one, found himself a candidate for election to the Ōita Prefectural Assembly. Satō won in that election in 1951 and in the two succeeding elections. After twelve years service he left the Assembly to run for election to the Lower House of the Diet. Aragane Keiji also won his bid for Mayor of Beppu in the election of 1951 and has been re-elected in each succeeding election, including that of April, 1967.

When Satō entered the Prefectural Assembly there were two main conservative parties active in Ōita Prefecture as well as on the national level. In the first years following the war, Satō

[6]

campaigned for candidates of one of these parties, the *Minshutō* (Democratic Party), of which Aragane was a leading member. When he ran for election to the Assembly, however, Satō switched his allegiance to the other major conservative party, the *Jiyūtō* (Liberal Party), and ran as an official candidate of that party. Until 1955 the Liberal Party was the strongest political party in Ōita Prefecture, as indeed it was nationally as well.[10] In that year occurred the merger of the Liberal and Democratic Parties and what had formerly been separate Prefectural Chapters of the two parties combined to form the Ōita Chapter of the Liberal Democratic Party.

The leadership of the "main-current" faction in the Prefectural Chapter[11] has since the creation of the LDP been made up of former Liberal Party members. The "anti-main current" has been led by leaders of the former Democratic Party. From 1947 to the present two men have dominated conservative Party politics in Ōita Prefecture, first as leaders of the Liberal Party and, after 1955, as leaders of the LDP chapter. Satō's rise from a thirty-one-year-old Prefectural Assembly candidate to a forty-three-year-old LDP-endorsed candidate for the Diet when he first stood for election in 1963 is largely the consequence of his relationship with these two men.

Iwasaki Mitsugu[12] has been involved in Ōita politics for over fifty years. He was born in 1894 in the town of Tsukumi, a

10 The postwar political history of Ōita Prefecture as it relates to Diet elections is provided in three newspaper series. One is a twenty-one part series appearing under the title "Sōsenkyo" ("General Elections") in the evening edition of the *Ōita Gōdō Shinbun* beginning on October 1, 1963. Other more recent ones appeared in serial form in the *Ōita Shinbun* and the *Yomiuri Shinbun* during January, 1967. On the national level the Liberal Party held a majority of seats in the Diet from 1949 to 1955. Its president, Yoshida Shigeru, was Prime Minister five times.

11 The terms main current (*shuryū*) and anti-main current (*han shuryū*) are used to identify factional alignments both on national and local levels. The use of the terms here refers to local factions, not to LDP main current and anti-main current factions at the national level.

12 Biographical information on Iwasaki is taken from Hasegawa Ryūichi, *Ōita Ken No Seijika,* (Ōita, 1966), pp. 42–49.

mountainous, cement-producing area in the southeastern part of the Prefecture, the son of a local politician and owner of a large cement manufacturing company. In 1933 he was elected to the Tsukumi Town Assembly and served for three consecutive terms. He was elected to the Ōita Prefectural Assembly in 1947, and following his re-election in 1951, the year in which Satō entered the Assembly, he was made Speaker, succeeding the above-mentioned Aragane Keiji. Iwasaki became President of the Ōita Chapter of the Liberal Party in the same year, and with the conservative party merger in 1955 became the Chairman of the LDP Chapter in the Prefecture. Since 1951 Iwasaki has been at the head of the most powerful political party in the Prefecture. Though two humiliating defeats to "independent progressive" Kinoshita Kaoru in the Prefecture Governor's race have lessened his prestige,[13] and though he has held no public elective office since 1959, Iwasaki stands in control of the Prefectural Party. In June 1967 he was elected President of the LDP Chapter for the ninth consecutive time.

Satō's basic strategy for obtaining LDP endorsement was decided in the early 1950s. It was to attach himself to Iwasaki and rely on him to champion his cause at the opportune moment. As Satō readily admits, he owes his political life to Iwasaki. For Satō, a party man or "pure politician"[14] without a career outside of politics itself, the financial support pro-

[13] An interesting discussion of Iwasaki and the Ōita L D P Chapter is included in Usami Shō, "Nōson No Tōshika," *Asahi Jānaru,* VIII (December 11, 1966), 20–25.

[14] The term "pure politician" is the translation for *tōjin* given by Scalapino and Masumi in their book *Parties and Politics in Contemporary Japan* (Berkeley, 1962). "Party man" or "party politician" is used here because, though narrower in meaning than Scalapino and Masumi's "pure politician," which includes all nonbureaucratic politicians, it better conveys the meaning of the term as used by Satō and his associates. They are the men who have come up in the political world "working for the party." That this usually means working for a politician or a certain faction rather than for the party organization as such would not appear unusual to anyone familiar with party organization in the United States.

vided by the Party Chapter's President proved crucial not only in the campaign but also through the twelve years Satō spent in the Prefectural Assembly. Iwasaki is an independently wealthy man and also has close relations with the important businessmen in the Prefecture. He has considerable control over the collection and dispersal of party funds in the Prefecture because of his position as Chapter President, and this substantial financial power largely accounts for his continued rule. Satō's campaign funds came almost entirely from Iwasaki and men who were brought into Satō's campaign by Iwasaki. Iwasaki's support also was vital in providing the link between Satō, locality-oriented and lacking strong ties at the national level, and the national party organization. The person who was to perform the function of championing Satō's cause in Tokyo was Iwasaki's close ally within the Prefectural Chapter, LDP faction leader Murakami Isamu.

Born in Ōita Prefecture in 1903, Murakami·was long the President of a very large and prosperous construction company in the Prefecture.[15] He was elected to the Diet in the first post-war election in 1946 and has been re-elected in every election since. In that same year he established the Ōita branch of the Liberal Party, formally became its President in 1947, and remained in that position until 1951, when he was succeeded by Iwasaki. Murakami was a member of the LDP faction of Ōno Bamboku until 1965, when Ōno's death split the faction in two. One part came under the leadership of former Speaker of the Lower House Funada Naka, and the other under the leadership of Murakami. Though his faction is small, Murakami is the only leader of a national LDP faction from Ōita Prefecture. In his years in the Diet Murakami has served as Transportation Minister, Construction Minister, and Director General of the Hokkaidō Development Agency.

Murakami's support for Satō was crucial not simply because it provided a necessary channel for Satō to the national party

15 For biographical information about Murakami, see Hasegawa, p. 171.

organization. Satō could have associated himself with any one of a number of people in the Prefecture for this purpose. The association with Murakami was valuable because it enabled Satō to avoid establishing close ties with incumbent LDP Diet members from his own district. This was crucial because of the intraparty rivalry fostered by Japan's electoral law.

The Japanese election law divides the country into 123 election districts which elect the 486 members of the Lower House. Each of these districts elects from three to five members,[16] with each voter voting for only one candidate. In a five-member district, for example, the five candidates who poll the highest votes are declared winners.

This electoral system gives rise to problems of party organization and campaign strategy that do not exist in systems where elections are held in single member constituencies or by a form of proportional representation. The combination of multimember districts with single entry ballots has a divisive effect on any party that runs two or more candidates in any one district. The intensity of intraparty rivalry may be best compared to that of a hotly contested Democratic primary in a one-party American southern state. There is a general tendency for LDP incumbents in any district to oppose the entrance of any additional LDP candidates into the race, the common-sense assumption being that another candidate will reduce the vote of the other candidates of the party. Except for those situations where the death of an incumbent or some other atypical situation leaves little doubt about the possibilities of success for the incumbents and a new candidate, incumbents feel their position threatened and endeavor to keep the district safe by keeping any in-party challengers out.

In all stable political systems incumbents are at a great advantage. In congressional elections in the United States in 1954, 1956, 1958, and 1960, over 90 per cent of those elected

[16] There is one exception. The island of Amami Ōshima elects only one member.

were incumbent members of Congress.[17] In the United States, however, a new politician can often challenge an incumbent of his party by entering a primary. In Japan, as is typical of most parliamentary systems, party endorsement is officially determined by a small party oligarchy. Where an incumbent opposed to the entrance in the race of a new candidate is not himself in a decisionmaking position in the party hierarchy, he calls upon his faction leader to oppose the endorsement of the new challenger. Since it is in their interest to keep loyal faction members in office, faction leaders are usually anxious to insure the re-election of their supporting incumbents.

For the man who wants to become a member of the Diet, there are three basic strategic options. One is to gain the favor of an incumbent from his district and inherit his support base when the incumbent vacates his seat. This strategy is known to have made an old man out of many a Prefectural Assemblyman. In Ōita Prefecture, local politicians involve themselves in intimate relationships with others higher up in the political hierarchy. Diet members direct slices of the national pork barrel to areas where they have strong support and aid local politicians financially at election time. The local politician in turn campaigns for a particular Diet member and becomes associated with his faction in the local political divisions within the conservative camp. Elective offices in Japan form a pyramid of prestige and power, with the Diet member sitting at the apex. The local politician enters into a close association with a Diet member in order to maximize his own position lower down in the structure (by becoming the "pipe," as the Japanese term it, via the Diet member, between the national government and his local constituency). By so doing, his own chances of ever entering the Diet become dependent on the good will, or the bad health, of the Diet member with whom he has associated. The avoidance of such ties with Diet members in his own

[17] Charles O. Jones, "The Role of the Campaign in Congressional Politics," in *The Electoral Process,* eds. M. Kent Jennings and L. Harmon Zeigler (New Jersey, 1966), p. 24.

district was one of Satō's major concerns during his years in the Prefectural Assembly.

The second strategic alternative is to run as an independent and, if elected, present one's own incumbency as reason for endorsement in the next election. Almost all of those elected to the Diet as independents are, in fact, LDP members who opted for this strategy. As seen above, however, very few independents have success at the polls in Diet elections. It is a drastic strategy both because of the odds against success and the strong possibility that if a man were to run against the wishes of the party and be defeated his political career would come to an abrupt halt.

The third alternative is for the fledgling candidate to align himself with party politicians strong enough to overcome incumbent opposition. This strategy is most fully employed by the nationally oriented and particularly the ex-bureaucrat candidate who can utilize his close association with men at the top of the party structure to overcome incumbent opposition. Unlike the local politician, the bureaucrat usually has not had to develop an intimate and compromising relationship with an incumbent from the district in which he plans to run. For such a candidate the strategy is to apply pressure from the top down. He must gain support within the national party organization first and then utilize this support to bring the relevant Prefectural Chapter into line.

This third alternative was the strategy adopted by Satō, but, because of his local rather than national orientation, the pattern was reversed. Satō's strategy was first to gain support on the local level sufficient to insure his recommendation by the Prefectural Chapter in spite of incumbent opposition. He sought to apply pressure from the bottom up: to overcome the opposition of the incumbents on the prefectural level first and then bring the battle to Tokyo.

Ōita Prefecture is made up of two electoral districts. The larger, First District, with the prefectural capital of Ōita city, elects four members to the Diet. Both Iwasaki Mitsugu and

Murakami Isamu have made their political careers in this district. The Prefecture's Second District is a three-member constituency within which Beppu is the largest city. With his support and loyalties lying with men across the bay in party headquarters in Ōita City, Satō sought to challenge the incumbents in the Second District.

Since 1947, when the first postwar Lower House elections under the present electoral system[18] were held, two conservatives and one socialist have been elected in Ōita's Second District in every election save one. Only in 1953 were three conservatives (two members of the Yoshida faction Liberal Party and one of the Progressive Party, a temporary successor to the Democratic Party) elected. Such a political history held out little hope for a victory of three conservative candidates in the district, and Ōita's Second District's history was not unique. At the time of the 1963 election there were forty constituencies that were three-member districts. In that election only four of these districts elected three conservatives (including LDP and conservative independents), while thirty of the districts, like Ōita's Second, elected two conservatives and one progressive. The other six districts elected two progressives and one conservative.[19] To Ōita's Second District incumbents, Nishimura

[18] Japan has experimented with a variety of electoral systems. The first elections under the Meiji constitution were held under a single-member constituency system. In 1900 the law was revised to provide for large districts (electing up to 13 members) with single entry ballots. In 1919 this system was abolished and the single-member constituency adopted once again. In 1925 the present-day system of medium-sized districts (electing three to five members) with single entry ballot voting was adopted for the first time. There were at that time 122 districts. The first postwar election of April 10, 1946, was held under the old large district system first adopted in 1900. The revision of the Election Law in 1947 reinstituted the system first adopted in 1925, and this has continued essentially unchanged to the present day.

For a concise history of the Japanese districting system, see Yomiuri Shinbun Seijibu, *Seitō* (Tokyo, 1966), pp. 230ff.

[19] Data taken from Fujiwara Hirotatsu and Tomita Nobuo, *Seijiaku E No chōsen* (Tokyo, 1967), pp. 212–13.

Eiichi and Ayabe Kentarō, the meaning of the statistics was crystal clear: there was no room in the district for another LDP candidate.

Nishimura Eiichi[20] was born in 1898 on the island of Himeshima, a small fishing village off the tip of the Kunisaki Peninsula in Ōita's Second District. Graduating in the Engineering Department of Tōhoku University, he entered the prewar Ministry of Transportation and Communication and became Division Chief (*kyokuchō*) before resigning in 1948. In that year he returned to Himeshima, and in the 1949 Diet election ran as a member of the Liberal Party and won. Nishimura has competed in every succeeding election and has lost once, in 1955. In his Diet career he has served in many posts in the government and became Welfare Minister in the second Ikeda cabinet. A member of the Satō Eisaku faction, he was made Construction Minister in Satō's cabinet reshuffle immediately preceding House dissolution in December of 1966.

While Iwasaki, Murakami, and Satō are locality-oriented types, Nishimura, an ex-bureaucrat, is a nationally oriented politician. The difference was to have an important impact on Satō's quest for party endorsement. Within the LDP ex-bureaucrats and former local politicians represent opposite poles in terms of political style. Former local politicians tend to look upon the ex-bureaucrat as haughty and removed from the people and see themselves as seasoned professionals in political matters, most in tune with the views of the electorate. The former bureaucrats, for their part, often look down upon the local politician type as crude in manner, inferior in education and intelligence, and untrained in the act of governing. They view themselves as an elite group of highly skilled administrators best qualified to deal with the complex problems of policymaking.

The conflict between bureaucrat and local politician is never far below the surface. Satō Bunsei attributes every ill of the

---

[20] For biographical data, see Hasagawa, p. 168.

LDP to its "dominance by inflexible bureaucrats," and Murakami Isamu, when Satō was finally elected to the Diet, congratulated his supporters for "electing another anti-bureaucrat party man." This antipathy has always been a factor in the relationship between Nishimura and the other leaders of Ōita's Liberal Party and later of the LDP Chapter. Apparently the only thing that prevented for so long a split between Nishimura and the locality-oriented Liberal Party leaders was the greater hostility of all of them toward the leaders of the Democratic Party than toward each other. The fragile bonds that tied Nishimura with the other leaders of the Prefectural Chapter were rent asunder when Iwasaki and Murakami, in spite of Nishimura's opposition, decided to sponsor Satō's candidacy for the Diet.

The other LDP incumbent Diet man from the district, Ayabe Kentarō, was born in 1890 in the city of Takamatsu on the island of Shikoku.[21] He came at a very young age to the town of Kitsuki in Ōita's Second District as the adopted son of a locally prominent family. Ayabe graduated from the Usa Middle School in the northern part of the district and went to Kyoto University's Law Department. He was elected to the Diet in 1932 as a member of the *Seiyūkai* and served during the war as Parliamentary Vice Minister of Naval Affairs. He was purged in 1946 but reappeared on the political scene soon after the signing of the Peace Treaty and the lifting of the purge restrictions. In 1952 he gave his support in the Diet election to his close friend, former Foreign Minister Shigemitsu Mamoru, signer of the Japanese surrender at the end of World War II.[22] Once depurged, Shigemitsu re-entered politics, became President of the Progressive Party, a temporary successor to the Democratic Party, and was elected to the Diet in 1952

[21] Hasegawa, p. 157.

[22] Shigemitsu was also purged by the Occupation authorities and spent two years in Sugamo prison as a war criminal. During this time he wrote his memoirs, *Japan and Her Destiny; My Struggle for Peace* (New York, 1958).

and again in 1953 and 1955. With Shigemitsu's death in 1957, Ayabe Kentarō decided to run for the Diet after a retirement of nearly fifteen years. Ayabe won in the election in 1958 and was re-elected in 1960 and 1963. He served as Transportation Minister in the second and third Ikeda cabinets. Though a member of the faction of Fujiyama Aiichirō, Prime Minister Satō Eisaku's main antagonist in the party presidential election in December of 1966, Ayabe was considered a moderate in the intraparty conflict. On December 3, 1966, he was appointed Speaker of the Lower House, only the second politician from Ōita Prefecture to have had the honor of that position.

Ayabe Kentarō, though from the same nonbureaucratic background as Iwasaki and Murakami, was the main antagonist of these two leaders of the Prefecture Chapter. While the bureaucrat-local politician split affected relations between the LDP leadership and Nishimura, the relationship between the leadership and Ayabe, a relationship hardly cordial even on the surface, was the legacy of the bitter fighting between the Liberal and Democratic parties in the postwar period up to their merger in 1955. After being depurged Ayabe served as President of the Prefectural Chapter of Shigemitsu's Progressive Party and then of the Democratic Party. Following the merger of the conservative parties, Ayabe's support continued to center around these former Democratic politicians. To an astounding degree Ōita politics are still dominated by battles between the Liberals and the Democrats of the Liberal-Democratic Party.

In the 1958 elections Satō, acting at the request of Iwasaki, ran the Beppu campaign for Nishimura Eiichi. Iwasaki had agreed that Satō should run for the Diet in the next election, and supporting Nishimura was intended to lessen Nishimura's opposition to Satō's endorsement. However, at the next election Satō was again stopped by Iwasaki. When the House was dissolved in 1960 Ayabe, it is alleged, told Iwasaki that if re-elected he would surely be made a cabinet minister and with that dream fulfilled would no longer oppose Satō's entering the race. Iwasaki agreed and told Satō to wait one more election and to give support to Ayabe in the November 1960 race. Satō hoped that his impartial work "on behalf of the party" would be rewarded when the question of his endorsement arose at the time of the next election. That time came when the House was dissolved in October, 1963. Contrary to Satō's hopes, however, both Ayabe and Nishimura vehemently opposed Satō's endorsement and used as their major argument the candidacy of another conservative, independent Noyori Hideichi.

Noyori was born in the city of Nakatsu, the childhood home of the great Meiji personality, Fukuzawa Yukichi, and the second largest city in Ōita's Second District.[23] He began study at Keiō University but left before graduation and proceeded to amass considerable wealth through the publication of a daily newspaper in Tokyo, the *Teito Nichinichi Shinbun* and a magazine, *Jitsugyō No Sekai*. In the prewar period he served one term, from 1932, in the Diet. Following the war he re-entered the political arena, well on the right. Religion and politics blended into one for him; good politics required a "spiritual recovery" that Buddhism, which Noyori saw as a kind of nostalgic nationalism, could provide. For several years in the period immediately following the defeat, Noyori, it is reported, "traveled from Hokkaidō to Kyūshū giving more than a hundred lectures, mainly at temples, on the nation's [need for] a spiritual recovery."[24]

He did more than lecture. In 1952 he returned to Ōita and ran for the Diet for the first time in twenty years. In his campaign speeches he called Japan's participation in World War II "a holy war to save the Asian race,"[25] and argued for constitutional revision to allow for Japanese rearmament and to restore the Emperor to his former position.[26]

In the 1952 election Noyori placed sixth among nine candi-

[23] Biographical information on Noyori is taken from Jinji Kōshinsho, *Jinji Kōshinroku*, 23rd edition (Tokyo, 1966).
[24] *Ibid.*
[25] *Ōita Gōdō Shinbun*, November 13, 1963, p. 1.
[26] *Ibid.*, November 6, 1963, p. 3.

dates and lost again in the following election in 1953, this time placing fifth among eight candidates. In the first election he ran as a member of the Liberal Party. In the second he ran as an Independent. In the following election, in February of 1955, he ran as a member of the Democratic Party, and for the first time in twenty-three years was elected to the Diet with an astounding vote of 65,412, the highest among the candidates. This was his one and only successful election to the postwar Diet. After being defeated in 1963 he retired, at the age of seventy-eight, from active politics.

Noyori was opposed to and opposed by nearly every other major conservative party leader in the district. He headed what is known as the "Prefecture's northern LDP" (*Kenboku Jimintō*), an isolated and personal political machine in the Nakatsu area. As an incumbent conservative Noyori received the endorsement of the LDP in the first post-merger election in 1958, but after losing in that election he was denied not only endorsement but also even a certificate of membership in the party.[27]

Though Noyori was unlikely to win a seat, incumbents Nishimura and Ayabe could argue with some persuasiveness that his candidacy would drain enough of the conservative vote away to make impossible the election of three LDP members in this three-member district. In the 1960 election Noyori received 42,330 votes, less than a thousand votes behind the third-place winner. Satō must wait, the incumbents argued, until Noyori retired from politics.

While the incumbents emphasized Noyori's candidacy in opposing Satō's endorsement, Satō emphasized the weakness of the incumbent who had won all his elections in the third spot on the ticket, seldom more than a few hundred votes ahead of the runner up.

Komatsu Kan had been the Socialist Party's candidate in Ōita's Second District since 1952. Born in 1914 in the town

27 Sōsenkyo Kaiko, *Ōita Gōdō Shinbun*, February 9, 1967, p. 1.

of Hiji in Hayami County, a town that borders the city of Kitsuki where Ayabe Kentarō makes his home, Komatsu attended Ōita Teachers College, and from 1939 to 1952 was a middle-school teacher.[28] Like many socialists, particularly in heavily conservative rural areas,[29] Komatsu built his support around the Japan Teachers' Union (Nikkyōso), affiliated union of elementary and middle-school teachers. Although the district is predominantly one of farmers, Komatsu had no significant organized support among the farmers and made little attempt to organize them.[30] He rose to power in the Prefecture's Socialist Party through his activities in the Teachers' Union. In 1952 Komatsu became Chairman of the Ōita Prefecture General Council of Labor Unions (Kenrōhyō) and was elected to the Diet in that year, barely squeezing into the third spot. His 25,780 votes were only 197 votes more than those received by the runner-up. Komatsu, however, hardly had time to furnish his new Diet office before the House was dissolved and new elections called only six months after the previous ones.[31] In this April 1953 election, Komatsu, running as a member of the Socialist Party-Left Wing, suffered a crushing defeat, coming in 11,000 votes behind the third-place winner. He made a comeback in the following election in 1955, once again winning in third place. He was re-elected in 1958 and 1960 as a candidate of the merged Socialist Party. In all his elections, Komatsu received the lowest vote among the winning candidates. In 1960 he received only 718 votes more than runner-up Noyori.

Komatsu has consistently been the weakest of the winning

28 Hasegawa, p. 161.

29 Cf. the chapter written by Ronald Dore, "The Socialist Party and the Farmers" in Allan Cole, George Totten, and Cecil Uehara, Socialist Parties in Postwar Japan (New Haven, 1966) particularly pp. 409–14.

30 Interview with Komatsu Kan, July 7, 1967.

31 During a meeting of the Lower House Budget Committee, the then Prime Minister Yoshida Shigeru called his Socialist Party interpellator a damn fool (baka yarō). This led to a nonconfidence motion and the "damn fool dissolution" (baka yarō kaisan).

candidates but he, nonetheless, has been a consistent winner, which the incumbent conservatives in the district emphasized. The district, they argued, has a tradition of electing one Socialist and there is no possibility for all three conservatives to get more votes than he, particularly as long as Noyori is in the race and taking votes that would otherwise go to the LDP candidates. Thus Satō should not be allowed to run. Satō, of course, emphasized Komatsu's weakness. Ayabe and Nishimura have strong and stabilized support and their victory could not be in doubt. Therefore his candidacy would be for the purpose of eliminating the socialist and electing three LDP members to the Diet. The party should not deny itself the opportunity to elect a full slate of party members, Satō argued.

The conflict between Satō plus his backers, Iwasaki and Murakami, and the Second District incumbents, Nishimura and Ayabe and their supporters, erupted into an open political struggle in October of 1963, when the Lower House was dissolved and new elections called.

The dissolution of the House had been expected for several months and a meeting of the Prefectural Chapter was to have been held in mid-September to determine the Chapter's recommendations for endorsement of LDP candidates. For weeks Iwasaki postponed the meeting, hoping to secure the agreement of the Second District incumbents to Satō's candidacy and thereby obtain a show of unanimity in the Chapter's meeting. Iwasaki's efforts proved fruitless, and, knowing he had majority support for Satō's endorsement, he finally called a meeting of the Chapter's Executive Board (sōmukai) for October 8.

Recommendations of the Ōita Prefecture LDP Chapter for endorsement of Diet candidates are determined by an Executive Board of approximately one hundred members comprised of LDP prefectural assemblymen, heads of the party's youth and women's groups, and chairmen of the branch organizations in the cities, towns, and villages of the Prefecture. The October meeting of the Executive Board saw a full-scale debate between opposing sides on the issue of Satō's endorsement.

The attack against Satō's endorsement was led by Utsunomiya Hidetsuna, a prefectural assemblyman from the Beppu
constituency and presumed successor to Ayabe.[32] Utsunomiya
argued that the LDP officials from the Second District alone
should determine the candidates to be recommended for LDP
endorsement in the district. He maintained that "having people from the First District decide the candidates to be endorsed
[in the Second] is like having Ōita Prefecture determine endorsements in Fukuoka.[33] Since the Nishimura and Ayabe
factions had an overwhelming majority of support among
party officials in the Second District, the consequences for Satō
of Utsunomiya's suggested method of recommending candidates were obvious. Utsunomiya also harped on the effect of
Noyori's candidacy on the conservative vote, and maintained
that Satō's candidacy would only imperil the chances of re-
electing the incumbents, men whose long years of service in
the Diet had achieved for them positions of influence that were
of great and direct benefit to Ōita Prefecture. Their re-election
should not be endangered by the futile attempt to elect three
LDP candidates.

Satō's supporters replied that Utsunomiya was proposing a
"Second District Monroe Doctrine" and that the entire Chapter should decide whom the Chapter recommends for endorsement. They argued that the election of three LDP members
was possible and that the incumbents, serving at the time as
Ministers of Welfare and Transportation, were in no danger
of being defeated. If it refused to recommend the endorsement
of Satō, his supporters argued, the party would be denying
itself a clear opportunity to expand its strength.

Political distribution of power in the Chapter rather than
the virtues of the arguments of the debate was crucial in determining Satō's fate; and that distribution tipped the scales
heavily in Satō's favor. By faithfully following Iwasaki's lead

[32] The October 8 meeting and the problem of endorsements in the Prefecture's districts are discussed in an article in the *Ōita Gōdō Shinbun*,
October 19, 1963, p. 2.
[33] *Ibid.*

for the previous twelve years, Satō could now reap the benefits of having the support of the leader of the main-current faction in the party Chapter. After acrimonious debate, the Executive Board recommended, by majority vote, that Satō as well as Ayabe and Nishimura be endorsed as official party candidates from the Second District.

Nishimura and Ayabe were not yet, however, defeated in their fight to keep Satō out of the race. The battle now moved to the Election Policy Committee (*senkyo taisaku iinkai*) of the national party organization, where the incumbents hoped to be more successful than they had been on the prefectural level. Satō, as a locality-oriented politician, had miniscule support on the national level compared with that commanded by cabinet ministers Ayabe and Nishimura, and it was here that his quest for endorsement faced the greatest challenge.

The endorsement of party candidates is determined by the Election Policy Committee of the national LDP organization. The Committee consists of fifteen members: the President and Vice-President of the party, the Secretary-General, and twelve members chosen by the party President.[34] In practice all faction leaders or their representatives sit on the Election Policy Committee. Obviously the Committee's decisions vitally affect every faction in the party, and the decisionmaking process is a bargaining process between faction leaders. Yet it is not simply an unregulated factional struggle. The party President and Secretary-General have considerable power to determine the total number of endorsements, thereby setting the boundaries in a sense to the bargaining process, and the Election Policy Committee operates on the basis of a number of party principles governing endorsement policy.

These general principles were defined in a document entitled "The Main Principles of Election Policy" adopted in February 1960.[35] The Committee was to be guided by five broad principles. The first is that only those candidates whose

34 LDP Party Law, Article 51.

35 Jiyūminshutō, "Senkyo Taisaku Yōryō," *Jiyūminshutō Jyūnen no Ayumi* (Tokyo, 1966), p. 266.

victory appears certain are to be endorsed. This might appear to be common sense, but some parties often run candidates who have no chance of success as a technique for increasing general party support. The Japan Communist party, for instance, runs one candidate in each of the 123 districts. The LDP rejected this approach in order to minimize the dangers of LDP candidates so dividing the vote as to defeat each other. The second is that under no conditions are more candidates to be endorsed in any one district than the number of seats the district holds. In other words, in a four-member district the Committee could endorse a maximum of four candidates. A third and crucial principle is that endorsement should be based upon the "incumbent first" principle. There is of course nothing unusual about a policy that aims at the re-election of incumbents. The point to be noted is that in the context of the Japanese electoral system it becomes a basic principle for determining how many, if any, additional candidates are to be endorsed. The burden rests upon the new candidate to convince the party that his candidacy would not threaten the incumbent's re-election. A fourth principle is that no person being prosecuted for a criminal offense is to be endorsed, with the exception of cases which involve an appeal from a lower-court decision which has found the defendant innocent. Finally, the Committee was to be guided in its actions by the principle that it should give serious consideration to the Prefectural Chapter's recommendations.

Satō had the recommendation of the Prefectural Chapter, but it was clear that without strong political support at party headquarters, incumbents Ayabe and Nishimura would block his endorsement. It was largely for this reason that in 1963 Satō joined the LDP faction of Ōno Bamboku.

The role the politics of party endorsement play in determining factional alignments of new candidates can hardly be overestimated. Though the reasons for factional shifts among Diet men are multifarious, the first commitment to join a faction is often related to the endorsement problem. For the aspiring Diet candidate the only way to effectively plead his case within the national party organization is to obtain the support of a faction leader. It is because of the relationship between party endorsement and factional alignments that there are, as a rule, no two members of the same faction from any one district. A new candidate seeking endorsement will solicit the support of a faction leader who does not yet have a member of his faction in the district in which he wants to run. In 1966, among the 117 election districts in the country, only fourteen had two or more Diet members from the same faction.[36]

For Satō there was little question which faction he would enter. Because of his ties with Iwasaki and Murakami he had to join the faction of Ōno Bamboku in which Murakami was a top lieutenant. Satō's struggle for party endorsement now became but a small part of the larger struggle for power among the faction leaders. The question was whether Ōno could overcome the opposition of Fujiyama Aiichirō (Ayabe's faction leader) and Satō Eisaku (Nishimura's faction leader) and obtain the endorsement of the party for Satō.

It is the practice of the LDP to announce its list of endorsed candidates in groups. The choices for "first endorsement" (daiichi kōnin) are those easiest to decide: cases of incumbents and others which raise no serious problems. Later on the "second endorsements" are announced and, finally, the most difficult cases are decided in a group of "third endorsements."

On October 16 the LDP announced its list of first endorsements. Satō was not included.[37] Several days later the list of "second endorsements" was announced. Again Satō's name was absent. Iwasaki at this point sent several people from the Prefectural Chapter to Tokyo to plead Satō's case, but the party leaders were still unable to reach agreement.[38] Finally, on October 26, just a few days before the campaign was to begin, the party gave Satō its official approval in its third set of endorsements.[39]

36 Fujiwara and Tomita, pp. 77–80.
37 Ōita Gōdō Shinbun, October 19, 1963, p. 2.
38 Ibid., October 24, 1963, p. 1.
39 Ibid., October 26, 1963, evening edition, p. 1.

Although Satō succeeded in obtaining party endorsement, the suspicions of the incumbents proved correct. The District failed to elect three LDP candidates. It was Satō, however, and not one of the incumbents that lost to Socialist Komatsu. For Satō the problem of party endorsement would have to be faced again when new elections were called.

In the 1963 election Ayabe Kentarō received 51,373 votes, highest among the candidates. Nishimura was second with 47,695, and Komatsu Kan, as in his four previous successful campaigns, took the third spot, this time with 46,287 votes. For Komatsu it was another narrow victory and for Satō, runner-up,[40] 1,657 votes behind Komatsu, a bitter defeat. Noyori Hideichi was fifth with 35,532 votes, and the Communist Party candidate, Tsuru Tadahisa, amassed a grand total of 3,270 votes.[41] One result of the election was Noyori's decision to finally retire from active politics.

It is an indication of the insecurity fostered by the multi-member districting system that, in spite of Noyori's retirement, incumbents Ayabe and Nishimura bitterly opposed Satō's endorsement when the House was dissolved in December of 1966 and new elections called for January 29, 1967. Although Satō's case for endorsement appeared much stronger in 1966 than it had in 1963, the weeks preceding the announcements of endorsed candidates were for Satō plagued by uncertainty, constant phone calls to and from supporters in Tokyo, and strategy meetings to discuss steps to be taken to insure endorsement.

Satō did not expect any serious problems to arise at the Prefectural Chapter level. He had already received the recommendation of the Chapter once before, Noyori was out of the picture, and the Iwasaki group was still in control of the

---

[40] Runner-up (*jiten*) is of special significance in Japanese Diet elections because of an Election Law provision that if a Diet member should vacate his seat within three months of election, the runner-up shall automatically succeed to it. See *Election Law*, Article 97.

[41] Ōita Ken Senkyo Kanri Iinkai, *Senkyo No Kiroku, Shūgiin Giin Sōsenkyo,* November 21, 1963 election (Ōita, 1963).

Party's executive posts. If the opposition of the incumbents in the end proved futile in 1963, it was hardly likely to be successful now.

On December 27 the House was dissolved and the Executive Board of the Ōita LDP Chapter met to determine recommendations for party endorsemen.[42] A resolution was quickly submitted that in the Second District recommendations for endorsement be given to Ayabe, Nishimura, and Satō and that recommendations for endorsement in the First District be awarded to the three incumbent Diet members. Unlike 1963, when Satō could muster only majority support, the resolution carried unanimously and Satō's fight for endorsement moved to Tokyo.

In 1955 the two conservative parties endorsed 537 people as official party candidates. In the first post-merger elections in 1958, the LDP endorsed 413 candidates. In 1960 the number of endorsed candidates fell to 399, and in 1963 to 359.[43] Although no figures are available as to how many candidates were considered for endorsement in the January 1967 election, it is known that at least 430 cases were expected to come before the national organization.[44] The Secretary-General of the party, Fukuda Takeo, asserted that the number of endorsed candidates would be kept below 350,[45] even though the number of Diet seats had been increased by nineteen since the previous election.

On December 29 the LDP Election Policy Committee met and decided on the "first endorsements."[46] The 312 candidates named included 260 incumbents, 31 who had never been elected to the Diet and 21 former Diet members. The second

[42] For an account of the meeting see *Ōita Gōdō Shinbun*, December 28, 1966, p. 1.

[43] Figure for 1955 taken from Lawrence Olson, *Dimensions of Japan* (New York, 1963), p. 87; figures from 1958–1963 taken from Jiyūminshutō, p. 275.

[44] *Ōita Gōdō Shinbun*, December 23, 1966, p. 1.

[45] *Asahi Shinbun*, December 22, 1966, p. 1.

[46] *Mainichi Shinbun*, December 29, 1966, p. 1.

endorsements were given on December 30, and a third list of endorsed candidates issued by the Election Policy Committee on December 31 brought the number of official LDP candidates to 342, the smallest number in the party's history.

Following his battle in 1963, Satō Bunsei's fight for endorsement in 1967 looked mild by comparison. Two developments, however, threatened Satō. On December 3 Ayabe Kentarō was appointed Speaker of the Lower House. It is customary for the Speaker to be on the Election Policy Committee and Ayabe, whose opposition to Satō's endorsement was unabating, thereby had the opportunity to press his case at the highest decision-making level. The second development was the violent anti-Satō (Eisaku) position adopted by a group of anti-main-current faction leaders and Satō Bunsei's close relationship with one of them, Nakasone Yasuhiro.

Nakasone, former Cabinet Minister and, as of January 1967, leader of his own faction in the Diet, is one of the leading exponents of the so-called New Right movement within the LDP, a movement which, though vague in policy proposals, is clear in its goal of wrenching power from the old oligarchy that has controlled the party and turning it over to a group of younger conservatives.[47] Satō came to know Nakasone in the early 1950s, and since that time has identified his views on national questions largely with those expounded by Nakasone. For a time he accepted the responsibility for propagating in Kyūshū the policy of which Nakasone is the leading if not the sole exponent: constitutional revision to permit the direct election of the Prime Minister.[48]

[47] The views of Nakasone and his faction members are expressed in the first issue of his faction's magazine, the "New Politics," Shinseidōshikai, *Shinsei* (August, 1967).

[48] In the final report of the Government's Committee on the Constitution, only two of the Committee's 38 members favored the adoption of the Nakasone Plan for the direct popular election of a Prime Minister. See Robert Ward, "The Commission on the Constitution and prospects for Constitutional Change in Japan," *The Journal of Asian Studies,* XXIV (May, 1965), p. 414.

Although Satō was a member of the Murakami faction, his friendship with Nakasone was well known, and in December of 1966 the supporters of Prime Minister Satō were not well disposed to anyone friendly with Nakasone.

In the months preceding House dissolution a series of scandals rocked the LDP.[49] The opposition parties demanded new elections in which the voters could demonstrate their disillusionment with the corrupt ruling conservatives, and a group of anti-Satō Diet members in the LDP formed a "party reformation league" (*shukutō renmei*) calling for a change in leadership. The demands for new elections finally became too vociferous to ignore and led to the so-called black mist dissolution (*kuroi kiri kaisan*) on December 27.[50] The demands for new party leadership reached a climax in the party's presidential election held earlier the same month. Anti-Satō factions for the most part centered their support on Fujiyama Aiichirō, but could not muster enough support to topple Satō. They did, however, greatly embarrass him and obtained for themselves an image of political purity that was to dominate the campaign speeches of many candidates, including Satō Bunsei. "Elect us, conservatives untainted by the ruling faction's black mist," the anti-Satō candidates pleaded, "and clean up the LDP."

It was this "civil war" in the party, as one newspaper article characterized it,[51] that most seriously threatened Satō Bunsei's chances for official endorsement. Satō feared he would suffer the same fate as the majority of new candidates in the Nakasone faction. Only three of eighteen members of Nakasone's

49 These scandals received almost daily front-page coverage in all major newspapers from the end of August, 1966, to election day in January 1967. The men involved and the situation in their districts are discussed in a series of articles in the *Yomiuri Shinbun*, "Mondai No Hito-Sono Senkyoku," December 8, 9, 11, 12, 13, 1966.

50 All House dissolutions in postwar Japan have nicknames that identify the immediate causes for the dissolutions. These are conveniently listed in Tsuji Kiyoaki, ed., *Seiji*, Vol. 1 of *Sengo Nijyūnenkan* (Tokyo, 1966), pp. 204–5.

51 *Asahi Evening News*, January 20, 1967, p. 1.

group received Party endorsement.[52] The incumbents from Satō's district are said to have stressed his disloyalty to the party as a major reason for denying him endorsement. Nishimura, it is to be remembered, is a member of the Satō Eisaku faction and was a member of the Satō cabinet at the time of dissolution. Nishimura and Speaker of the Lower House Ayabe Kentarō, having access to the high councils of the party, pressed their case against "new rightist" Satō Bunsei.

On his side, Satō had the support of his faction boss, Murakami. Unfortunately for Murakami, but in a sense fortunately for Satō, the Murakami faction failed to have any faction member appointed to a cabinet post in either of Prime Minister Satō's two cabinet reshuffles preceding the December dissolution. Although disgruntled, Murakami supported Satō Eisaku in the presidential election but insisted on endorsement for all his faction's candidates, including Satō Bunsei, as a price for his support. Murakami's power was augmented by his relationship with Iwasaki, who controlled the Prefectural Chapter's vote in the presidential election. This also was put onto the scales to tilt them in Satō's favor.

Satō also received the backing of political commentator Mitarai Tatsuo, a native of Ōita Prefecture and a confidante of many LDP leaders.[53] Mitarai urged Satō's endorsement in discussions with the party President and Secretary General and following one of these meetings called Satō in Beppu to inform him his endorsement was assured.

On the evening of December 29 Satō returned home from a campaign strategy meeting to find a telegram from the Secretary-General asking him to appear at party headquarters the following morning to receive his certificate of endorsement and the three million yen in campaign funds that go with it. When

[52] *Asahi Shinbun,* December 31, 1966, p. 2.

[53] The author was introduced to Mitarai by Satō Bunsei in the fall of 1966. Thereafter, Mitarai, with his intimate knowledge of LDP politics in both Ōita Prefecture and Tokyo, proved to be an invaluable source of information.

party President Satō Eisaku handed him the certificate of endorsement, he remarked that "A lot has passed but now that you are endorsed you are to abstain from making anti-party speeches and you are to campaign in harmony with your elders from the District, Ayabe and Nishimura." Satō Bunsei returned to Beppu saying the party President's remarks made him feel he was being awarded a kindergarten graduation diploma. The fight for endorsement, however, was now history and Satō could concentrate on the fight for election victory.

Satō's struggle for party endorsement is illustrative of a number of important themes in Japanese politics. The split between ex-bureaucrat and local politician, the antipathy between Liberal and Democrat in the Liberal Democratic Party, the relative importance of prefectural and national party organization, and the role of factions in the endorsement process all came into play in Satō's rise from prefectural assemblyman to Diet member.

A crucial theme is the intraparty competition generated by the multimember district single entry ballot system. Incumbent opposition to his candidacy was the major obstacle to Satō's endorsement and the need to overcome incumbent strength was Satō's major problem in the campaign, as we shall see in the following chapters. In deciding endorsement policy the party is torn by the desire to insure the re-election of incumbents and the desire to increase party strength by bringing new candidates into the race. For the incumbent there is the constant fear that the appearance of a new LDP candidate can result in his own defeat regardless of the total LDP vote received by the candidates in the district. For the party there is the fear that infighting among its candidates can so scatter the LDP vote that opposition parties will elect more candidates than is commensurate with their percentage of the popular vote.

Keeping in mind what has been said about the conflicts generated by the multimember single-entry ballot system, it is instructive to look again at the figures concerning LDP endorsement policy with the other data included in the following table.

Table 3

LDP Performance in General Elections, 1958–1967

	A Number of endorsed candidates	B Number of successful candidates	C $\dfrac{B}{A}$	D % of popular vote
1958	413	287	69.4%	57.8%
1960	399	296	74.1	57.6
1963	359	283	78.8	54.7
1967	342	277	80.9	48.8

The above chart indicates not merely LDP endorsement policy but also a basic dilemma facing the party. The LDP percentage of the popular vote has been declining with every election since the formation of the party. (This is true even if one includes candidates who ran as independents and joined the party following election.) In 1958 LDP candidates received 57.8 per cent of the vote; and in 1967 the party slid below majority support for the first time, getting 48.8 per cent of the vote.

In the face of this declining support the LDP has endorsed fewer candidates with each succeeding election in the hope of maximizing popular support and insuring the re-election of its incumbents. As the table shows, this policy has been very successful up to the present. In 1958, when it endorsed 413 candidates, only 69.4 per cent were successful. In 1967, with 342 candidates, 80.9 per cent won.[54] As the success rate ap-

[54] It is interesting to note that these trends were continued in the December 1969 election. The L D P reduced its endorsed candidates to 327. With 288 candidates winning, the success rate increased to 88.0 per cent, while the popular vote percentage continued on its slow decline, falling to 47.7 per cent.

proaches 100 per cent, this strategy of constantly reducing the number of candidates reaches its ultimate limit. The LDP can hardly reduce its endorsed candidates further without refusing endorsement to some incumbents. Unless the party can reverse the trend in the popular vote, it will suffer serious losses as the endorsed candidates divide the smaller vote and defeat each other. This is the dilemma posed by the electoral system. The fears of incumbents of losing an election because of the entrance into the race of a new candidate of the same party are often justified. In 1966 Ayabe Kentarō opposed Satō's endorsement with good reason. Ayabe was to lose the election.

II

Campaign Organization
in Rural Areas

▟ IN CERTAIN SYSTEMS of representative government the official endorsement of a major political party can be the crucial factor in determining a candidate's chances of electoral success. In some southern states in the United States, for example, the nomination of the Democratic Party in effect means success at the polls. In the single-member constituencies of Britain, candidate fortunes are highly dependent on shifts in political party popularity.[1] In Japan, because of the effects of the multimember districting system, the relationship between political party strength and individual candidate success is not as direct as in some other countries. A district with strong LDP support will still see a vigorous battle between the LDP candidates for the conservative vote and declines in party popularity will only exacerbate the intraparty conflict as the candidates fight among themselves for the anticipated smaller conservative vote. One consequence of the intraparty conflict generated by the electoral system is that candidates must rely on personal campaign organizations in their endeavor to mobilize support sufficient to insure election.

The Second District of Ōita Prefecture consists of four cities, seventeen towns, and three villages. The towns and villages are grouped into five counties (*gun*). The two cities of Beppu and Nakatsu, with 42 per cent of the district's electorate, represent the urban component of the constituency. The other two cities are typical of the "rural cities" that have resulted from postwar amalgamations of towns and villages. The city of Kitsuki has

---

[1] See Richard Rose, *Politics in England* (Boston, 1964), pp. 147–50.

Listening to a Candidate at a Joint Speech Meeting

Courtesy of Ōita Gōdō Shinbun

over 60 per cent of its labor force engaged in the primary sector of the economy and Bungo Takada 56 per cent of its labor force. Taken together, these two cities and five counties represent the rural component of Ōita's Second Electoral District. They have a population of 282,794, 62 per cent of the total population of the district, and their labor force accounts for 60 per cent of the district's total. The accompanying chart indicates the high proportion of the labor force engaged in the primary sector of the economy, which in Ōita's Second District means almost exclusively agriculture.[2] Of the district's 278,584 voters, 162,250 or 58 per cent live in these areas.

It is almost axiomatic to say that a candidate for public office organizes his campaign in line with what he perceives to be the most rational behavior for obtaining the support of the electorate. The axiom is somewhat misleading in that a person is never completely free to act in accord with his rational judgments. For one thing, an election law might prohibit certain activities a candidate perceives as rational. For another, as social psychologists have long pointed out, individual perception is not merely a response to stimuli in the environment but is dependent in part on assumptions the individual brings to a particular situation. "This implies that the meanings and significances we assign to things, to symbols, to people and to events are the meanings and significances we have built up through our past experience, and are not inherent or intrinsic in the 'stimuli' itself."[3]

Japan's first experiences with parliamentary elections occurred when the country was dominated by an agricultural economy and a predominantly rural society. Strategies of support mobilization in rural areas were developed over a long

[2] In agriculture, 62.4 per cent; 0.5 per cent in forestry and hunting; 2.6 per cent in fishing. Figures compiled from Ōita Ken, *Shōwa 40 nen Kokusei Chosa, Ōita Ken Shūkei Kekkahyō* (Ōita, 1967).

[3] Hadley Cantril, "Perception and Interpersonal Relations," in *Current Perspectives in Social Psychology,* eds. Edwin P. Hollander and Raymond G. Hunt (New York, 1967), p. 284.

Table 4

Selected Population Figures for Ōita's Second District

Area	Population	Voters	Employed persons	Percentage of employed persons in primary[a] sector	Percentage of employed persons in secondary[b] sector	Percentage of employed persons in tertiary[c] sector
ŌITA PREFECTURE	1,187,474	738,951	555,703	42.1	17.9	40.0
Beppu	118,938	78,071	56,863	7.3	19.1	73.6
Nakatsu	58,371	38,263	27,312	28.6	23.9	47.5
Bungo Takada	25,138	15,377	12,953	56.4	11.7	31.9
Kitsuki	25,248	15,853	12,070	60.8	8.2	31.0
City Total	227,695	147,564	109,198	38.3	15.7	46.0
NISHI KUNISAKI COUNTY						
Ota	3,756	2,285	1,933	82.8	2.2	15.0
Matama	6,291	3,966	3,348	73.9	7.9	18.2
Kagachi	6,382	3,783	3,182	63.9	13.1	23.0
County Total	16,429	10,034	8,403	73.5	7.7	18.8
HIGASHI KUNISAKI COUNTY						
Kunimi	9,641	5,992	5,026	70.1	8.3	21.6
Himeshima	3,865	2,257	2,056	58.9	13.4	27.6
Kunisaki	21,982	13,746	11,473	65.6	7.8	26.6
Musashi	6,684	4,080	3,560	78.7	3.8	17.5
Aki	13,759	8,424	7,158	74.1	6.2	19.6
County Total	55,881	34,499	29,273	69.5	7.9	22.6

		HAYAMI COUNTY				
Hiji	20,120	12,729	9,576	55.9	12.6	31.5
Yamaga	13,612	8,108	6,776	65.9	11.1	23.0
County Total	33,732	20,837	16,352	60.9	11.9	27.2
		SHIMOGE COUNTY				
Sankō	6,581	4,043	3,604	70.2	8.6	21.2
Honyabakei	6,484	4,085	3,296	65.9	9.7	24.3
Yabakei	9,486	5,533	4,694	71.0	8.9	20.1
Yamaguni	6,789	4,041	3,030	62.5	13.0	24.6
County Total	29,340	17,702	14,624	67.4	10.1	22.5
		USA COUNTY				
Innai	8,615	5,224	4,321	75.5	6.8	17.7
Ajimu	13,040	8,113	6,668	77.1	3.5	19.4
Ekisen	6,897	4,291	3,602	62.3	11.0	26.7
Yokkaichi	22,475	14,166	11,437	60.6	10.4	29.0
Nagasu	17,621	10,922	8,089	46.3	17.7	35.9
Usa	8,377	5,232	4,011	54.8	14.0	31.2
County Total	77,025	47,948	38,128	62.7	10.7	26.6
District Total	440,102	278,584	215,978	62.1	10.7	27.2

a agriculture, forestry and hunting, fisheries   b mining, construction, manufacturing
c wholesale and retail trades, finance, insurance and real estate, transportation and communication, electricity, gas and water supply, services, government.

Compiled on the basis of data in: Ōita Ken, *Shōwa 40 nen Kokusei Chōsa, Ōita Ken Shūkei Kekkahyō* (Ōita, 1965); Sōrifu Tōkeikyoku, *Ōita Ken No Jinkō* (Tokyo, 1967); Ōita Ken Senkyo Kanri Iinkai, *Senkyo No Kiroku, Shūgiin Giin Sōsenkyo*, January 29, 1967 election (Ōita, 1967).

period of time and to a considerable degree became formalized. Although Japan is no longer a predominantly rural society, the strategies developed in an earlier period are still utilized and are naturally employed with the greatest frequency in those areas of the country that are still highly rural. The conservative politician who enters into the competition of Diet elections approaches the problem of creating strategies of support mobilization with a perception conditioned by decades of previous conservative politician experience. Satō, a professional politician trained by older professional politicians in one of Japan's rural prefectures, perceived the challenges of the rural electorate with a number of assumptions that are no longer, as Cantril writes, necessarily "inherent or intrinsic in the 'stimuli' itself" but no less real for this reason. The rural hamlet, or *buraku*, in his view, is highly integrative, cohesive, and hierarchical, a pattern Japanese sociologists characterize by the generic term *kyōdōtai*. The existence of such "traditional" communities made imperative certain campaign styles and strategies not rational in more urban areas. In a specifically political sense, Satō's perception of the rural electorate was dominated by two concepts: that of the "hard vote" and its corollary, the "gathered vote."

The term "hard vote" (*koteihyō*) is common to both popular and academic writings on politics in Japan, but few scholars have attempted systematically to analyze its meaning. One group of scholars dismissed the problem by defining the hard vote as one "difficult to move."[4] A "hard vote" means specifically a vote that goes consistently and repeatedly to a particular person as a consequence of personal ties (*en* or *enko*). These ties may be direct (between the candidate for political office and the voter) or indirect (between the supporter of a candidate for political office and the voter). In discussing the concept of the hard vote, Japanese lay great stress on the role of *giri* or obligation in the political system. A voter will cast

[4] Kobayashi Naoki, Shinohara Hajime, and Sōma Masao, *Senkyo* (Tokyo, 1960), p. 91.

[38]

CAMPAIGN ORGANIZATION IN RURAL AREAS

his vote for a certain candidate in order to return a favor received from that person or to repay an obligation to a third party who is supporting the candidate. Votes become "hard" for the politician who reaches the voter through a web of personal relationships. A Diet member who continues to serve year after year gradually builds up personal relationships with a large number of voters in his district and with local politicians, business leaders, and others who in turn have intimate ties with numbers of the electorate. At election time the persons brought into this web of personal relationships are expected to vote for the politician at the web's center.

Implicit in much of the discussion of the "hard vote" is the idea that such behavior is somehow uniquely Japanese. On the whole Japanese are very self-conscious about the influence a supposed "feudalistic" sense of obligation has on voting behavior. In the 1963 local elections, for example, one of the slogans used by the Ōita Prefecture Election Management Committee was "My vote will not be sold for a bribe or given away because of a sense of traditional obligation" (*baishū ya giri jya urenai kono ippyō*), the implication being that bribes and obligations are equally "undemocratic." While the particular form obligation takes in Japan may originate in traditional Japanese values, the phenomenon itself is universal. This is what the German sociologist Robert Michels meant when he spoke of the "masses' sentiment for gratitude" in reference to the perpetuation of oligarchies in political parties.[5] The "norm of reciprocity" ("people should help those who have helped them") is universal.[6] What is unique about Japan is not the existence of the norm but the extent to which it has been encouraged by traditional patterns of social organization and institutionalized and articulated in terms of specific modes of social behavior.

The concept of the hard vote has certain obvious conse-

[5] Robert Michels, *Political Parties* (New York, 1962), p. 92.

[6] Alvin W. Gouldner, "The Norm of Reciprocity: A Preliminary Statement," in *Social Psychology*, p. 278.

quences for campaign strategy. If the rural voter votes in accordance with demands placed upon him by personal relationships, the candidate for political office can hardly hope to obtain support by the attraction of his political ideas or the power of his campaign oratory. Satō saw little point in going to the countryside to make speeches. His time, he felt, would be better spent in the urban areas of Beppu and Nakatsu, where direct appeals to the electorate would have greater effect than in the hard vote rural areas of the district. The most rational strategy for mobilizing rural support was the building of an organization of men who held positions in local society that involved them in the kind of personal relationships necessary to reach the voter, men who had the power to "gather the vote" (*hyō o matomeru*).

The concept of the gathered vote flows inexorably from that of the hard vote. Votes are hard because of a personal relationship that impels the voter to vote a certain way. This relationship is often not with the candidate himself but with one of his campaigners. The concept of gathering the vote is predicated (as is that of the hard vote) on the perception of the hamlet as a cohesive community. The ability of a hamlet to function in harmony is often referred to with the phrase *matomari ga ii;* the *buraku,* in Dore's apt translation, "hangs together."[7] Within such a community there is assumed to be a nucleus of decisionmakers, a political elite that leads the community as a unit. There are no writings that deal explicitly and at length with decisionmaking in local communities in Japan that are on the order of such studies as Dahl's study of New Haven[8] or Hunter's study of "Regional City."[9] But the works that do deal with the subject of community power structure invariably indicate that decisions are made by a "power elite" in the Hunter sense of the term rather than by a plural-

[7] Ronald P. Dore, *Land Reform in Japan* (London, 1959), p. 386.

[8] Robert A. Dahl, *Who Governs; Democracy and Power in an American City* (New Haven, 1961).

[9] Floyd Hunter, *Community Power Structure; A Study of Decision Makers* (New York, 1963).

istic leadership such as Dahl describes in New Haven. The emphasis on *matomari*[10] itself implies a great degree of unity in the making of a broad range of community decisions.

When this concept of *matomari* is applied to the specific issue of voting, it refers to the ability of the community leaders to influence voting behavior, to "gather" the vote for a chosen politician. The personality or platform of the candidate is at best peripheral to whether the vote is gathered or not. The person who can gather the vote is regarded as being capable of delivering it to whomever he wishes.[11]

For a politician like Satō who approached the problem of mobilizing the support of rural voters within a perception grid dominated by concepts of the hard and gathered vote, the crucial strategic problem was the recruitment of men capable of gathering significant numbers of votes. It was this endeavor, rather than a direct appeal to the voters, that dominated Satō's activities in the rural areas of the district.

From the beginning of Japan's parliamentary system to the dissolution of the political parties in the wartime years, it was to the landlord class that conservative politicians turned to mobilize the vote of the rural electorate. As one of Japan's most eminent rural sociologists, Fukutake Tadashi, has written, "[I]t would be little exaggeration to say that in Japanese villages before the war only landlords played any part in national politics."[12] Until 1925, when universal manhood suffrage was granted, the mass of farmers did not even have the right to

[10] *Matomeru* is a transitive verb form meaning to gather, to collect, to arrange. *Matomari* is the noun form usually translated as unity, consensus, arrangement, agreement.

[11] The use of campaigners who can gather votes by the power of their own personal connections has led to the use of the term "election broker." As Ronald Dore remarks, it is a technique also much used by rural-based socialist Diet members, a view my own observations of socialist politicians in Ōita would corroborate. See Ronald P. Dore, "The Socialist Party and the Farmers," in *Socialist Parties in Postwar Japan,* Allan B. Cole, George O. Totten, Cecil H. Uyehara (New Haven, 1966), pp. 414–15.

[12] Fukutake Tadashi, *Japanese Rural Society,* transl. Ronald P. Dore (Tokyo, 1967), p. 189.

vote. After being granted suffrage a great number of them voted in accordance with the wishes of local landlords with whom they were related. In the prewar period "if the landlord would support you, the votes of the farmers within his domain would, as a matter of course, come with his support. There was no need to deal directly with the individual farmers. . . . [V]otes could easily be gathered."[13] The modeling of landlord-tenant relations on the pattern of family organization, with its emphasis on deference, obedience, and loyalty to the head of the family, gave the landlord extraordinary power to control the voting behavior of his tenants and, because of his high status in the community, significant influence over the voting behavior of less wealthy farmers. While one might be somewhat skeptical of Fukutake's sweeping assertion of the total control exercised by landlords over voting in rural areas, there is no doubt that the landlords did command enormous influence and that they were central to the campaign strategies of Diet candidates. Fukutake expresses a view often uttered by politicians nostalgic for the easier campaigns of the prewar period when he writes that "[The farmer] simply voted for the [Diet] candidate supported by the landlord with whom he had the closest connections. As for parliamentary politicians, they had no need to make any direct appeal to the farmers as such; it was enough for their election if they could mobilize the support of landlords."[14]

In the postwar period various Occupation-sponsored reforms effected drastic changes throughout Japan. In particular the extensive land reform dispossessed the class that had been the major support of the conservative parties in rural areas. The consequences of this development for the strategies of candidates for public office were obviously far reaching. Either the politician would have to reject the strategy of relying on men to gather the vote as being irrational in the absence of a power-

[13] Fukutake Tadashi, " 'Jimoto Rieki,' O Seiritsu Saseru Mono," Interview with Ishikawa Hideo, *Asahi Jānaru*, IX (February 26, 1967), 95.

[14] Fukutake, *Japanese Rural Society*, p. 190.

ful landlord class or else he would have to find another group to replace the landlord in performing this electoral function. In fact the politician did both. On the one hand he created new strategies for reaching the voter. The mass membership *kōenkai*, which is discussed in a later chapter, is the most striking example of this. On the other hand, he turned to a different group to perform the function of the landlord: the locally elected politician. In Satō's case at least it was reliance on this group in the rural communities of the district rather than the utilization of other campaign techniques that dominated his campaign strategy.

There are obviously tremendous differences in the power of a landlord over a tenant and that of an elected official over his constituents. Nonetheless, the similarities in the political role performed by these groups in rural areas are pointed to both by political scientists in explaining in part the reasons for continued conservative dominance and by conservative politicians in rationalizing a strategy of using local elected politicians to gather the vote.

Political scientist Matsushita Keiichi forwards the thesis that the landlord has been replaced in postwar Japan by a new "ruling class," the *yakushokusha* or the officials' class. Although the great majority of these officials—mayors, assemblymen, heads of agricultural cooperatives, and so on—"are formally chosen through democratic elections, they should be regarded as forming the new ruling class in the countryside."[15] Local political bosses, able to exert pressures on the residents of a community similar to those formerly exerted by the landlords, now function as the support base of conservative party candidates. The reason for conservative party success in elections, argues Tokyo University Professor Ishida Takeshi,

is, in brief, because of its use of an obviously apolitical (*hiseijiteki*) traditional order which has the local bosses at its summit. . . . In

[15] Matsushita Keiichi, *Gendai Nihon No Seijiteki Kōsei* (Tokyo, 1964), p. 132.

short, the conservative party does not gain votes by heightening the political interest of the electorate and organizing this from below, but on the contrary receives its votes through the cohesive order's power to inhibit heightened political interest on the part of the people.[16]

The reasons that local politicians can perform the functions of gathering the vote for Diet candidates are all predicated on a view of the rural community, of the *buraku*, as being in fact a "cohesive order" (*kyōdōtai*). Within such a community, and in the vacuum created by the expropriation of the landlords, the locally elected politician has become the person most strategically situated to do favors for the community's inhabitants and to expect in return the acceptance of his political leadership.

In the towns and villages of Ōita's Second District a candidate for the local Assembly often needs no more than two or three hundred votes to be elected. Such politicians usually have their support concentrated in one section of the town and have extensive ties of friendship, kinship, and obligation with their supporters. An assemblyman elected repeatedly over a number of years builds up a stable group of supporters who become his "hard votes." When that politician lends his support to a candidate for the Diet, he attempts to "gather" his own hard votes for the politician with whom he is associated.

The local politician functions to gather the vote by basically two methods. The first is to ask voters to support a particular Diet candidate as a favor to him, the local politician. Such an appeal can be effective for a variety of reasons. A local politician, because of the great dependence of local municipalities on the national government for subsidies and grants-in-aid, must have good relations with a member of the Diet if he is to provide valuable services to his own constituents. He needs to demonstrate to the Diet member his effectiveness as a supporter to insure a continuation of benefits for his constituents

16 Ishida Takeshi, *Sengo Nihon No Seiji Taisei* (Tokyo, 1961), pp. 87–88.

and to secure the Diet member's financial aid for his own local Assembly election. Thus he can argue with his own supporters that support for a particular Diet candidate is essential for his own continuation and effectiveness in office. In this sense, the local politician is not a representative of what Ishida refers to above as an "obviously apolitical traditional order." On the contrary, he is appealing to the voters' very real concern for economic and political benefit.

Commonly, however, the local politician, much as the pre-war landlord, requests a vote for a certain Diet candidate as a repayment of obligation owed to him by the voters. It is quite common in Japan for people to feel that the politician who has managed to get, for example, a desired road built in their hamlet did them a favor rather than carried out his duty as the representative of the constituency. They accept the notion that they are obligated to him much as they assume that the politician himself has incurred an obligation to someone higher up in the political hierarchy in order to have the road built. The politician can cash in, in a sense, on these obligations to achieve his goal of gathering votes for the Diet candidate. There are innumerable incidents, like the one I witnessed while walking down a village street with a town assemblyman supporting Satō. As we were walking an elderly farmer approached from the other direction and greeted the assemblyman. The politician returned the greeting and reminded the man that he was supporting Satō in the election and hoped the farmer would too. "Why, of course," responded the farmer spontaneously, "I am so indebted to you, sure I'll vote for Satō."

If the first method by which the local politician can gain votes for the Diet candidate is his own personal appeal to numbers of his constituents, the second is the similar appeal possessed by the staff of his own political machine. Like the Diet candidate himself, the local politician has a group of supporters who run his election campaign. In the case of a town or village assemblyman this "staff" may not number more than a few people, but mayors, prefectural assemblymen, and

[45]

powerful leaders in local Assemblies often have highly developed personal organizations that extend down through the local Assemblies to the hamlets and comprise large numbers of people.

The relationship between the leader and the followers of these political organizations, particularly in rural areas but generally through the society at large, is characterized by patterns of organization and the prevalence of values associated with the family system. The extension of familism to nonfamily groups in the society takes the generic form called *oyabun-kobun.* "In such groupings, organization and authority follow closely the models of the family, whether of the individual household or of the extended 'house.' The head is the *oyabun,* or *oyakata* (literally, 'father role') and the subordinates are *kobun,* or *kokata* (literally, 'child role')."[17] "Persons of authority assume obligations and manifest attitudes toward their subordinates much as if they were foster parents, and conversely the subordinates behave dutifully and hold feelings of great personal loyalty toward their superiors."[18] "Characteristically, the head is the benevolent father, the subordinates are loyal and obedient children; and the relation between them is not only functional, specific, and economic, but personal and diffuse as well."[19]

The *oyabun,* a prefectural assemblyman for instance, provides a variety of services and benefits to his *kobun.* He may, for example, be their source of funds for campaigns to local Assemblies. He may, as Iwasaki did with Satō, groom a *kobun* for high political office. In return the leader is the recipient of obedience and loyalty from his followers. When he decides to throw his support behind a particular candidate for the Diet, his organization of followers becomes, as a matter of course,

---

[17] Herbert Passin, "Japanese Society," *International Encyclopedia of the Social Sciences* (New York, 1968), p. 243.

[18] John W. Bennett and Iwao Ishino, *Paternalism in the Japanese Economy* (Minneapolis, 1963), p. 40: quoted in Passin, p. 243.

[19] Passin, p. 244.

part of the candidate's campaign organization. The support of one powerful politician in any particular area can result in the support of a network that extends through the entire town or village. Satō's organization in Bungo Takada, described in the following chapter, is an example of this type of campaign organization. In the "ideal model," so to speak, of a campaign organization, the local politician in one's support will have considerable influence to gather the vote of numbers of the electorate, and his organized followers, often being lesser politicians themselves, will have a similar influence over other members of the constituency. This power to gather the vote is not limited exclusively to the local politician. Heads of agricultural cooperatives, presidents of organizations such as the Chamber of Commerce, and men of high social standing such as dentists and doctors are also utilized in election campaigns for similar purposes.[20] It is the group of local elected politicians, however, that is most extensively utilized in the campaign organization of Diet candidates.

It is essential to stress that the assemblyman's support is largely an empty promise without the active participation of his personal organization. This is one point many commentators fail to take into consideration when they criticize Diet candidates for the large amount of money they give local politicians for their support. The effective assemblyman usually keeps only a small amount of campaign funds for himself and directs the rest down among his staff.[21] The ineffective assemblyman who does pocket the money is usually not given the opportunity to be ineffective more than once. These local politicians can of course demand a good price for their support because the Diet candidate is so very much dependent on them. To successfully fulfill his function, however, the local politician has to allow a considerable portion of the money re-

[20] The role of a variety of voluntary associations in the campaign is discussed in Chapter VII.

[21] The uses of campaign funds distributed to local politicians is discussed further in Chapter VIII.

ceived to filter down through his own personal organization of supporters.

Rural areas have of course not been immune to changes that have occurred in Japanese society since the end of the war, and politicians have not remained ignorant of these changes and their possible effects on voting behavior and campaign strategies. Satō's perception of the rural electorate and of rational strategies of support mobilization is neither simple nor unambiguous. He is aware of the different degree of political influence of the postwar local politician and the prewar landlord and realizes the limits of a strategy of relying on community notables to deliver the rural vote. Yet he is also aware of the high regard paid to deference, obligation, and harmony in rural areas, and thus the utility of a campaign strategy that is rationalized by such factors. Although some attempts were made to organize support directly among the voters rather than rely entirely on local notables, the overwhelming thrust of Satō's rural strategy was in the direction of gathering the hard votes of local political elites. The prevalence of traditional patterns of group behavior and, as is discussed later, the strength of LDP incumbents in rural areas and Satō's own urban orientation, militated strongly against any radical departure from the tradition-sanctioned strategy described above.

Some degree of modification of this strategy to accord with changed conditions has of course occurred. Satō, in calculating the number of votes a particular local politician can deliver to him, for instance, does not assume that all the people who voted consistently for that politician (that is, his hard votes) can be delivered to a Diet candidate on command. Satō, as a rule of thumb in estimating his support in any particular rural area, calculates that the local politician in his support would provide roughly between one-fifth and one-third the number of votes received in his own election. Some of his supporters will simply dislike the Diet candidate; others will be obligated to another Diet candidate or his supporter; still others will not be interested enough to vote. Allowing for all these contingencies, Satō calculates that a mayor, for example, who has been re-elected several times with a stable vote of say five thousand, will provide between 1,200 and 1,400 votes to the Diet candidate he is supporting. Thus, the more support the Diet candidate has from prefectural, city, and town assemblymen, mayors, and other elected officials the more votes he can expect to receive.

Such calculations are not unique to Satō. One newspaper wrote of the role of local politicians in Diet campaigns in the same terms of delivering a percentage of their own vote to the candidate but set the figure higher.

A prefectural assemblyman with 10,000 votes in his own election can deliver half or 5,000 votes in a Diet election. The same rule applies to city assemblymen. If the candidate can win over city, town, village and prefectural assemblymen who are involved in everyday activities, votes can easily be predicted. That is why it is said that the battle to win a Diet seat is settled in the battle for local assemblymen support in the year preceding the election.[22]

The concept of a Diet candidate's support being based on the vote that is delivered by political machines of local politicians makes understandable certain usages of the term *jiban,* usually translated as support base or bailiwick. It is common to hear talk of the "transferring" of a *jiban* or of "receiving" a *jiban.* Inukai Tsuyoshi, one of Japan's prewar political leaders and the holder of a so-called iron *jiban* in Okayama Prefecture, wrote to a follower in 1902 that "I gave half of my *jiban* to Nishimura Tanjirō. I am holding the other half, plus two *gun* in the Bizen area."[23] When Inukai died his son "inherited" his *jiban.* Despite the changes that have occurred in Japanese society, the same quote could be made today without anyone thinking strangely of it. When Satō entered the Prefectural Assembly he "inherited" the *jiban* of Aragane Keiji,

[22] "Kono Ippyō De Kiri O Harae" (5), *Mainichi Shinbun,* January 6, 1967, p. 1; quoted in Sōma Masao, *Nihon No Senkyo* (Tokyo, 1967), p. 124.

[23] Quoted in Richard K. Beardsley, John W. Hall, and Robert E. Ward, *Village Japan* (Chicago, 1959), p. 425.

and when he left he "transferred" it to his chosen successor Shutō Kenji. Whereas Inukai asked landlords supporting him in part of the district to support Nishimura Tanjirō, Satō had the men in his organization go to work for Shutō. It is implicit in such procedures that the supporters of a politician have a loyalty to that politician which takes precedence over personal feelings toward the new candidate they are being asked to support, and that they will be able to deliver their "hard votes" to the candidate of their choice.

The fight for votes in Ōita's Second District's rural areas was in large part a fight among the conservative candidates—Ayabe, Nishimura, and Satō—for support of local politicians. In this fight Satō was in the least advantageous position. Being the only nonincumbent candidate, he was faced with a situation in which most of the district's political leaders were already supporters of one or the other of the two conservative incumbents.

Ōita's Second District had fifteen prefectural assemblymen, all of whom were associated with particular Diet candidates. Of this number Satō had, at the time of the 1967 election, the open support of only one (his successor in the Assembly, Shutō Kenji). He had the partial, unpublicized support of one other and the support of a former assemblyman. The case of the "shadow" support of the one assemblyman is interesting in reflecting the practice of dividing one's *jiban* much as Inukai Tsuyoshi did sixty years ago. This prefectural assemblyman, from the city of Nakatsu, was a close ally of Iwasaki, and through that connection was brought into Satō's campaign. Being a member of the former Liberal Party, he and the members of his organization had long supported Nishimura, who, as has been mentioned, was also a member of this party. Afraid of alienating Nishimura because of the importance of Nishimura's support in his own Prefectural Assembly election, and required to do something for Satō because of his close relationship with Iwasaki, the assemblyman took an ostensibly "neutral" position in the Diet race. Quietly he delegated members of his organization, "divided his *jiban*" in the Japanese phraseology, to work for the two candidates. Three of his *kobun,* all members of the Nakatsu Assembly, were "given" to Satō.

The district also elects twenty-four city, town, and village mayors. Satō had the open support of only the mayor of Yamaguni in the northwestern corner of the district and indirect support from two others. The same pattern applies to Speakers of local Assemblies, another position considered a seat of political power. Satō had the full support of only one Speaker in the district, the partial support of one other, and the support of one former Speaker.

Satō, therefore, was in the position of having to try to "eat into" the *jiban* (*jiban ni kuikomu*) of the incumbents. The limited success he had in this effort was due almost entirely to LDP leader Iwasaki's influence over many politicians in the district. As a nonincumbent, Satō lacked the power to do favors for local politicians on a scale that could compete with the power of the incumbents. His defeat in the 1963 election made many politicians wary of switching support to a candidate who might well lose the election and leave them without any pipeline to the Diet. Some assemblymen who had supported him in 1963 refused to do so in 1967, and many others made clear that they could not continue to support him in another election if he were defeated again in 1967.

One newcomer to Diet campaigning, when asked how he tried to organize his support, responded by saying that "I asked help of my relatives, friends, and former classmates and started out building an organization."[24] Satō's organization was built in much the same way. In some areas, such as Kitsuki and part of Higashi Kunisaki County, former classmates of the Kitsuki Middle School dominated the campaign effort. Kitsuki, mentioned above as a typical "rural" city with over 60 per cent of its labor force of 12,000 engaged in the primary sector of the

[24] "Uchiyabure, Sanban Henchō" (2), *Asahi Shinbun,* January 11, 1967, p. 1.

economy, is an amalgamation of seven villages. There was one man in each of these villages responsible for Satō's campaign. Over-all responsibility was in the hands of a relative of Satō, forty-one years old, a twice-elected member of the City Assembly, and a graduate of the city's middle school. Of the six other campaign managers, four were Satō's classmates at the school. Another was his senior at the school by one year. The sixth man, sixty-one years old, was from the village where Satō's mother was born and was a long-time friend of the Satō family. The extraordinary degree of attention Satō gave to maintaining his school ties, attending alumni meetings, contributing generously to the alumni fund and to special projects, and in other ways maintaining his association with the group are indications of the high value he placed upon his former schoolmates as a source of electoral support.

In other places relatives were important organizers of support and, in many of the towns, friends associated with the LDP prefectural youth group led the organization. Satō's own political machine, as that of a prefectural assemblyman, was limited largely to Beppu, the constituency from which he was elected. During his years in the Assembly he served as President of the party's youth group in the Prefecture. It was the membership of this group that provided the basis for building a district-wide machine. Satō was succeeded as youth group President by Kiyohara Fumio, who ran Satō's campaign in Bungo Takada, and Kiyohara was in turn succeeded by Shutō Kenji, the man Satō designated as successor to his seat in the Prefectural Assembly. Members and former members of this group proved to be the crucial and sometimes only organizers of support for Satō in several of the towns of the district.

The only place where Satō had no organization at all was the island village of Himeshima, the birthplace of Nishimura. In the 1967 election 98 per cent of the island's electorate of 2,257 went to the polls and the 95 per cent of those voting faithfully cast their ballot for Nishimura. Nishimura received 2,140 votes, Socialist Komatsu was second with 54 votes, Ayabe third with 6, and Satō and the Communist party candidate each received 3 votes.[25]

In each of the other twenty-one cities, towns, and villages that comprise the rural sector of the Second District, Satō engaged in an organized campaign effort. The majority of men at the head of these area organizations were local assemblymen or former assemblymen at the time of the 1967 election. Twelve were members of the local Assemblies, while three had been former members. The six non-office-holding campaign managers included three medical doctors, one dentist, one veterinarian, and one merchant who was president of the local association of merchants. Among this group of twenty-one supporters, two were in the thirty-year-old age group, fourteen were in their forties, and five were over the age of fifty-five. Among the assemblymen the average age was forty-three, somewhat younger than Satō himself.

Satō's campaign organizations in the district's rural cities, towns, and villages followed a general pattern. His support, as is typical of the traditional organizational structure employed by conservative politicians, was organized on a *chiiki* or geographical basis. Each city, town, and village has a campaign organization that deals directly with the candidate and his headquarters and is independent of the organizations in the other cities, towns, and villages. This is the so-called vertical approach to campaign organization—the creating of independent support groups in each administrative area. It is in contrast with the organization of Socialist Party politicians who, because of the support of labor unions, are seen as using a "horizontal" approach. The labor unions which are used as the candidate's campaign organization have a membership which fans out over the district and cuts across *chiiki* lines.

[25] As an ironic note to the Japanese government's campaign for high voting rates, the walls of the office of Himeshima's mayor (who has always been elected uncontested) are covered with plaques won in the competition for the highest voting rates and lauding the high level of political consciousness of the island's electorate.

Every town in the district is the result of amalgamations of smaller towns and villages, most of these amalgamations taking place in the period of the so-called amalgamation boom following the passage of the Law for the Promotion of Amalgamation of Towns and Villages in 1953. The amalgamated areas, which are referred to as "former villages" (*kyūmura*), remain significant administrative and social units and form an important level for Satō's campaign organization. Below the former villages are the *buraku,* the hamlets which form the basic level for the organization of campaign support. Satō's support group in any of the towns in the district is organized along the lines of these basic administrative and social divisions: the town, the former village, and the *buraku.*

At the head of the organization in a town is the town *sekininsha,* Satō's campaign manager for that particular area. As his title (the "responsible person") implies, the *sekininsha* is responsible for organizing the campaign and delivering the vote. In general he is the only person in the town organization accountable directly to the candidate, and he is also the only one whose degree of success can be judged by the candidate with some measure of accuracy. While each town has several polling centers, votes are counted only at the town level. Thus the candidate cannot know, for instance, how many votes he received in a particular former village.[26] The candidate sets a goal for the town and the *sekininsha* is responsible for deliver-

[26] It is often said that candidates do in fact know how many and even which individuals voted for them in each *buraku*. Campaigners may "station themselves near polling booths and watch the facial expressions of voters as they come and go. Those who have not obeyed instructions are likely to give themselves away when so confronted." See Kyōgoku Junichi and Ike Nobutake, "Urban-Rural Differences in Voting Behavior in Postwar Japan," *Economic Development and Cultural Change,* IX, Part 3 (October 1960), p. 173. The reliability of this and other similar techniques is questionable and the campaigner is likely to exaggerate his success in delivering the vote when he reports to the candidate's headquarters. The only reliable information at the candidate's command is the records of voting statistics for the entire vote-counting area.

[54]

ing the agreed-upon number of votes. Commonly there is only one person in a town who holds this position in Satō's organization. Partly this is due to a desire to clearly define the lines of accountability and in part a desire to keep the number of men who deal directly with the candidate's headquarters as few as possible so as to minimize the risks of the headquarter staff or the candidate himself being implicated in an Election Law violation. Particularly after the official campaign has begun, the *sekininsha* is usually the only campaigner from a town to deal with the candidate and receive campaign funds directly from his headquarters. He in turn is responsible for distributing campaign funds to the other men in the town organization.

Below the *sekininsha* are the "former-village" campaign managers. In a town that is, for example, the amalgamation of four villages there will usually be four former-village campaign managers owing responsibility directly to the town *sekininsha*. In some areas, such as the town of Kunisaki, discussed in the following chapter, several people are placed at this level of the organization. Only in a few cases do campaigners at this level or below deal directly with the candidate's headquarters. In consultation with the town *sekininsha,* the former-village-level campaign managers develop the organization in their areas and are given a vote quota to be filled. These former-village managers, in turn, are responsible for organizing the campaigners in the *buraku* within their respective villages. Ideally a former-village campaign manager will have subordinate *buraku* campaign managers in each *buraku* responsible for recruiting campaigners and delivering a set vote to him. In Satō's case, while some towns had such *buraku* managers, the more usual practice was for all *buraku* campaigners to deal directly with the former-village-level campaign managers.

The structure of the typical town organization, accordingly, is that of a pyramid, with commands passing down from the candidate's headquarters to the town *sekininsha,* from him to the former-village campaign managers, and from them to the campaigners in the *buraku*. Each level of organization sets quotas to be filled by the level immediately below. Through this process the candidate's quota for the town is so divided that at the bottommost *buraku* level a campaigner may be responsible for obtaining four or five votes. This structure, with minor variations, is representative of those used by conservative party Diet politicians. The town, former-village, and *buraku* are as fundamental to Japanese political organization, as are the county and ward to political organization in the United States.

The structuring of a campaign organization in this fashion has certain consequences for the mobilization of electoral support. For one thing, the channeling of communications in the structure through vertical lines that become increasingly narrow as they approach the candidate's headquarters makes it extremely difficult for the candidate at the top of the structure to gain reliable information about the organization on its lower levels. In some areas the candidate is not familiar with anyone but the town *sekininsha*. In almost all areas knowledge of campaigners is confined to those on the *sekininsha* and former-village campaign manager levels. The men campaigning in the *buraku* are an unknown quantity. As a consequence the candidate, particularly a new candidate first building an organization, cannot accurately judge the strength of his organization or identify its weak points. The election results, as remarked above, describe only the candidate's strength in the entire town. They do not indicate which areas within the town are weak and which are strong.

The local politician who leads a town organization has a vested interest in keeping the candidate ignorant of his supporters on the lower levels. The value of the local politician, as has been noted, is the personal organization he commands in his local area. A well-developed organization reaches down into each of the former villages and into nearly every *buraku*. The politician at the head of such a structure is, as a rule, reluctant to share detailed information with the Diet candidate he supports as to who comprises the campaign organization. By keeping the membership rolls secret he insures the candidate's dependence on his continued support. By divulging information on the *buraku* campaigners, the position of the *sekininsha* would be endangered not particularly in the imminent election but in the long run as the Diet member approaches the *buraku* campaigners with New Year cards, gifts for various occasions, and so on in an attempt to obtain their support directly and to lessen the chances of a local politician changing his support to another candidate and taking all his campaigners with him.

In December of 1966, in a futile effort to gain some information on his organized strength in the countryside, Satō held a meeting in Beppu attended by the *sekininsha* from each town and village in the district. For each of the areas Satō's staff had drawn up charts listing the names of the amalgamated towns and villages in the particular area and of the *buraku* in each of these subdivisions. Space was left under the name of each *buraku* for the *sekininsha* to fill in the names of the men campaigners, the women campaigners, campaigners among young voters, and those, such as dentists, barbers, and the like, having ties with various organized groups. The opposition of the *sekininsha* to filling in the charts was unmistakable. Most said they would need time to get complete information and agreed to fill in the charts within a week or two. Most of the charts were never completed and even those which were gave little idea of the extent of Satō's organizational strength.

One consequence of this is that the Diet candidate's campaign organizations in the several towns become largely autonomous units, separated not only from the organizations in other towns but also from the candidate himself. The relationship between the candidate and his town organization becomes not so much a delegation of authority as a total relegation of responsibility. The candidate attempts no control over campaign methods or strategy within the particular area. These problems are left to the town *sekininsha* and the other leaders of the town organization. The candidate's main responsibility is to set the quota of votes for the town in consultation with the *sekininsha* and to provide the campaign funds. The way his supporters campaign is their own business, and there is plenty of room for differences in "style." Because the visibility of the candidate himself is so minimal, his image in the various towns of the district varies considerably with the type of person that leads his organization in any one area.

The vertical pattern of organization has another serious consequence for campaign strategy in that it tends to cluster support within highly restricted areas of a particular town. One example will suffice to demonstrate this point.

The town of Honyabakei in Shimoge County had an electorate at the time of the 1967 election of 4,085. Satō's *sekininsha* in Honyabakei is forty-year-old Sakamoto Tosuke, town assemblyman and head of the Shimoge County LDP youth group. Like many of Satō's supporters, Sakamoto became friendly with Satō while the latter was serving as chairman of the Prefectural youth organization. In the 1963 election Satō received 554 votes in Honyabakei, fourth among the five contenders. Following that election the organization was made considerably stronger. Sakamoto brought into it the chairman of the Shimoge County LDP women's group and four other town assemblymen, as well as several former town assemblymen and people active in an informal way in the town's politics. This expanded organization plus the retirement of Noyori Hideichi, who had received 1,039 votes in the town in 1963, led Satō to set a goal of 1,200 votes from Honyabakei in the 1967 election. The result of the election, however, was that Satō received 784 votes, third among the four candidates. Satō's failure to achieve his goal is intimately related to the practice of local politicians having their own supporters clustered in highly restricted geographical areas of the town.

Honyabakei, which became a town in 1959, is an amalgamation of four villages. One of these villages has an electorate of approximately 700 and another of 600 voters. The electorate in the third village numbers 1,300, and there are 1,400 voters in the fourth. Almost all of Satō's supporters are concentrated in the village of 1,300 voters. The youth group and women's group chairmen, the most active supporting assemblymen, and the great majority of the other supporters all live within the eighteen *buraku* of this one amalgamated village. It was in these eighteen *buraku* that the "hard votes" of Satō's supporters were clustered. Satō's organization was in fact not an organization of the town of Honyabakei as much as it was an organization of one of the town's "former villages." It is probable, if Satō's organization was effective at all, that the great majority of his 700 votes came from the 1,300 voters of that one area. The failure of his organization to have influence in the other villages, particularly the largest one with over 1,400 voters, was a consequence of the support base of the local politicians that staffed it.

One important effect of the *chiiki* or area-based campaign organization is that it militates against its own expansion because of what may be termed its "inward-looking" nature. The men who make up the organization are local people intimately familiar with the voters in their areas. A local politician can drive around his area and point out house by house who votes for whom in local Assembly, Mayoral, Prefectural Assembly, and Diet elections. There is a strong tendency to identify the Satō supporters and mark everyone else off as the "hard votes" of other candidates. Those who are known to have supported Ayabe or Nishimura or important campaigners of either of the two incumbents are considered inaccessible to Satō, and there is consequently little attempt made to bring such voters over to his support. One of Satō's major problems in recruiting participants for a large women's meeting[27] was that those whom the *sekininsha* invited were invariably those already known to be Satō supporters. This tendency of the organiza-

[27] See Chapter VI.

tion to turn in upon itself is quite probably a significant factor in accounting for the stability of the votes of incumbent Diet members in rural areas. The supporters of each candidate are identified and regarded as unapproachable by the campaigners of another candidate. It is, in fact, often regarded as less than polite to try to "steal" them.[28] Without immigration into Ōita's rural areas the population is largely one of long-time residents whose political allegiances are well known to the local politicians. Since these are the men who control the Diet candidate's campaign organization, little attempt is made to obtain the support of voters whose allegiances are to the campaigners of a different candidate.

A further important consequence of reliance on local politicians operating within the pyramid structure described is to involve the Diet candidate intricately in factional disputes and divisions on the local level. Any town in the district will have at least two and often more factions among its politicians. If the leader of one of these factions became Satō's *sekininsha* for the town, the other people recruited into the organization would also generally be of the same faction. It is difficult to imagine a member of one local faction serving as a campaign manager on the former-village level in a structure where he has to work through an opposing faction leader acting as *sekininsha* in order to deal with the Diet candidate. In some cases Satō attempted to build a multiheaded organization with separate channels for different factions, but this most often got him into trouble with one faction or another. The Diet candidate usually has to take sides in factional disputes in the towns and consequently limits himself to the support of only one element in the local conservative power structure. This

---

[28] Paul Dull relates how when he asked a local campaigner if he ever visited voters in *buraku* and villages not part of his *jiban* to solicit votes for the candidate he was supporting, he "looked shocked and said no. When asked why, he said because he had self-respect." Paul S. Dull, "The Senkyoya System in Rural Japanese Communities," *Occasional Papers*, No. 4, Center for Japanese Studies (Ann Arbor, 1953), p. 36.

relationship between the Diet candidate and local factions, though limiting in some ways, is also responsible for Satō having been able to obtain support among some local politicians. In places where incumbents Ayabe and Nishimura had the support of the main local factions, Satō was able to draw the support of politicians opposed to the leadership of the major factions and as a consequence opposed to the Diet candidates supported by them.

The description provided above of rural campaign organization is abstracted and simplified for the purpose of analysis. In practice, there were variations in strategy in different towns and villages of the district depending on particular local circumstances. More important, there was present in Satō's approach to the rural voter an undertone of concern for what he and some of his most important supporters sometimes suspected to be an outmoded strategy. Yet whatever doubts Satō felt about the utility of a strategy of relying on local leaders to deliver the vote were for the most part resolved in favor of a continuing use of the traditional strategy. New approaches to organize support directly among the electorate were seen as being too costly in money and time and largely futile because of the incumbent conservatives' strong and long-nurtured bastions of support in the rural parts of the district. For Satō, innovation in strategy and direct appeals to the electorate were to be made in the urban components of the constituency. Changes in rural strategy would await future elections.

Within the pattern of rural campaign organization sketched above there were, as has been noted, significant variations. An amplification of some of the points discussed and an indication of something of the complexity of the organization may be perhaps best provided by a description of two of Satō's campaign organizations that represent polar extremes within the general pattern. These two organizations form the subject of the following chapter.

[61]

III

Campaign Organization
in Rural Areas:
Two Case Studies

⌘ THE CITY OF BUNGO TAKADA is, as mentioned earlier, one
of Ōita second District's rural cities, the result of an
amalgamation of eleven towns and villages. Bungo Takada's
population, as is true of all the rural areas in the district, has
been decreasing at a geometric rate since 1950.[1] In 1965 it stood
at 25,138. Of a labor force of 12,953, 56.4 per cent is engaged
in the primary sector of the economy. There are only 1,522
people engaged in the secondary, industrial, and manufacturing sector, and labor union strength stands at 1,421 members.
Bungo Takada's eligible voters numbered 15,377 in January,
1967.[2]

In the nine postwar Diet elections (that is, from the election
of April, 1946, through that of November, 1960) Bungo
Takada, as Takada Town through the 1953 election and
Bungo Takada City thereafter, invariably gave its three top
votes to two conservatives and one progressive candidate. In
1963, for the first time in the postwar period, the conservative
candidates took all three top positions in the Diet race in

[1] There was a 2.8 per cent decrease between 1950–1955; 7.6 per cent between 1955–1960; and 11.1 per cent decrease between 1960–1965. Ōita Ken,
Kokusei Chōsa Ni Yoru Shi-chō-son Betsu Jinkō No Trend, mimeo (Ōita,
1967).

[2] Data obtained from: Ōita Ken, *Shōwa 40 nen Kokusei Chōsa, Ōita Ken
Shūkei Kekka Hyō* (Ōita, 1967); Sōrifu, *Ōita Ken No Jinkō* (Tokyo, 1967);
Ōita Ken Shōkō Rōdōbu Roseika, *Rōdō Kumiai Meikan* (Ōita, 1966);
Ōita Ken Senkyo Kanri Iinkai, *Senkyo No Kiroku,* January 29, 1967 elec-
tion (Ōita, 1967).

Bungo Takada. Ayabe and Nishimura received an almost equal number of votes and Satō was third in the city, with eighty-one more votes than Socialist Komatsu and twenty-two votes less than Nishimura.[3] In the next election in 1967 Satō emerged with the top vote in the city.

In the three years from his defeat in the 1963 election to the calling of the Diet election for January 1967 Satō did not make any speeches in Bungo Takada nor make any other significant attempt to directly attract the votes of the electorate of that city. He did not have to. In 1963 Satō set a goal of 3,000 votes for Bungo Takada and was delivered 2,993; in 1967 he set a goal of 3,500 votes and received 3,564. The man responsible for delivering this vote to Satō was Kiyohara Fumio.

Kiyohara, then forty-three years old, former city assemblyman, Satō's successor as chairman of the Prefectural LDP youth group, and a member of the Iwasaki faction in the Ōita LDP, ruled over a powerful political machine in Bungo Takada. Although young and not a holder of elective office since 1963, Kiyohara was generally regarded as a powerful local boss in the city. What is commonly referred to and what Kiyohara himself proudly calls the "Kiyohara *taisei*" (the Kiyohara regime or structure) is one of the major political forces in Bungo Takada.

In 1954 Kiyohara's father, who had served for twenty years as a member of the Takada Town Assembly, retired from politics. His thirty-year-old son, with the help of his father's supporters, was elected to the Assembly in the following election. With the aid of his father's former supporters, he expanded his influence, and after success in two city Assembly elections (in 1955 and 1959) he prepared to run for the Prefectural Assembly in the following election in 1963.

In 1963 it was expected that the incumbent Governor, Kinoshita Kaoru, would not stand for re-election and that LDP Chapter President Iwasaki would win in an uncontested race.

---

[3] The votes were Ayabe, 3,217; Nishimura, 3,015; Satō, 2,993; Komatsu, 2,912.

As the election approached, Kinoshita announced his intention to run again, and the LDP found itself with a difficult fight against this popular "independent progressive" who had been governor since 1955. Like Satō Bunsei, Kiyohara owed his rise in the political world of the Prefecture to LDP Chapter President Iwasaki. It was with Iwasaki's support that he decided to enter the race for the Prefectural Assembly, and it was Iwasaki's campaign difficulties that forced him to withdraw. The election for the Prefectural Assembly and governorship are held on the same day. Had Kiyohara run for the Assembly he would have been forced to stay in Bungo Takada campaigning for his own election and would have been able to do little for his mentor Iwasaki. The success of Iwasaki being the most important consideration, Kiyohara withdrew from the Assembly race and campaigned throughout the Prefecture on behalf of the LDP Chapter President in his position of chairman of the youth group.

As in his one previous encounter with Kinoshita, Iwasaki proved unable to topple the popular incumbent. While a disaster for Iwasaki, the election in some ways proved beneficial to Kiyohara. In later talking about the election, Kiyohara stressed only his enormous sacrifice for his political boss Iwasaki. Nonetheless, he did win a seat for the third time in the City Assembly, the two weeks following the governor's election being sufficient time to campaign for the 589 votes that elected him. Furthermore, Kiyohara's withdrawal from the Prefectural Assembly race in order to support Iwasaki further ingratiated him with the President, a point that cannot be overemphasized because of Iwasaki's power to aid favored subordinates financially.

When Kiyohara's close friend and predecessor as chairman of the LDP youth group, Satō Bunsei, ran for the Diet in 1963, Kiyohara took control of the Bungo Takada campaign. The chance to work as *sekininsha* for a Diet campaign was of considerable value for Kiyohara in preparing for the next Prefectural Assembly race in 1967. Satō's goal of 3,000 votes was

[64]

more than five times as great as Kiyohara's vote in the City Assembly. The campaign for Satō allowed him to activate the machine he was building on a scale the City Assembly election did not require or permit. In a sense the campaign for Satō served as a dress rehearsal for his own coming Prefectural Assembly campaign.

In the Diet election Kiyohara supported Satō; in the Governor's race he worked for Iwasaki; and in Bungo Takada's mayoral election in 1963 he was the man who "made the mayor" (shichō o tsukutta). When he was a member of the City Assembly Kiyohara was part of a local political faction led by the then mayor Sakai. When he resigned before the 1963 election, Sakai gave his support to a man named Mizunoe in the mayoral race, and the Kiyohara organization, much as in Satō's Diet race, took control of Mizunoe's campaign.[4]

In any Japanese election one of the greatest fears of the candidates is that an arrest for an Election Law violation will start a chain reaction. The man on the lowest level of the organization will tell who he received money from, that man will be arrested and pressured into telling who further up in the structure gave him his campaign funds, and if somebody does not stop the process the violation eventually reaches up to the candidate. In the Bungo Takada mayoral election in 1963 large numbers of Mizunoe's supporters were arrested for Election Law violations. After the election ended with Mizunoe's victory, the police continued to make arrests, pushing further and further up in the organizational structure until they reached Kiyohara, Mizunoe's sekininsha for the campaign. Kiyohara refused to tell who gave him the money he distributed among the campaigners. He was subsequently convicted of violating the Election Law, was forced to vacate his seat in the Assembly, and had his voting rights suspended for five years. Thus he was disqualified from running in the Prefec-

4 The discussion of Bungo Takada is based largely on a long interview with Kiyohara and several of his supporters at Kiyohara's home in Bungo Takada in May 1967.

tural Assembly election four years hence. After sacrificing his own Prefectural Assembly race to support Iwasaki in the 1963 governor's election and being disqualified from running for the Prefectural Assembly in 1967, Kiyohara is waiting and building for the 1971 Prefectural Assembly election, eight years behind his original schedule for winning a Prefectural Assembly seat.

At the heart of Kiyohara's organization in Bungo Takada is a group of sixteen men, all young, all influential politically, and all owing political allegiance to Kiyohara. One element in Kiyohara's organization is the group of older men whose support he inherited from his father. The other is this group of younger men whose support Kiyohara has cultivated during his nearly fifteen years of activity in Bungo Takada politics. The group includes the eldest sons of the mayor and the former mayor, two city assemblymen, the city's deputy mayor (*joyaku*), five city office division chiefs (*kachō*), and the chairman of the city's Agricultural Cooperative Union, a man yet in his thirties who is the youngest man in such a position in the Prefecture.

The Agricultural Cooperative chief, along with five other members of this group, were present the day I visited Kiyohara's home. While we were talking about their activities on behalf of Satō's Diet campaign, the union chief made it a point to emphasize, in Kiyohara's presence, that the support they gave Satō had nothing to do with their attitude toward Satō personally. "We support Satō and brought others into the campaign on Satō's behalf because we thought Satō's success would be of benefit to Kiyohara's political future." If Kiyohara were to support somebody else for the Diet, I was told, they would all support that new candidate immediately. "Don't make any mistake about it. Satō gets the vote here not because any of us care about Satō but because we all care about Kiyohara."

In addition to building an organization of young politicians intensely loyal to him personally, Kiyohara has been very solicitous of the older politicians of Bungo Takada who were closely associated with his father. Formally at the head of his

[66]

organization in each of ten of the eleven former towns and villages of the city is an older man who has the title of Kiyohara's *sekininsha* for the area. Kiyohara himself heads the organization in the eleventh village. Under these men the organization fans out in the manner described in the previous chapter, with campaign managers and campaigners in each of the *buraku*. Brought into the Satō campaign by the Kiyohara organization, in addition to the group of sixteen young men and the ten elderly *sekininsha,* were ten other city assemblymen, twelve women that Kiyohara sent to Satō's women's meeting in Beppu,[5] and an unknown number of men in the *buraku* who did the campaigning—Bungo Takada style.

Satō does not have an organization of supporters in Bungo Takada. He has one supporter, Kiyohara. He relies on him to mobilize his own personal supporters in Bungo Takada and to deliver the vote. Such a relationship allows Satō to view the campaign there as though he were an outsider to the whole process. Satō describes the campaign methods and organization in the city as rare (*mezurashii*), outrageous (*hidoi*), and old fashioned (*furui*), indicating not so much criticism as amazement and admiration for Kiyohara's ability to play the political game in Bungo Takada so successfully. Satō's own impression is that buying of votes is probably greater in Bungo Takada than anywhere else in the district. There is a story local Takada politicians tell of how on the last nights before an election you can know who have not been paid for their votes by driving around the city after eleven o'clock (when farmers are usually already asleep). Those who still had their lights on were waiting for a visit from a campaigner. One of Kiyohara's supporters, who owns a small dry-goods store, remarked that he can always tell the going rate for a vote in any election by the cost of the extra things his steady customers buy at election time.

Old-time politicians still talk of "reading the vote" (*hyō o*

5 See Chapter VI.

yomu), meaning to predict the vote. In the folklore of Japanese campaigning a candidate is able to work out on the abacus a few days before the election the vote he will receive with almost perfect accuracy. In Satō's case the only place where such "reading" of the vote was accurate was in Bungo Takada. In both the 1963 and the 1967 elections there was less than a seventy-one vote discrepancy between the vote read and the vote delivered. Because the vote can be accurately predicted, the campaign in Bungo Takada costs somewhat less per vote than in many other areas in the district. The major problem of strategy was deciding how many votes to aim for. Both Kiyohara and Satō agree that Satō could have gotten 4,000 votes in 1967 if he had asked Kiyohara to deliver that amount rather than the 3,500 votes he did ask for. The price per vote rises geometrically, however, as the vote goal is pushed higher, and, in the end, it was decided that the extra 500 votes could not be afforded.

Without Kiyohara's support Satō, in his own estimation, would have received the lowest vote among the Diet candidates in the city. With Kiyohara's support he received the highest. Whether the cause and effect relationship between Kiyohara's support and Satō's vote is as direct as both Satō and Kiyohara believe is not demonstrable. Satō is convinced of such a relationship, however, and this conviction reinforces his belief in the soundness of his basic campaign strategy: rely on powerful local politicians to deliver the vote in rural areas and concentrate campaign activities directed at the general electorate in the more urban sectors of the district.

Bungo Takada is one of the few areas in the district where Satō's campaign is run by a highly developed political machine. In most areas he had to rely on the weakest elements among local conservative politicians to organize his campaign.

The county of Higashi Kunisaki neighboring Bungo Takada is the stronghold of LDP incumbent Nishimura Eiichi. It consists of four towns and one village, the island of Himeshima where Nishimura was born. As was mentioned in the preceding chapter, Himeshima votes overwhelmingly for Nishimura, some 95 per cent of those voting writing the name of the famed native son on the ballot in the 1967 election. Within the county, Nishimura's vote declines the further one moves away from Himeshima, but for the county as a whole, with an electorate of 34,499 and a voting rate of 87.21 per cent in the 1967 election, Nishimura receives nearly one out of every two votes cast. Higashi Kunisaki is, in short, Nishimura territory, and it was within this framework of political realities that Satō had to develop his own organization of supporters.

The largest town in Higashi Kunisaki County is Kunisaki, with an electorate in 1967 of 13,746. In his Diet elections Nishimura has always received the top vote in Kunisaki. In the elections of both 1963 and 1967 he received 46 per cent of the total vote in the town.

In the elections of 1958, 1960, and 1963, Ayabe Kentarō received the second highest vote. In the 1963 election 22 per cent of those voting cast their ballots for Ayabe. In 1967 his vote decreased substantially, from 2,721 in the previous race to 2,038, 17 per cent of the 11,778 votes cast. Together, Nishimura and Ayabe have obtained between 63 and 74 per cent of the total vote in Kunisaki in the four general elections since 1958.

Socialist Komatsu Kan, until the 1967 election, had received the third highest vote in Kunisaki, and his percentage of the vote has increased steadily over the years. In 1958 he received 10 per cent of the vote; in 1960 this increased to 14 per cent; in 1963 he received 15 per cent; and in 1967 he replaced Ayabe as the second highest vote getter in the town, polling 20 per cent of the votes cast. Why Komatsu's vote should have increased so significantly in this heavily agricultural and politically conservative area is beyond the scope of this study. It is sufficient here to note that such socialist strength was not perceived by Satō as a challenge to his assumptions about the rural electorate. On the contrary, he attributes such success largely to Komatsu's ability to mobilize support in much the

[69]

same manner as the conservatives, relying on local people who could request support for Komatsu as a favor to themselves.[6]

Last among the contending candidates[7] in both the 1963 and 1967 elections in Kunisaki was Satō. In the 1963 election he received 1,571 votes. In 1967 this increased to 1,789, 15 per cent of the total vote. Satō's weakness in Kunisaki is representative of his general performance in the rural areas of the district. Bungo Takada represents the exception. It was one of only three areas in the rural sector of the district to give Satō the top vote. By contrast Satō placed fourth in eight towns.

In terms of its economy, Kunisaki is much like the other agricultural towns that spread out to the north and west of the main city of Beppu. Farming engages 63.2 per cent of its labor force. The secondary sector accounts for only 7.8 per cent, with the remaining labor force in the tertiary sector of the economy. In terms of campaign organization, Kunisaki is also representative of Satō's support through much of the district. Although each town has its unique characteristics, an understanding of the Kunisaki organization provides a general view of Satō's rural campaign organization.

Satō's *sekininsha* for Kunisaki was thirty-six-year-old Kiyonari Fumito.[8] Kiyonari was for several years active in the

[6] Komatsu himself, in discussing the question of his rural support, gives primary credit to the ability of members of the Japan Teachers' Union (*Nikkyōso*) to "gather" the vote of people in their communities. Next in importance, he believes, was his ability, because of fifteen years in the Diet, to gradually dissociate himself from the image of the Socialist Party as being "red." "I don't like the Socialist Party but Komatsu is a good guy" is Komatsu's own explanation of his increasing support among generally conservative farmers. He largely dismisses the idea that his vote represents any significant support for the Socialist Party or dissatisfaction with the LDP. Interview, July 7, 1967.

[7] Communist Party candidate Tsuru received 157 votes in 1967 in Kunisaki, and nowhere received enough votes to be considered a serious contender in the election.

[8] Kunisaki is an area in the district where I spent a considerable amount of time. In August of 1966 I lived for several days at the home of Kiyonari and met and interviewed most of Satō's supporters in Kunisaki. A close

national organization of local area youth groups (the Japan Seinendan Council) and served as a part-time secretary to Satō's faction boss, Murakami Isamu. In 1966 he was elected for the first time to the Kunisaki Town Assembly in a by-election called to fill a seat vacated by the death of one of the assemblymen. Like Satō and Kiyohara in Bungo Takada, Kiyonari was deeply indebted to and closely associated with LDP Chapter President Iwasaki, and was one of the leading young conservatives in the Second District opposed to the factions of Nishimura and Ayabe.

Kiyonari's position as *sekininsha* for Kunisaki was in itself an indication of Satō's weakness in this area. Where other candidates placed prefectural assemblymen, mayors, or other men politically powerful in this position, Satō had to rely on a young freshman of the Town Assembly.

As in all the other towns of the district, Satō's campaign organization in Kunisaki was a pyramid structure spreading out from the town to the "former village" to the *buraku*. Unlike the organization in Bungo Takada, there was no one in the Kunisaki organization with a developed political machine such as possessed by Kiyohara. Consequently, the organization was much more complex and much less integrated than the Bungo Takada one. Kiyonari could not simply delegate an already established machine to go to work for Satō. He had to actively recruit campaigners throughout the town. For both Kiyonari and Kiyohara the position of *sekininsha* in a Diet campaign was valuable precisely because of the opportunity it provided to expand one's own political power. Kiyohara, as we saw, used the 1963 Diet campaign as a means to activate his

---

friendship with Kiyonari greatly facilitated my research. Following the Diet election Kiyonari undertook to gather data at my request on the nature of the town organization. The discussion of the Kunisaki town organization is based on the taped interviews made while living in the town and the detailed information Kiyonari compiled and presented in written form under the title *"Shūin Senkyo Soshiki Taisei—Kunisaki Machi"* ("The Organizational Structure For the Lower House Election—Kunisaki Town").

machine to a degree not allowed by City Assembly elections. Kiyonari, similarly, was planning to challenge the two conservative prefectural assemblymen from the county (one a supporter of Nishimura and the other a backer of Ayabe) in the April 1967 local elections. Running Satō's campaign gave him the chance to expand his organized strength throughout the town in preparation for the Prefectural Assembly campaign.

In the Kunisaki organization three other Satō supporters in addition to Kiyonari were placed on the *sekininsha* level of organization. They were men of considerable stature in the community, men whose influence extended not only to their respective *buraku* or village but also through the entire town. Kiyonari's youth and lack of high position made it awkward, in terms of hierarchical sensibilities, to have them work under Kiyonari in order to campaign for Satō. Unlike the commanding position of Kiyohara in the Bungo Takada organization, Kiyonari's main function was to act as liaison between Satō's headquarters and the other major campaigners in the town. The other three men are fifty-three-year-old Takami, owner of a construction company, former supporter of Ayabe, and the only incumbent assemblyman in addition to Kiyonari among Satō's supporters; Ōta, Chairman of the Kunisaki Chapter of the Prefecture's Bamboo Association, sixty-two years old and formerly a Nishimura supporter; and Kuribayashi, Vice-President of the Ōita Prefecture Dental Association, fifty-six years old, and also a former Nishimura supporter. Ōta and Kuribayashi are responsible for the so-called horizontal strategy in Kunisaki town, organizing support for Satō not only in their own *buraku* but also among the members of their organizations throughout the town. Ōta and Kuribayashi as well as Kiyonari supported Satō in both 1963 and 1967. Takami first supported him in 1967. Thus at the top town level of the organization there are four *sekininsha,* with Kiyonari acting as liaison between the town and Satō's headquarters.

In 1954 six towns and villages amalgamated to form the town of Kunisaki. These six amalgamated areas form the next

[72]

level for organizing Satō's supporters. One of these "former villages" is that of Miura. Satō's campaign in this village is in the hands of two men. One, thirty-six years old, is a farmer and President of the local Tobacco Producers' Union. A former supporter of Nishimura, he switched support to Satō in 1963 at the request of his close friend and former classmate, Kiyonari. The other village manager is also a former Nishimura supporter, fifty-nine years old and a distant relative of Satō.

Miura Village contains seven *buraku*,[9] in each of which are one or more men responsible for organizing the campaign on this lowest level of organization. Five of the seven *buraku* have two such campaign managers each; one has three, and one has one manager. Seven of these fourteen men are in their thirties, three in their late twenties, one is fifty-five, and three are in their early sixties. The average age is forty-three. One man is a former supporter of Noyori, and all the others previously campaigned for Nishimura.

Each of these fourteen *buraku* campaign managers is responsible for recruiting a group of people in his *buraku* to

[9] There is a problem of classification regarding this bottom level of campaign organization. In the Tokugawa period the *buraku* were for the most part independent village units and were generally called villages (*mura*) by the inhabitants. In 1888 these *buraku* were combined into larger administrative units known as *mura* and the *buraku* became a subdistrict of the new administrative villages. In some cases these subunits (in Japanese referred to as *gyōseiku* or administrative wards) combined several small *buraku*. What are referred to as *buraku* in our discussion are in fact these administrative wards of the Meiji period. Though they contain up to eight separate agricultural settlements, they are generally regarded as single *buraku*. Therefore, in agreement with Fukutake Tadashi, the *buraku* as a physical settlement and basic social unit and the *buraku* as an administrative ward of the *mura* (which in Kunisaki are today the six amalgamated villages) are considered as being "by and large identical." Fukutake Tadashi, *Nihon Nōson Shakairon*, (Tokyo, 1966), pp. 95–98. This book has been translated into English by Ronald P. Dore as *Japanese Rural Society* (London, 1967). See pp. 87–89. For another useful discussion of the use of terms *buraku* and *mura*, see Kida Minoru, *Nippon Buraku* (Tokyo, 1967), esp. pp. 8–10.

campaign for Satō. There are nineteen men who actively campaigned (in addition to the town, village, and *buraku* managers), and fifteen of them are concentrated in four of the seven *buraku*. Their average age is thirty-nine. All are farmers. Only one had formerly actively campaigned for another candidate, Ayabe Kentarō in this case. Miura Village has 1,958 voters, and it is estimated by Kiyonari that 300 voted for Satō in the 1967 election.

It has been mentioned in the previous chapter that there is often a great imbalance in the strength of Satō's organized support among the "former villages" of a particular town. In Kunisaki this imbalance is quite evident. The village of Tomi, for instance, with its 2,544 voters, has practically no organization of Satō supporters. On the village level the campaign is conducted by a close friend and former classmate of Kiyonari named Imamura, a former supporter of Noyori, and by fifty-five-year-old Ichii, a friend of Imamura and Kiyonari who had not actively supported any candidate before Satō entered the race. Both men supported Satō for the first time in 1967. Tomi consists of eleven *buraku*. In six of these there are no organized Satō supporters. Imamura is the only active campaigner in his own *buraku,* and Ichii has the aid of two men, aged thirty-three and thirty-five, in his *buraku*. One other *buraku* has two campaigners aged fifty and sixty, both members of the Dental Association and brought into the campaign by Association Vice President Kuribayashi. The two remaining *buraku* have one campaigner each, farmers aged forty-one and forty-two. According to Kiyonari, both Nishimura and Ayabe's campaign managers for the county are from this village and there is no room for Satō to move in. In Kiyonari's estimation Satō received no more than 100 to 150 votes from Tomi's 2,544 voters in the 1967 election.

The village of Kamikunisaki with its 1,113 voters is the home of Takami Takashi, the only incumbent assemblyman beside Kiyonari to support Satō in the town. Takami ran for the first time for the Town Assembly in the April, 1963 election and won with the highest vote (741 votes) among the twenty-eight candidates. In the immediate Diet election thereafter, in November of the same year, he lent his support to Ayabe Kentarō. Takami developed a close friendship with Kiyonari in the Town Assembly; a friendship bolstered by their both being "anti-establishment" (that is, anti-Nishimura) freshmen assemblymen. Through Kiyonari, Takami was introduced to Satō. The two men met several times, and at a dinner in Beppu in September of 1966, hosted by Satō with Kiyonari, Takami and six of Takami's staff attending, Takami's support for Satō in the coming election was obtained.

In the previous chapter it was mentioned that local politicians generally attempt to keep the Diet candidate ignorant of their own support base and away from their constituencies in the hope of assuring their continued value to the campaign. In Bungo Takada Kiyohara was typical of this type of strategy. When asked if Satō had come to the city to give speeches his response was "What for? There's no need for him to come. I'm here." Takami's approach was different. As a first-term member of the Assembly, not yet in control of a machine like Kiyohara's, more was to be gained than lost by having a Diet candidate come to meet his constituents. The meeting would serve as valuable publicity for the local politician. People who had not supported Takami would come to a meeting in which Satō was to speak simply because of the change in pace from routine farm life this occasion represented. Takami would gain exposure to voters he had not been able to attract before—and all at the financial expense of Satō. Takami consequently urged Satō to come to Kamikunisaki. On two occasions in the months preceding the election Satō spoke at parties in the village arranged by the assemblyman.

Takami is listed on the organizational charts as one of the town *sekininsha* for Satō's campaign, and there are five other campaign managers on the Kamikunisaki "former village" level. Four of the five had campaigned for Kiyonari in his

Assembly election and were brought into Satō's organization mainly through this connection. The fifth is a relative of Satō. Two were formerly supporters of Ayabe and two of Nishimura and one had not worked on behalf of any other candidate before Satō entered the race. Three of the five supported Satō for the first time in 1967. Two are in their thirties, two in their forties, and one is sixty years old. There average age is forty-six.

Kamikunisaki Village has three *buraku*. There are one or more campaign managers in each of these responsible to one of the campaign managers on the "former village" level. In Naributsu *buraku* there are four men who lead the *buraku* organization, the most important being a sixty-five-year-old former Nishimura supporter and mayor of Kamikunisaki Village before it amalgamated. There is one other former Nishimura supporter and the other two men were formerly campaigners for Ayabe. Under these men is a group of eleven *buraku* campaigners. The eldest is eighty and President of the elderly people's club and the youngest is twenty-six and President of the local youth club. Three are women, two of whom have served as women's club President. The average age of the campaigners is forty-four.

The *buraku* of Michi has two campaign managers, one a sixty-year-old former supporter of Nishimura and the other thirty-nine years old and a former campaigner for Ayabe. Below these two men on the organizational chart are eight *buraku* campaigners, all male and, excepting an eighty-year-old elderly people's club President, with an average age of thirty-four.

It is a common practice in rural areas in Japan for a *buraku* or a couple of *buraku* to put forth one candidate for the local Assembly as the *buraku* representative. The small competition rate in local Assembly election is due to this practice of having *buraku* "delegates" chosen by a "*buraku* recommendation" (*buraku suisen*) before the election is held. The data in Table 5 indicate the low competition rate for election to Second District town and village Assemblies in the April 1967 elections. In

[76]

the thirteen towns and villages that held elections at that time, 266 candidates vied for 215 seats, a ratio of 1.24 candidates to each seat.

Town Assemblyman Takami is the "delegate" of Nakada *buraku* in Kamikunisaki Village. Takami lives in Nakada and his organized supporters are in this *buraku*. Unlike Kiyohara, whose political influence spreads throughout the city of Bungo Takada, Takami's influence is largely confined to Nakada. Here it is overwhelming. Satō's support organization in the *buraku* is the organization of Takami.

Kamikunisaki Village provided Satō with his greatest support in the town. In addition to the support given by Takami,

Table 5

Competition Rate in Town and Village Assembly Elections

Town or village	Number of seats	Number of candidates
Himeshima	12	13
Kunisaki	22	28
Musashi	16	17
Aki	20	24
Hiji	22	32
Yamaga	20	28
Ōta	12	15
Matama	16	18
Kagachi	14	16
Sanko	16	21
Honyabakei	16	17
Yabakei	15	20
Yamaguni	14	17
Total	215	266
Ratio	1	1.24

Data obtained from: Ōita Ken Senkyo Kanri Iinkai, *Senkyo No Kiroku, Ōita Kengikai Giin Senkyo,* April 15, 1967 election, *Shi-chō-son Gikai Giin Senkyo,* April 28, 1967 (Ōita, 1967).

it was in this village that Satō met with the electorate at Takami's request, one purpose being the expansion of Takami's influence into the other two *buraku* of the village. The combination of assemblyman support and direct exposure to the electorate gave Satō an estimated 300 votes in the 1967 election, nearly one-third of the total votes cast in the village, assuming that 87 per cent (the voting rate in the town as a whole) of the village's 1,113 voters went to the polls.

The village of Toyosaki, with an electorate of 1,223, is the only one of the six villages of the town in which Satō has the active support of a former campaigner for socialist Komatsu Kan. A friend of Kiyonari and a self-proclaimed liberal conservative who supported Komatsu because of the lack of a young and modern conservative candidate, forty-year-old Yoshitake switched support to Satō at the time of the 1963 election. Yoshitake was a farmer and seller of fertilizer rather than a labor union member, and his support meant little in providing an inroad to socialist supporters. Along with Yoshitake are three other managers at the village level, one former Ayabe and two former Nishimura supporters.

Toyosaki village consists of four *buraku*. There is at least one Satō campaign manager in each of them and a total of nine men on this level of organization. Five are former Nishimura supporters, four formerly worked for Ayabe, and their average age is forty.

The *buraku* campaigners consist of thirty-one people, including two women. Supporters range in age from twenty-nine to sixty-three, with the average age being thirty-nine. Nineteen were former campaigners for Nishimura, seven for Ayabe, and two for Komatsu. Three had not been involved in another candidate's campaign.

Satō's vote in this village is estimated at 250, or nearly 25 per cent of the total estimated vote. Kiyonari's explanation for Sato's relative strength here is an interesting one: "Satō has benefited by the reaction of many people to the growth of bossism (*bosuka*) among Nishimura's managers in the village." Satō was able to gain considerable support because of the voters wanting to put the bosses "in their place" by not voting for Nishimura.[10]

One of the six areas that amalgamated to form the present-day town of Kunisaki was the area that before amalgamation was called Kunisaki Town. This is the largest of the six amalgamated areas and accounts for nearly half of the electorate with its 5,926 voters. It is the urban nucleus of the town of Kunisaki and is an area where Satō has few active supporters. Satō's campaign managers for the area include two men mentioned at the beginning of the discussion, the representatives of the bamboo and dental associations. Three others are the owner of a gasoline station, the owner of a newspaper delivery service, and one of his workers. Four of the five formerly supported Nishimura and campaigned for Satō in both 1963 and 1967. The fifth supported Satō for the first time in 1967 and was formerly a campaigner for Ayabe.

The former town consists of four administrative subdivisions, and there are nine men at this level of the organization. Six were formerly Nishimura and three Ayabe supporters. They are all farmers, none hold elective office of any kind, and their average age is forty-five.

Under these managers are a group of forty-one campaigners. The number includes four women. The average age is forty-two. Thirteen had formerly campaigned for Nishimura and one had supported Ayabe. The rest had not actively taken part in the Diet campaign before supporting Satō. Occupationally, twenty-eight are farmers, two are dentists, seven retail merchants, two fishermen, one a producer of bamboo, and another in the construction business.

These fifty-five people are spread out very thinly among the area's nearly 6,000 voters and, with 70 per cent of their number being farmers, are particularly weak among the salaried and nonagricultural class in this, the center of town and heart of

10 Kiyonari, "*Shūin Senkyo Soshiki Taisei—Kunisaki Machi.*"

its limited secondary and tertiary sectors of the economy. Traditionally conservative party-supporting merchants, to the extent that they are organized, are almost entirely in support of Nishimura. The small number of unionized laborers are mobilized on behalf of the campaign of Komatsu. The consequence is that Satō receives exceedingly little support. Kiyonari estimates Satō's vote among the 6,000 voters in the area at no more than 550.

The sixth village is that of Asahi, the home of Kiyonari and the smallest of the amalgamated areas, with an electorate of 1,036. There are two campaign managers on the village level and twenty campaigners in the village's three *buraku*. All of these twenty men and two women supporters are supporters of Satō by way of being supporters of Kiyonari. All are farmers. The two women are fifty-four and fifty-five years old, and the average age of the men is thirty-six, precisely the same age as Kiyonari. This statistic is not coincidental. It emphasizes the nature of Satō's Asahi village support as being the friends and supporters of Kiyonari. Fourteen of the campaigners formerly worked for Nishimura's campaign, two for Ayabe, and the remaining seven had not campaigned for any other candidate. Nishimura is considered to have the support of the older voters and Satō's support is centered around a group of young men aligned with Kiyonari. An estimated 250 Asahi voters, or approximately 27 per cent of the estimated number of votes cast, went to Satō in the 1967 election.

Several aspects of Satō's Kunisaki campaign organization are of relevance to the general issue of campaign strategy in rural areas. For one thing the organization of the campaign reflects the difficulty of a new LDP candidate moving into an area dominated by the supporters of an incumbent candidate of the party. Kiyonari, when asked to note down what he considered to be important features of Satō's campaign in Kunisaki, wrote the following as being of the most significance. "Because the area is Nishimura's homeground as well as a base of support for Ayabe, Satō supporters are treated as heretics in spite of Satō's endorsement by the party. Because of this there are extremely few supporters holding public office. There are few supporters who are long-time members of the [conservative] party."[11] The lack of elected public officials among Satō's supporters is striking. Kiyonari and Takami were the only campaigners to hold public office. Satō had no support among former or incumbent assemblymen except for these two, no support among local LDP officials, nor among officers of the agricultural cooperatives in this predominantly agricultural area. There are several reasons for this absence of officials from the campaign. When Satō entered the race most of the officials were already associated with Nishimura or Ayabe, and there was little Satō could offer to lure them into his own camp. Furthermore, those officials who wanted to support Satō could be, and in several cases clearly were, inhibited or stopped from doing so by the enormous pressures Nishimura supporters could bring to bear on these isolated mavericks.

The data concerning Satō's campaign organization in Kunisaki illustrate the extent to which the struggle for organized support is an intraparty struggle among the LDP candidates. The fight for the support of elected officials was but one element in this larger struggle. For the 118 people who had switched support from another candidate to campaign for Satō, 84 had formerly supported Nishimura, 29 Ayabe, 2 Noyori, and 3 had supported Komatsu. In other words, only 3 of 118 supporters had formerly campaigned for a progressive party candidate.

There is a high correlation between former Nishimura supporters and those who campaigned for Satō in both 1963 and 1967 and Ayabe supporters and those who first joined the Satō campaign in 1967. Satō and Nishimura were both members, as has been discussed, of the Iwasaki led Liberal Party

[11] Kiyonari, "*Shūin Senkyo Soshiki Taisei—Kunisaki Machi.*"

before the conservative merger. When Satō entered the 1963 race most of those who supported him were former Liberal Party members closely associated with Iwasaki and supporting Nishimura in the Diet as the Liberal Party candidate. Among Liberal Party Nishimura supporters, those who could be brought over to support Satō were recruited in 1963. Satō's town *sekininsha* in Kunisaki in the 1963 election, Kiyonari, Kuribayashi, and Ōta, had all been Nishimura supporters before Satō entered the race. Because the campaign organization is built up at the lower levels by those higher in the local organization, it was to be expected that in 1963 the great majority of Satō supporters recruited by his three top *sekininsha* in Kunisaki should also have been former Nishimura supporters. The case of Ayabe's supporters is, however, significantly different. Ayabe had his support centered around members of the former Democratic Party, and there was little opportunity for Iwaskai to bring these men into Satō's campaign or for Satō to appeal directly to them. Satō's own ties during the years he spent in the Prefectural Assembly were largely with former Liberal Party members. Very few of Satō's supporters in Kunisaki in 1963 were brought over from the Ayabe camp. By 1967 the situation was significantly changed. There was a general feeling that Ayabe had had his day and some people, like assemblyman Takami, who had supported Ayabe in 1963, decided to jump off what they saw as a rapidly sinking ship and support another candidate. Interestingly, in Kunisaki Satō was in a good position to benefit from this movement of support away from Ayabe. Those people who had supported Ayabe in this Nishimura stronghold had become what can be called anti-establishment in that they were opposed to the ruling faction that backed Nishimura. Their enemies were Nishimura supporters and their change of support, accordingly, largely went to Satō by virtue of his being the other anti-establishment LDP candidate.

An analysis of the reasons why the men in Sato's organization decided to support him discloses the highly indirect nature

[82]

of his support on the village and *buraku* levels. Connections with other men in the organization, particularly with Kiyonari, resulted in their support for Satō. When asked why they were campaigning for Satō the response of nearly everyone invariably involved a relationship with another of the men in the organization: because he was a classmate of Kiyonari or a member of the Takami group or because his friend Kuribayashi had asked him to take part. The reasons given for the support of sixteen "former-village" level campaign managers divided as follows: five because they were close friends of Kiyonari; two because they were Kiyonari's classmates; two because they had supported Kiyonari in the Town Assembly election; one (Matsumoto) because he is a relative of Satō and a friend of Kiyonari; two others because they were asked to do so by Matsumoto; two more because they were asked to do so by one of the men who had been recruited by Matsumoto; one who was related to one of Satō's uncles and was asked to campaign by him; and one because of the help Satō had given him with a particular business problem when Satō was still in the Prefectural Assembly.

When one brings this down to the *buraku* level the reasons for people joining the campaign become even more remote from the candidate. One example will suffice. One of the campaign managers for the "former town" of Kunisaki was a thirty-six-year-old former classmate of Kiyonari named Hatano. He attributed his support for Satō to being Kiyonari's classmate and a member of the Prefectural Table Tennis Association, of which Satō was President. In the *buraku* where he lives there were seven main campaigners. The reasons for their participation in the campaign were as follows: one because he was a classmate of Hatano and Kiyonari; one because he was a close friend of another campaign manager in the former town; one for having graduated the same middle school as Satō; and four because of their membership in the local *buraku* Volunteer Fire Brigade, of which Hatano was chief (*danchō*).

In spite of overwhelming evidence of the indirect relationship between the Diet candidate and his local campaigners, there is an intriguing aspect to Satō's organizational support on the *buraku* level that cautions against overemphasizing the lack of direct ties between candidate and supporter. On the town and village manager levels, almost all of Satō's supporters previously campaigned for other candidates. On the level of *buraku* campaigners, however, few had previously taken an active part in another candidate's campaign. One possible explanation is that when asked by a man higher in the pyramid to support Nishimura or Ayabe, they complied with their vote. But when asked by the same man to support Satō they complied with their active support. There is a subtle fugue being played between personal relationships on the local level and the appeal of individual candidates.

The data also indicate that Satō's supporters were chiefly middle-aged men. One hundred fifty-five of the 209 supporters were in the 30- to 49-year-old age bracket. There were eleven supporters in their twenties and thirteen past sixty. Thirty supporters were in their fifties. The average age of the supporters was forty-three, and eleven were women. The data for Kunisaki support a general impression in the district as a whole that the age of the candidate's support group correlated closely with the age of the candidate. The data for Kunisaki lend support to the results of an NHK public opinion survey which indicated that men between the ages of 30–49 favored Satō.[12]

In terms of occupation the overwhelming majority of Satō's supporters were farmers. Although farmers account for 63.2 per cent of Kunisaki's labor force, they made up 81 per cent of Satō's organized supporters (170 out of 209 campaigners). Small retail and wholesale merchants, another traditional source of conservative support, accounted for sixteen of the

12 The results of an unpublished NHK public opinion poll were made available to the author by Kudō Takashi, editorial writer for the NHK Ōita Broadcasting System.

remaining thirty-nine supporters. Members of the Dental and Bamboo associations, the two most important groups among those voluntary associations supporting Sato,[13] accounted for twelve supporters (five dentists and seven bamboo growers). The remaining eleven included two fishermen, four people in the construction business, two owners of manufacturing enterprises (one of house furniture, the other of sake), the wife of a priest, a village postmaster, and a local town office official. Satō had no organized support among salaried workers, unionized or not. Although he received the official recommendation of various occupational groups,[14] no members of these groups were found among his supporters except the above-mentioned bamboo growers and dentists.

To Satō the way to mobilize the support of the rural electorate was to rely on locally powerful politicians to gather and deliver the votes. Satō's inability to gain the support of this element in Kunisaki and in most other areas did not cause him to consider alternative strategies for obtaining votes in such places. It forced him instead to put his major effort into gaining the support of the electorate living in the more urban sectors of the district. For Satō the rural areas were made up of voters largely "hard" for the incumbent candidates. In order to win he would have to maximize his support in other areas and particularly in his hometown—the resort city of Beppu.

[13] See Chapter VII.
[14] *Ibid.*

Sato's Staff at Campaign Headquarters

IV

Campaign Organization in Beppu: Utilizing the Neighborhood Associations

AN LDP DIET MEMBER often has support in his district concentrated in a limited geographical area of which his home town is the center. In Ōita's Second District this division of conservative strength is striking. Figure 1 shows the percentage of the vote received by Nishimura, Noyori, and Ayabe in each city and county in the 1963 election. Around 60 per cent of the total vote of each candidate was obtained in areas surrounding his home town, and there is little overlap in areas of major support. Noyori, for example, received 66 per cent of his total vote from his home town city of Nakatsu and the adjacent counties of Shimoge and Usa while Nishimura received 59 per cent of his vote from the counties of Higashi and Nishi Kunisaki and Usa and the city of Bungo Takada. The support of all three candidates overlaps in Usa mainly because there was no candidate from the county in the race. Even within the counties there is a tendency for the vote to decrease the further the town from the candidate's native town or village. In Higashi Kunisaki County, for instance, Nishimura in 1963 obtained 95 per cent of the votes of Himeshima. In the town nearest to Himeshima he received 64 per cent of the vote. This decreased to 46 per cent in the next town, 44 per cent in the following one, and 41 per cent in the town furthest from his birthplace. When data for all candidates are combined this concentration of support is placed in striking relief. For purposes of contrast, Figure 2 combines Satō's vote

[87]

Figure 1

Geographical Concentration of Support of
Noyori, Ayabe and Nishimura[a]

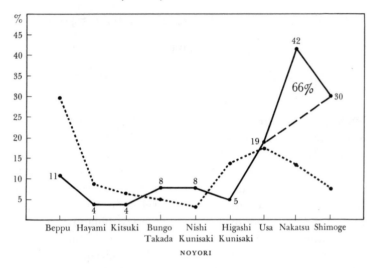

1a

in the 1967 election with the votes of the other three conservatives in the 1963 election.

There are several reasons for conservative politicians having a high concentration of votes in narrow geographical areas. For one thing, in rural areas particularly, a great deal of pride is taken in the "local boy who made good," and there is a strong feeling that one should vote for the local candidate precisely because he is a native son. Furthermore, in an electoral system where the voter is faced with several candidates from the-same party, the location of the homes or birthplaces

[a] Continuous line indicates percentage of vote in each city and county received by candidate. Area marked by dotted line is the percentage of the candidate's total vote received in that area. Dotted line indicates the percentage of the district's electorate in each area.

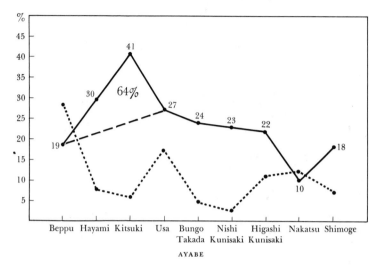

AYABE

1b

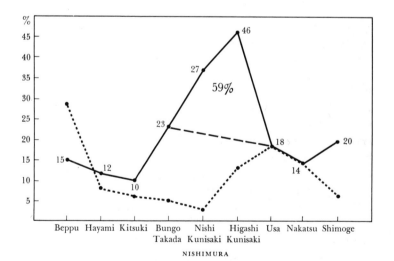

NISHIMURA

1C

Figure 2

*Distribution of Primary Support for the
Four L D P Candidates*

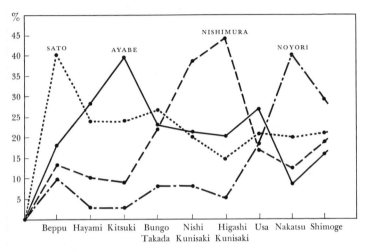

of the candidates become meaningful criteria for choosing among them. It seems "natural" if you are going to vote for an LDP candidate to vote for the one who is from the same area as you. Third, the use of separate area organizations in the several towns and villages to deliver the vote through a web of interpersonal ties leads conservative politicians to concentrate their activities in their home areas because of the already existing ties they can build upon. Thus these areas see the greatest effort to get out the vote for the candidate. A fourth reason is that the concentration of support reflects a strong strain of localism in the Japanese electorate.

There is a variety of data to show that Japanese on the whole show a greater concern about local than national elections, a consequence probably both of a greater interest in local problems and, in the rural areas, "the strong village solidarity and the idea that voting is regarded as an obligation to the com-

Figure 3

Popular Vote in Elections in Ōita Prefecture in 1963

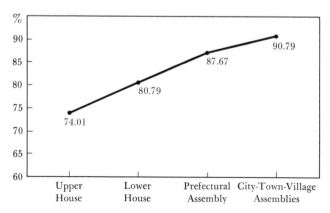

munity."[1] Figure 3 indicates the differences in voting rates in national and local elections in Ōita Prefecture in 1963.

More relevant than voting rates to the question of localism is the literature of survey data, which suggests that large numbers of Japanese consider the "benefit of their locality" (*jimoto rieki*) the major consideration in choosing the Diet candidate they vote for. A poll conducted in 1965 in Satō's home city of Beppu asked voters to choose from a list the one reason they felt most important in deciding for whom they voted in elections. (See Table 6. The type of election was not specified.) The largest single group (27.3 per cent) chose as the most important reason "Because he is a person who will work for the development of the city." A significantly higher proportion of supporters of the LDP and supporters of no party (which usually indicates supporters of LDP candidates) chose this reason than did supporters of progressive parties.

[1] Jōji Watanuki, "Patterns of Politics in Present Day Japan," in *Party Systems and Voter Alignments, Cross-National Perspectives,* eds. Seymour M. Lipset and Stein Rokkan (New York, 1967), p. 462.

Table 6

Reasons Cited Most Important by the Beppu Electorate in Deciding Which Candidate to Vote for

	Total (N-433)	Conservative Party supporters (N-130)	Support no party (N-215)	Progres- sive Party supporters (N-56)	Won't say which party they support (N-32)
A	0.7%	0.8%	0.9%	0.0%	3.1%
B	1.8	3.1	1.9	0.0	0.0
C	0.9	0.0	0.5	1.8	6.3
D	20.4	32.3	8.4	35.7	28.1
E	2.1	1.5	1.9	3.6	3.1
F	4.6	2.3	6.6	3.6	3.1
G	27.3	21.5	34.4	14.3	21.9
H	19.2	17.7	22.8	8.9	18.8
I	19.2	11.5	9.3	5.4	6.3
J	0.0	0.0	0.0	0.0	0.0
K	4.6	1.5	3.3	16.1	6.3
L	1.2	0.8	1.4	0.0	3.1
M	6.9	6.7	7.4	8.9	0.0
N	0.7	0.0	0.9	1.8	0.0

Code:

A—Because he is a relative or friend
B—Because he has the recommendation of my *buraku* (*buraku suisen*)
C—Because he has a high education
D—Because I support his party
E—Because he often does favors for me
F—Because everyone says he is a good person
G—Because he is a person who will work for the development of the city
H—Because he has an attractive personality
I—Because he has ability
J—Because he is of a good family
K—Because he is a representative of my place of business or my occupation
L—Because I was asked to by a powerful person (*yūryokusha*) or by a friend
M—Miscellaneous
N—No Answer

Source: Ōita Ken Senkyo Kanri Iinkai, *Moderu Chiku Ni Okeru Akaruku Tadashii Senkyo Undō No Jittai—Yōron Chōsa No Gaiyō* (Oita, March 1965), pp. 53-55.

In another poll Beppu voters were asked whether they were mainly interested in city, prefectural, or national politics. Fifty-five per cent said city politics were the most important. When asked what was the second most important to them the largest number (49.6 per cent) said prefectural politics. Asked which of the three was of least concern, 64.9 per cent indicated national politics.[2]

In a nationwide poll conducted after the 1967 election voters were asked whether they chose the candidate they voted for chiefly because of what he could do for their home area or for their particular occupation or mainly because of what he could do for the entire nation. Unfortunately for our purposes, the poll combines both occupational and local interests. Nonetheless, the responses are worth considering (see Table 7). In spite of the fact that the question was loaded (it strongly hinted that in a national election the good of the entire nation is the "right" answer), some 30.4 per cent of the sample considered local or occupational interests more important than national concerns. A group comprising 40.9 per cent said national concerns were paramount. Another 18.5 per cent said both were important, and when asked to make a choice the majority of these said non-national concerns were most crucial. Among those who voted for LDP candidates, 36 per cent thought local or occupational issues most important, while only 24.4 per cent of those who voted for the opposition parties thought so. While those in large metropolitan cities expressed an overriding concern with national issues (63.6 per cent), a much smaller percentage of people in small and medium-sized cities (39.5 per cent) and in rural areas (31.0 per cent) were

[2] Complete responses were as follows: most important: city politics—55%, national politics—25.4%, prefectural politics—4.4%, other—15.2%; second most important: prefectural politics—64.9%, city politics—10.2%, national politics—9.7%, other—15.2%; third most important: national politics—49.6%, city politics—19.6%, prefectural politics—15.5%, other—15.3%. Ōita Ken Senkyo Kanri Iinkai, Ōita Ken Akaruku Tadashii Senkyo Suishin Kyōgikai, *Moderu Chiku Ni Okeru Akaruku Tadashii Senkyo Undō No Jittai—Yōron Chōsa No Gaiyō* (Ōita, March 1965), p. 63.

Table 7

Influence of National, Local and Occupational Concerns on Voting in Diet Elections

"When you voted for a candidate in this past election, were you mainly concerned with choosing a candidate who would work hard for the benefit of your local area or for the benefit of people who work in the same occupation as you, or were you mainly concerned with choosing the candidate who would work hard for the benefit . . . of the entire nation of Japan?"

For those who answer "both": "If you have to choose between them, which one is most important?"

| | A | B | Consider Both | | | |
			C	D	E	F
TOTAL (N = 2163)	30.4	40.9	9.4	6.8	2.3	10.2
7 metropolitan cities	17.1	63.6	4.6	6.3	1.1	7.3
small & medium size cities	31.1	39.5	10.0	7.8	1.8	9.8
towns and villages	36.1	31.0	11.1	5.6	3.7	12.4
AGE						
20–29	33.9	38.3	9.4	6.8	2.9	8.7
30–39	29.2	43.4	10.1	6.6	2.2	8.6
40–49	30.6	43.9	8.8	7.0	1.2	8.4
50–59	26.5	42.4	11.4	7.1	2.3	10.4
60–over	32.6	33.4	7.0	6.5	3.5	17.0
EDUCATION						
primary	38.6	25.6	7.3	3.2	2.2	23.1
old high primary; new junior high	34.3	35.7	10.9	7.5	1.8	9.8
old middle; new high school	24.1	50.1	9.1	7.6	2.6	6.4
old higher & technical; new univ.	16.4	63.2	5.3	6.6	4.6	3.9
OCCUPATION						
self employed:						
agriculture; forestry; fishing	45.6	24.2	15.8	2.8	3.7	7.9
merchant, service trades	28.3	39.4	11.8	10.2	3.1	7.1
other self employment	20.0	50.0	16.7	6.7	3.3	3.3
employed:						
total	25.9	51.8	8.6	6.9	1.4	5.4
administrators, managers	10.0	70.0	10.0	7.5	—	2.5
technical; white collar	22.0	58.5	8.3	6.5	1.4	3.2
laborers	31.4	43.4	8.7	7.1	1.6	7.8

[94]

	A	B	Consider Both C	D	E	F
family workers:						
agriculture; forestry; fishing	41.8	20.6	9.8	5.7	2.1	20.1
merchant; service, others	33.0	36.4	6.8	4.5	4.5	14.8
housewives	26.8	43.4	8.0	8.4	1.7	11.7
others, unemployed	30.2	39.6	5.5	3.8	3.3	17.6
POLITICAL PARTY						
LDP	36.0	33.7	10.5	7.2	2.9	9.6
J S P–D S P–J C P–Kōmeitō	24.4	52.5	8.7	6.1	1.3	7.1
JSP	26.4	49.6	8.8	6.7	1.5	7.0
DSP	19.1	55.9	9.6	7.4	1.5	6.6
JCP	12.5	75.0	9.4	—	—	3.1
Kōmeitō	21.7	60.9	5.8	1.4	—	10.1
Independent & Minor Parties	26.9	34.6	15.4	11.5	—	11.5
Others	—	60.0	20.0	—	—	20.0
Don't Know	26.5	30.5	5.5	7.0	4.0	26.5

Code:
A—considered the benefit of my locality or occupation
B—considered the benefit of the entire nation
C—If I must choose I considered the benefit of locality or occupation
D—If I must choose I considered the benefit of the nation
E—If I must choose I don't know
F—Don't know
Source: Kōmei Senkyo Renmei, *Shūgiin Giin Sōsenkyo No Jittai,* (Tokyo, March 1967), pp. 18–19.

concerned with such issues. Among occupational groups farmers were the most influenced by non-national issues, some 46 per cent saying their vote was determined by local or occupational concerns. In contrast, only 24 per cent believed national interests determined their vote.

The dominant position of Satō's conservative opponents in separate areas of the district and the tendency of the electorate to favor local candidates and be concerned with local issues were two of the most important factors in determining Satō's campaign strategy. Both Nishimura and Ayabe had strong support in "hard vote" rural areas and there was little Satō could do to move in on that support. To win the election he would have to maximize his support in those areas outside the strongholds of the incumbents. Of these the most populous were the two largest cities in the district, Beppu and Nakatsu.

Nakatsu, with a population of 58,371, is famous as the childhood home of Fukuzawa Yukichi.[3] When Fukuzawa left Nakatsu in 1854 it was a rural castle town that watched over endless acres of lush forest to the west and rice paddies to the east and south stretching all the way down the Tokugawa fief of Bungo to the area of hot springs that was later to be known as Beppu. One hundred years later, Nakatsu was the second largest city in the district, fourth largest among the Prefecture's ten cities, and sixth among the cities of Ōita Prefecture in productive income.[4] The primary sector of its economy accounts for somewhat less than a third of its labor force (29 per cent). Its secondary sector, largely engaged in the manufacture of textiles and lumber, accounts for almost one-quarter (24 per cent), with the rest of its labor force in the tertiary sector. But what Fukuzawa referred to as a "secluded town on the coast of Kyūshū"[5] was in the 1960s as secluded in a political sense as it had been in the waning years of the Tokugawa Shogunate. For as long as most people care to remember the politics of Nakatsu had been controlled by Noyori Hideichi, who was born in Nakatsu when Fukuzawa was forty-eight years old. In the postwar Diet elections, Noyori

[3] Fukuzawa, much to the dismay of Nakatsu residents, attributed the journey to Nagasaki which embarked him on a career that was to make him one of the most famous personalities of the Meiji period as being due to "nothing more than to get away from Nakatsu." Fukuzawa Yukichi, *The Autobiography of Fukuzawa Yukichi,* trans. Eiichi Kiyooka (Tokyo, 1960), p. 22

[4] Ōita Ken, *Chiiki Betsu Kenmin Shotoku (Seisan Shotoku)* (Ōita, 1967).

[5] Fukuzawa, p. 2.

always received the highest vote in the city, obtaining nearly one of every two votes cast by the city's electorate. In his last unsuccessful Diet campaign in 1963 he received 12,261 of the 29,305 votes cast in Nakatsu.

With his retirement following that election, all the candidates rushed in to try to obtain as large a share as possible of the vote of the 40 per cent of the Nakatsu electorate that had voted for Noyori in 1963. Satō's own hopes for Nakatsu were fairly conservative. In 1963 he received 3,000 votes in the city. In the 1967 election he aimed at doing a little better than doubling that vote, hoping to obtain between 6,500 and 7,000 votes. Nakatsu is at the other end of the district from Satō's home town of Beppu and he was little known among the city's inhabitants. Most of the local political leaders who had supported Noyori went over to Ayabe and Nishimura. Satō visited the city several times a month to meet with his supporters, discuss the campaign, and try to attract new support. The 25 per cent of the Nakatsu vote aimed for was calculated to provide 10 per cent of his total vote. Another 40 per cent, in Satō's strategy, had to be obtained from his *jimoto,* his own home area, the city of Beppu.

In 1889, with the promulgation of the city-town-village system, a small area of gushing mineral springs and hot sands that stretch out into the Inland Sea on the northeastern tip of Kyūshū Island became the village of Beppu. Five years later its status was changed to that of a town. In 1907 occurred the first amalgamation between Beppu and a neighboring village, and in 1924 Beppu city was created. Further amalgamations with neighboring towns and villages in 1935 and 1936 brought Beppu to its present size of 136.48 square kilometers. In the first national census in 1920 Beppu was recorded to have 6,339 households and a population of 28,647 people. By 1935 the population had risen past 62,000. The city was spared bombing during World War II and its population in the period from 1940 to 1947 jumped from 67,000 to 97,000. All the cities, towns, and villages in rural Ōita Prefecture witnessed a population increase in this period,[6] but only in Beppu and Ōita city did the population continue to rise after the postwar readjustment. With a population of 121,359 in 1966, Beppu is the home of one out of every four people in the district and of 28 per cent of the district's electorate.

Several characteristics of Beppu's population set the city apart from all other areas of the district. One characteristic, indicated above, is Beppu's increasing population. In twenty years, from 1947 to 1967, the population of the city increased by nearly 30,000. The other twenty-three cities, towns, and villages of the district have all been experiencing rapid population decline at least since 1955. A second characteristic of the population is a relatively large number of youth. Because it is one of Kyūshū's major resort areas, Beppu attracts young people from the surrounding rural areas. Compared to the 9,463 people between the ages of ten and fourteen, there are 13,331 people in the fifteen to nineteen-year-old age group.[7] Nakatsu is the only other area in the district to show this demographic pattern.[8] The other two cities and the five counties of the district are all experiencing population decline rather than increase in the fifteen to nineteen-year-old age group. Another population characteristic of note is the large female population. Beppu has 67,781 women and 53,578 men. The city's ratio of 80.3 males per 100 females is the lowest in the Prefecture.

Economically, Beppu is overwhelmingly service-trade oriented.[9] Most of the city's workers engage in occupations that cater to the seven to eight million people who visit the city annually.

[6] Between 1940 and 1950 the prefecture's population rose from 972,975 to 1,222,999. Data on population trends are taken from Ōita Ken, *Kokusei Chōsa Ni Yoru Shi-chō-son Betsu Jinkō No Trend* (Ōita, 1965).

[7] Ōita Ken, *Shōwa 40 nen Kokusei Chōsa, Ōita Ken Shūkei Kekka Hyō* (Ōita, 1965).

[8] 6,004 in the 10 to 14 group; 7,219 in the 15 to 19 group.

[9] Data concerning Beppu's economy obtained from Beppu Shiyakusho Kikakushitsu, *Beppu-shi Tōkeisho* (Beppu, 1967).

Table 8

Decrease in Farm Households in Beppu

	Number of farm households 1960	Number of farm households 1965	Decrease	Rate of decrease
Beppu	2,117	1,750	367	17.3%
Ōita Pref.	128,683	117,939	10,744	8.3
Counties	79,906	73,804	6,102	7.6
Cities	48,777	44,135	4,642	9.5
Ōita City	4,540	3,800	261	5.7

The primary sector of Beppu's economy engages 7.2 per cent of the city's working population of 56,940 persons fifteen years old and over. Fewer people are involved in the production of primary goods in Beppu's economy than in the economies of any of the other cities and counties of the district or Prefecture.[10] The rate of decrease of farm households in Beppu, as the above chart indicates, is the highest in the Prefecture. This, is should be noted, indicates a decrease of households, not population. Population decrease is much greater in the rural areas but decrease in houses tends to be low because the family maintains the farm while some of its members leave to work in the cities.[11] In a sense decrease of farm households is a better index of urbanization than decrease of farm population because giving up the house indicates a decision to permanently give up farming as a livelihood. While some of the outlying parts of Beppu are agricultural, the city is a nonrural, nonagricultural area.

[10] Sorifu Tōkeikyoku, *Ōita Ken No Jinkō* (Tokyo, 1967).

[11] This is a pattern that has led to the coining of the phrase the "three chan" ("*sanchan*"). The farm is run by the grandfather (*ojiichan*), grandmother (*obaachan*), and the young wife (*Okaachan*), while her husband is away working in the city.

Table 9

Party Support of Voters in 1967 Diet Election

"What party does the person you voted for [in the 1967 general elections] belong to?"

	LDP	JSP	DSP	JCP	Kōmeitō	Ind. & minor	Others	Don't know
TOTAL	50.0	28.3	6.3	1.5	3.2	1.2	0.2	9.2
7 metropolitan cities	36.1	29.3	12.8	4.6	7.6	0.5	0.5	8.4
small & medium size cities	48.6	32.1	5.5	1.2	3.0	1.1	0.2	8.3
towns and villages	59.6	21.9	4.1	0.3	1.1	1.7	0.1	11.1
AGE								
20–29	42.5	34.9	7.1	2.4	2.9	2.1	0.5	7.6
30–39	41.0	38.4	5.9	2.2	2.7	0.9	0.2	8.8
40–49	49.1	31.4	6.2	0.2	4.1	1.4	0.4	7.2
50–59	60.9	17.4	6.6	1.8	3.3	0.3	—	9.3
60–over	61.9	12.9	5.9	0.9	2.9	0.9	—	4.7

EDUCATION							
primary	57.9	13.6	4.7	1.9	3.2	1.6	—	17.1
old high primary; new junior high	52.9	25.7	4.9	1.3	3.2	1.1	0.2	10.6
old middle; new high school	46.1	33.0	8.0	1.4	3.1	1.6	0.1	6.6
old higher & technical; new univ.	42.8	28.9	10.5	3.3	3.3	0.7	0.7	9.9
OCCUPATION							
self employed:							
agriculture; forestry; fishing	70.2	14.4	3.7	0.5	0.9	2.3	—	7.9
merchant, service trades	66.5	15.7	5.9	0.8	4.3	0.4	—	6.3
other self employment	63.3	18.3	10.0	—	3.3	—	—	10.0
employed:							
total	35.3	41.4	7.2	2.4	4.0	1.0	0.5	8.3
administrators, managers	55.0	17.5	12.5	2.5	2.5	2.5	—	7.5
technical; white collar	32.5	44.4	8.3	1.4	2.2	1.4	0.7	9.0
laborers	35.3	41.7	5.5	3.2	5.8	0.3	0.3	7.8
family workers:							
agriculture; forestry; fishing	64.4	13.9	3.6	1.0	1.5	2.6	—	12.9
merchant, service, others	55.7	22.7	6.8	1.1	1.1	1.1	—	11.4

Source: Kōmei Senkyo Renmei, Shūgiin Giin Sōsekyo No Jittai, pp. 36–37.

Secondary industries in the city employ 19.2 per cent of the labor force. The construction industry, like all industry in Beppu, is composed predominantly of small firms. Of 302 firms employing 3,539 people, there are only five firms of over 100 workers, and none that employ over 300. There are only 645 workers in firms employing between 50 and 99 workers, and the majority of workers are in firms that employ less than thirty people each. Manufacturing industries employ 4,690 people or 10.07 per cent of the labor force. There are only 847 people employed in firms of more than fifty people. Sixty-two per cent of the people employed in this sector are engaged in the production of foodstuffs and bamboo products. The bamboo industry is of particular note because it accounts for 22 per cent of the workers in manufacturing industries. It is a highly traditional industry with few large firms and with many of the artisans working at their homes and being paid by the piece rather than with fixed wages. Beppu, although it does not have a rural economy, does not have an industrial one either. The secondary sector is characterized by small firms employing few workers and engaged in construction and small-scale manufacturing.

Nearly three out of every four workers in Beppu are engaged in the tertiary sector of the economy, primarily to serve the needs of tourists. Thus there are 16,906 people working in hotels, dance halls, movie theatres, and bars, and other similar occupations that go by the name "water trades." There are 15,004 people working in wholesale and retail trades. The tertiary sector, like the industrial sector of the economy, is characterized by a large number of small firms each employing small numbers of workers. The 15,000 workers in wholesale and retail trades, for example, work in over 3,000 firms for a ratio of less than five people per firm. The service trades have a ratio of less than eight people to each of the 2,308 places of business.

Figures for all sectors of the economy combined show that there are 44,999 people employed in 7,357 places of work, of which 5,404 (73 per cent) employ less than five people each and 6,417 (90 per cent) of the total employ less than ten people apiece. There are only four places employing over 300 people. Eighty-one per cent of these workers (1,257 of 1,558 people) are employed by Beppu's three large hospitals. Nearly 10,000 people in the labor force are employers or work in family businesses. Beppu, in standard Japanese classification, is a medium-sized city with a labor force employed in small and medium-sized enterprises that engage primarily in service trades.

These characteristics of the population and the economic structure of the city had important consequences for Satō's campaign strategy. For one thing, the small-firm nature of the economy, the large number of self-employed and family workers, and the lack of a significant industrial sector and large-scale enterprises provided a solid base of support for conservative party politicians. As Table 9 indicates, L D P candidates generally throughout the country gain more votes the more rural the area (36 per cent in metropolitan areas, 49 per cent in small and medium-sized cities, 60 per cent in rural areas) and have greater support among self-employed people, employers, and family workers than among employed white-collar and blue-collar workers. Although the data in this poll do not break down responses of workers according to size of enterprise, L D P support is greater among workers in small and medium-sized firms, such as predominate in Beppu, than among those in large-scale enterprises.[12]

Data on various elections held in Beppu indicate the overwhelming support for conservatives in the city. Beppu has had one mayor, independent conservative Aragane Keiji, since 1951. Nearly all of the city's assemblymen are conservatives. In the 1963 Assembly elections Beppu elected twenty-seven candidates of the LDP and three independent conservatives to fill thirty of the Assembly's thirty-six seats.[13] In the Diet election of the same year 77 per cent of those voting in Beppu

12 Watanuki, p. 452.

13 The six others included three members of the Kōmeitō (then the Kōmei Seiji Renmei), two Socialists, and one Communist.

voted for conservative candidates. On the other hand, labor unions, the major source of organized socialist support, are weak. Fifty-nine unions exist in the city, with a total membership of 9,232.[14]

This conservative dominance had one obvious implication for Satō's strategy: the campaign in Beppu would have to be largely a family fight. The challenge was not so much one of taking votes away from the only socialist candidate as it was one of getting a big piece of the conservative pie.

In addition to the electorate voting predominantly conservative, the service trade economy and the growth, mobility, and large female composition of Beppu's population are responsible for the presence of a large number of what are generally referred to as "floating votes" (fudōhyō).

In the Japanese context the concept of the floating vote carries with it an implicit comparison with traditional voting behavior in rural areas; an implicit comparison with the "hard vote." The concept of the hard vote, as has been discussed, reflects traditional modes of social behavior, an emphasis on consensus and hierarchy. In contrast to this, the "floating voter" is the person who leads an urban existence away from the communal pressures of village life. Living alone or with only his immediate, rather than extended, family in an apartment in a city, he has little sense of attachment to the area he is living in, no deep personal ties (enko) with leaders of his new and perhaps transient community, and consequently little sense of obligation to vote in accordance with the wishes of local community leaders. The floating voter is the unattached voter, the anonymous urban dweller to whom appeals in terms of obligation, community consensus, and the like are unavailing.

Because the hard vote represents the traditional norm in Japan, the concept of the floating vote has a fundamentally disparaging tone. Contrary to being regarded as the vote of

[14] Ōita Ken Shōkō Rōdōbu Rōseika, *Rōdō Kumiai Meikan*, (Ōita, 1966).

the independent voter who is politically aware and values his ballot, the term floating vote "carries with it the nuance that it is the vote of people whose political consciousness is low; a vote that will be cast indiscriminately."[15] Here one has an interesting example of the influence of traditional values on the use of universal political concepts. Within the traditional Japanese cultural milieu the hard voter was the man to be respected, a man who showed proper concern for the norms of community consensus and village harmony. The floating voter is a maverick, a product of the divisive effects of urbanization and the breakdown of traditional standards of correct social conduct. Deploring the prevalence of this view, the Asahi newspaper article quoted above goes on to implore its readers to "recognize, however, that within the floating vote there are votes of criticism . . . and votes arrived at by independent thought. These are rather the floating votes of people who have opinions."

In Western societies, the use of the term floating vote or independent vote is reserved for those "who do not make the same [party] choice at two successive elections."[16] In Britain or the United States the floating voter is the man who is free of *party* attachments; in Japan it is the person who is free of certain kinds of *personal* attachments. Consequently, there is no contradiction involved in talking of "conservative party floating voters" in Japan. The major problem posed by the floating voter is not that you cannot appeal to party loyalties but that you cannot reach him through a web of traditional, established networks of personal relationships.

The concepts of the hard vote and the floating vote form the fundamental inputs in Satō's perception of rational campaign strategies. If the problem in the rural areas was to build

[15] *Asahi Shinbun,* January 28, 1967, p. 1. See article entitled "Fudō-Hihanhyō in "Konnichi No Mondai."

[16] H. Daudt, *Floating Voters and the Floating Vote, A Critical Analysis of American and British Election Studies* (Leiden, 1961), p. 7.

an organization of men who could "gather the hard vote," the challenge presented by Beppu's nearly 80,000 voters was to create strategies for "catching the floating vote."

The basic problem faced by Satō in Beppu was how to appeal to a largely anonymous electorate. There are several alternative strategies one can envision a candidate adopting to meet this problem. One, probably the first to come to the mind of Americans, is for the candidate to appeal directly to the voters through the mass media, political rallies, and the like. In Japan the prohibition of pre-election campaigning and severe restrictions on the type of campaigning allowed during the official campaign period severely inhibit the use of such an approach.[17] A second possible strategy is to employ the same type of organization as used in rural areas, relying on local leaders to gather and deliver the vote. Obviously in Beppu the electorate was too large, the economic structure too urban, and patterns of social intercourse that rationalize such an approach too minimal for such a strategy to be effective. The rural campaign organization was for gathering hard votes, not for mobilizing the support of the floating voters. A third strategy would be to rely on political party organization to mobilize the vote. This strategy could not even be entertained by an LDP candidate running in a district where other men of the party were also candidates and where the party organization, to the extent that it existed, was split among the several official candidates.

With these alternatives largely eliminated, Satō's approach to the problem of mobilizing the support of the Beppu electorate was in the form of what may be analyzed as three general strategic responses. One was to appeal directly to the voters during the short official campaign period within the limits of the election law. The conduct of this appeal is discussed in Chapter VIII. The second strategy was to create a personal city-wide organization of supporters with basically three func-

<hr>

[17] See Chapters VI and VIII.

tions. The first of these was to gather and deliver the vote of the small percentage of the electorate susceptible to such appeals. This sector was envisaged as being made up of old and long-time residents of the city, relatives, close friends, and people indebted to members of the organization. The second function was to provide a city-wide network of campaigners that would appeal for votes, not on the basis of any particular personal relationships, but simply with the idea that a voter, particularly the floating voter whose "political consciousness is low" and who will cast his vote "indiscriminately," to quote again from the *Asahi* article, will tend to vote for the candidate he has been asked to vote for. The third function was to provide a means of access for the candidate himself to meet the voters, not through publicized rallies or other activities that would be flagrant violations of the Election Law's ban on pre-election campaigning, but through small neighborhood meetings arranged by members of the organization. This last function of the machine is the bridge with the third major strategic approach adopted by Satō: the creation of a mass-membership organization that would provide various activities for large numbers of the electorate and bring them into direct contact with the candidate. This use of a *kōenkai,* or supporters' organization, is discussed in the following chapter.

The present-day city of Beppu, as mentioned above, resulted from repeated amalgamations between an area known as Beppu village and neighboring villages and towns. The boundaries of these areas are largely the boundaries of the eleven school districts *(kōku)* into which the city is divided. In a general way these school districts correspond to the villages amalgamated in rural towns. While the sense of identification with these formerly independent areas has to a great extent dissipated with the passage of time and the entrance of outsiders, the school districts still maintain some degree of social identity and cohesiveness. For a Prefectural Assembly or Diet or Mayoral candidate, that is, a candidate who campaigns

Table 10

Beppu's Population by School Districts

School district	Number of households	Population	Male	Female	Number of chōnai
Noguchi	4,503	14,808	6,559	8,249	9
Kita	2,953	11,118	4,203	6,915	14
Aoyama	2,798	10,785	5,289	5,496	7
Minami	3,499	11,440	4,955	6,485	12
Nishi	3,566	12,327	5,531	6,796	9
Hasuda	3,953	13,705	6,320	7,385	20
Ishitake	3,627	13,312	6,084	7,228	10
Asahi	2,182	8,549	3,788	4,761	17
Kamegawa	3,848	14,731	6,634	8,097	13
Minami Takeshi	1,562	6,901	3,004	3,897	5
Higashiyama	232	1,262	592	670	5
Beppu Total	32,709	118,938	52,977	65,961	121

throughout the city,[18] they form convenient subdivisions of the city for the organization of campaign activities.

The school districts are, however, large units, as Table 10 shows. Only three districts, all on the outskirts of the city, have a population of less than 10,000. For purposes of campaign organization, Satō concentrated his activities within the smaller units of which the school districts are composed, the *chōnai* or neighborhoods.

Each of the school districts, as indicated in the last column of the Table 10, is comprised of a number of *chōnai*. These are areas which have long histories as units of social organization, many having been the *buraku* of Beppu's amalga-

[18] Although City Assembly elections are officially citywide, practically all candidates limit their campaigning to a small section of the city, usually encompassing several contiguous neighborhoods. Rarely does a City Assembly candidate make a significant effort to gain votes in more than one school district.

mated villages. In each of the city's 121 *chōnai* is a *chōnaikai* or neighborhood association. In Satō's building of a city-wide organization the neighborhoods and the neighborhood associations played a central role.

In the prewar period and particularly during the war years Ōita Prefecture is alleged to have developed one of the country's most thorough systems of neighborhood associations and their subdivision, the *tonarigumi*.[19] During those years the neighborhood association served as an instrument for imposing the control and demands of the central government on the populace. Until the American Occupation following Japan's defeat in World War II, neighborhood associations were active throughout the country, although they had never been established in law except for a short period following a revision of the Local Government Law in 1943.[20] In 1947, as part of the decentralization and general democratization policies of the Occupation, the neighborhood association and the *tonarigumi* were banned.[21] The system could not easily be destroyed and "continued to exist, sometimes in altered form, despite the 1947 government ordinance banning it. With the lapse of the ordinance in 1951 the neighborhood associations reappeared quickly and became very active in local elections at that time."[22] According to one source, even during the period when they were banned, neighborhood associations were active in 86 per cent of the country's cities, towns, and villages. As of August, 1956, such associations were functioning in 98 per cent of these areas.[23]

In Beppu the *chōnaikai* system was officially reconstituted in

[19] Usami Shō, "Nōson No Tōshika," *Asahi Jānaru*, VIII (December 11, 1966), 20.

[20] Matsushita Keiichi, *Gendai Nihon No Seijiteki Kōsei* (Tokyo, 1964), p. 224.

[21] Kobayashi Naoki, Shinohara Hajime and Sōma Masao, *Senkyo* (Tokyo, 1960), p. 80.

[22] *Ibid.*, p. 80.

[23] *Gendai Nihon No Seiji Katei,* ed. Oka Yoshitake (Tokyo, 1966), pp. 348–349.

1953 under a new name, the *Jichikai* or Self-Governing Councils.[24] Officially the *chōnaikai* are not established in law and coexist with the Self-Governing Councils which are legally part of the city's administrative structure. In fact, however, they are identical. The terms *chōnaikai* and *jichikai, chōnaikaichō* (Neighborhood Association President) and *jichiin* are used interchangeably.

The 121 *Jichiin*, the presidents of the councils, are appointed by the mayor from the names of three candidates submitted by the neighborhood association. The recommendations are decided by a general meeting of the association or by its *kumichō*, the leaders of the subdivision of the association (*kumi*) that correspond to the old *tonarigumi*. The largest number of households[25] under the supervision of any one council head (that is, the largest number of households in any one *chōnai*) is 950 and the smallest is 23.[26] There are an average of thirteen *kumi* in each *chōnai* and there are 1,593 *kumichō* in the 121 neighborhoods.[27]

The system of Self-Governing Councils is the old neighborhood association in new clothing. Organized among the 32,709

[24] The discussion of Beppu's *Jichiin* system is based on documents provided the author by the Beppu city office: Beppu Shiyakusho, *Jichiin Setchi Kisoku*, mimeo. (Beppu, ?);*Jyūmin Gyōsei Soshiki No Chōsa*, mimeo. (Beppu, October 1, 1965).

[25] The members of the neighborhood associations are households, not individuals.

[26] The term of office of the association presidents is two years and the salary a nominal 25,000 yen annually. In addition, they receive administrative funds of 120 yen per household up to 200 households and 70 yen for each household over 200. The average number of households in a neighborhood is 256, which provides 27,920 yen in administrative funds.

[27] Above the *chōnai*, in each of the city's eleven school districts, are three officers of the Association of Self-Governing Councils, a district captain (*shibuchō*) and two assistant captains (*fukushibuchō*). These thirty-three officers in turn elect the President (*kaichō*) and five Vice-Presidents (*fuku-kaichō*) of the association. The Beppu association is further federated with those of the ten other cities of the prefecture in the Ōita Prefecture Federation of Self-Governing Councils (*Ōita Ken Jichi Rengōkai*), created in 1963.

households of the city, its formal and legal purpose is to serve as an arm of the city's administrative structure; its traditional and overriding purpose is to serve as the common social organization of the neighborhood's residents.

In all the areas of the Second District outside Beppu, Satō's organized support is no older than the campaign preceding his first Diet race in 1963. As a prefectural assemblyman Satō needed an organization only in the city, which elected him to three consecutive terms in the Assembly. Although he endeavored to expand this organization when he entered the Diet race, the enormous problem faced in the rest of the district of recruiting supporters was not faced in anything near the same magnitude in his home city. The Beppu organization that ran Satō's campaign for the Diet in the elections of 1963 and 1967 was the same organization that had been responsible for three campaigns to the Prefectural Assembly.

The men who comprise Sato's organization in Beppu all have one thing in common: they are all, without exception, active members of their neighborhood associations. *Chōnaikai* in Beppu and, according to the limited data available, throughout the country are dominated by supporters of the conservative party. This includes both the association leadership and the type of people who most actively participate in the association's activities.

The control supporters of the L D P hold over local neighborhood associations has led one author to suggest that it is the neighborhood associations "that carry the load of the L D P organization at its extremities."[28] While this perhaps gives the L D P more credit than it deserves for having any kind of organization on the grass-roots level, it does reflect the extraordinary degree to which the leadership of neighborhood associations is in the hands of conservatives. In Beppu the *chōnaikai* are not organs of the L D P as such. Rather, they are organizations of people generally sympathetic to conservative policies and conservative party politicians; organizations

28 Matsushita, *Gendai Nihon*, p. 219.

Table 11

Political Participation of Beppu Electorate according to Types of Meeting Places

"At what type of meeting did you hear about, or take part in a discussion of, *kōmei senkyo* (fair elections)?"

	1	2	3	4	5	6	7	8	9	DK–NA
TOTAL (N = 122)	24.6	23.0	0.8	4.9	2.5	17.2	1.6	13.9	10.7	0.8
men	30.0	20.9	1.5	—	—	17.9	—	19.4	10.5	1.8
women	18.2	25.5	—	10.9	5.5	16.4	3.6	7.3	10.9	1.8
AGE										
20–29	12.0	44.0		4.0		4.0		12.0	24.0	
30–39	20.0	36.0	4.0		4.0	12.0		8.0	12.0	4.0
40–59	18.8	12.5		15.6	3.1	21.9	6.3	21.9		
50–59	42.1	15.8			5.3	31.6		5.3		
60–over	38.1	4.8				19.0		19.0	19.0	
EDUCATION										
primary	54.5	9.1			9.1	9.1		9.1	9.1	
middle	35.0	12.5	2.5	7.5		25.0	5.0	7.5	5.0	
high	13.5	28.8		5.8	3.8	17.3	17.3	11.5	1.9	
university	15.8	36.8				5.3		21.1	21.1	
OCCUPATION										
agriculture; fishing	50.0		7.1	21.4		21.4				
manufacture and service	17.2	31.3		1.6	1.6	18.8		17.2	12.5	

	1	2	3	4	5	6	7	8	9	DK–NA
tranportation and communication										
no particular occupation	34.6	3.8		3.8	7.7	19.2	3.8	11.5	15.4	
other	15.4	30.8		7.7	7.7	7.7	7.7	15.4	7.7	7.7
POLITICAL PARTY SUPPORT										
Conservative	27.9	4.7	2.3	2.3		27.9	2.3	18.6	14.0	
Progressive	10.5	63.2		5.3	5.3	15.8			5.3	
Won't Say	7.7	15.4		15.4	15.4	15.4		15.4	23.1	
None	31.9	25.5		6.4	4.3	8.5	2.1	14.9	6.4	8.0
LENGTH OF RESIDENCE										
less than one year	(1)					(1)			(1)	
1–2 years	(2)	(2)		(1)				(2)		
2–5 years	(2)	(3)			(1)	(1)		(2)	(1)	
5–10 years	23.5	41.2		11.8	3.9	11.8		15.8	5.9	
over 10 years	15.8	23.7		7.9	2.6	18.4	5.3	15.8	10.5	
from before the war	28.7	11.8	1.7	1.7		16.9		11.8	11.8	1.7

Code:

1—Neighborhood association meeting
2—Meeting at place of employment
3—Meeting of neighborhood youth association
4—Meeting of neighborhood women's club
5—PTA meeting
6—Meeting held at a local public hall
7—Meeting of women's group
8—Meeting sponsored by the Fair Election Movement
9—Other
DK–NA—Don't Know; No Answer

Figures in parenthesis are absolute numbers, given where respondents were too few to make percentages significant.
Source: Ōita Ken Senkyo Kanri Iinkai, Ōita Ken Akaruku Tadashii Senkyo Kyōgikai, *Akaruku Tadashii Senkyo Undo Nō Jittai, Yoron Chōsa No Gaiyō* (Ōita, March 1965), p. 40.

that can conveniently be used by L D P politicians in mobilizing electoral support.

The results of a poll conducted in Beppu give some indication of the type of people who are particularly involved in the city's neighborhood associations. The poll, both because of the size of its sample and the indirect relationship between the question asked and the issue of participation in the *chōnaikai,* is cited as representing only the most general tendencies among certain groups in regard to participation in the *chōnaikai.* The survey asked voters if they had ever taken part in any meeting that discussed the clean election movement. Those who answered yes (122 out of 433) were then asked where such discussion took place. The responses to this question are reproduced in Table 11. The results of the poll suggest that the *chōnaikai* is an important association predominantly for those people of the city who are long-time residents, over the age of fifty, of primary and middle school education, and supporters of the conservative party or of no party (which, as already mentioned, usually indicates supporters of conservative party candidates). The "no particular occupation" category of workers can probably be interpreted as referring to retired men and housewives. Except for the rather small percentage of women participants indicated in the poll, the profile of active *chōnaikai* members that emerges corresponds with that observed by the author in the course of numerous *chōnaikai* meetings attended over a period of a year.[29]

29 The percentage of conservative party supporting voters active in the *chōnaikai* is undoubtedly much greater than is indicated by the poll. A couple of months before the election I spent several days with the Chairman of the International Bureau of the Socialist Party, Matsumoto Schichirō, in his home district in Fukuoka Prefecture, a heavily industrial area in which progressive party candidates win a majority of the popular vote in Diet elections. In discussing the organization of his campaign Matsumoto remarked that he could not "get into" the *chōnaikai* because they were conservative party supporting associations. He rather had to concentrate on local labor unions to approach the electorate. In Beppu as well the *chōnaikai* are social clubs that attract mainly the active conservative sector of the electorate.

For the conservative candidate the *chōnaikai* provides an ideal base upon which to build a campaign organization. There he could find politically interested and conservatively inclined voters, people intimately familiar with their local neighborhoods who could appeal for the support of friends and acquaintances, and men who could provide, through their leadership positions in the associations, opportunities for the candidate to meet with large numbers of conservative voters in the city.

It is important to note that in Satō's perception, and commonly among Japanese, the electorate is divided into two camps: the conservative (*hoshu jin'ei*) and the progressive (*kakushin jin'ei*). Satō saw little merit in a strategy that would involve a considerable amount of his time in appealing to progressive camp voters. Thus the lack of any attempt to address labor unions or in other ways to attempt to attract the support of the identifiably progressive sector. Beppu votes overwhelmingly conservative and for a conservative party politician the problem was to maximize support within the conservative camp. That access to the electorate provided by the *chōnaikai* leaders would mean largely access only to conservative voters was accordingly not seen as particularly disadvantageous.

Satō has organized support in each of the city's 121 neighborhoods. In each there is a small group of men who are responsible for recruiting other campaigners and directing the campaign. As with the leaders of the town organizations, the *sekininsha*, there are similarly one or two men, generally referred to as *sewanin*, who lead these neighborhood organizations. At the time of the 1967 campaign there were 235 such *sewanin* in Satō's organization. Approximately 215, according to the estimate of Satō's secretary, had served in that position for at least ten years and some since Satō first ran for the Prefectural Assembly in 1951. At the time of the election thirty-eight of the city's neighborhood association presidents, again according to Satō's secretary, were part of his personal organization. Less than twenty others were known to support the other LDP candidates, and the rest were considered neutral in the election. The term of office of neighborhood association presidents is two years and many of Satō's *sewanin* not holding that position at the time of the election had held it at one time or another in previous years. All of his *sewanin* had served as *kumichō*, leaders of the small units of houses that together comprise the neighborhood associations.

With most of his supporters long involved in his campaigns, Satō's Beppu organization was dominated by middle-aged and elderly men. In rural areas where he had to build a completely new organization Satō's appeal was mainly to younger politicians. But in Beppu his political machine was fairly old and displayed many traits common to long-established personal political organizations: a tendency for the members to become entrenched in their positions, jealous of their prerogatives and indifferent to the problem of infusing new blood.

Some of the men recruited to serve as Satō's *sewanin* were part of Mayor Aragane's political machine and were delegated by him to organize Satō's first election campaign. Although the passage of time has worked a natural attrition on this group of supporters, they still form a sizeable portion of Satō's *sewanin*. The rest of these supporters represent a heterogeneous mix of personal friends, relatives, and people active in the neighborhood associations who want a native son of the city in the Diet. Satō has few supporters who can strictly be referred to as his *kobun*. He has such a relationhip with Shutō Kenji, who succeeded him in the Prefectural Assembly and with a few other of his younger supporters who have ambitions of entering elective politics. The lack of such intimate familial ties reflects the fact that the members of Satō's neighborhood organization are not professional politicians or men with the ambition of becoming politicians. For the great majority of them campaigning is a kind of sport; interesting and, because of the extreme restrictions on campaign practices embodied in the election law, often adventurous work that requires relatively little of the supporters' time.

The *sewanin* have only limited functions to perform. Unlike the head of a town organization with the responsibility for gathering and delivering the vote, the neighborhood *sewanin* serve mainly as a channel of communication between the candidates's headquarters and the neighborhood's residents. During the few weeks of the actual campaign they are expected to actively seek votes but outside of the official campaign period they function primarily to keep Satō's headquarters informed on developments in the neighborhood: occasions of births, marriages, and deaths, for instance, so Satō can send a suitable gift or greeting. They keep Satō informed on meetings within the neighborhood, those of the neighborhood association, its women's club or elderly people's club, and so forth where Satō or one of his staff may make an appearance or send a gift. For a year preceding the 1967 election a major responsibility of the *sewanin* was to arrange for special meetings between Satō and the neighborhoods' residents.[30]

Because Satō's neighborhood supporters are not elected politicians responsible to a constituency, the rewards they demand for supporting Satō are of a much different order and more easily fulfilled than demanded by local elected officials. Small material benefits are constantly being provided by Satō headquarters staff. His staff is always ready to help the *sewanin* with any problem from getting the fine for a speeding ticket reduced to getting their children into high school. The *sewanin* are constant recipients of greeting cards of one sort or another that Satō sends out periodically, and each receives in August a mid-year gift (*chūgen*) and in December a year-end present (*seibo*). More important than such material rewards is the abstract reward of being treated as the central members of a team responsible for getting a man elected to the Diet. The title of *sewanin*, the private confidential con-

[30] See below, pp. 122–25.

[117]

ferences, the right to talk to third parties of "Bunchan" (a diminutive formed from Satō's first name, Bunsei) in the familiar form of speech rather than the honorific, the responsibility, the prestige, and for many the fun and adventure their role in the organization provides would appear to be the most significant rewards for their activities on Satō's behalf.

Rewards of this kind are sufficient to maintain the support of people for whom serving in Satō's neighborhood organization is done as a hobby or a favor or for very limited personal benefit, but they were not sufficient to obtain the support of Beppu's elected officials. Despite the fact that Beppu was his home town, Satō had as little success in obtaining the support of local politicians in the city as he did in other areas. While many politicans could see Satō's election as beneficial to Beppu in the long run, few could afford to break their ties with those already in the Diet. As of January 17, 1967, one week before election day, Diet candidate support among the thirty-five members of the Beppu City Assembly divided as follows: Ayabe Kentarō—seventeen; Nishimura Eiichi—seven; Satō Bunsei—four; Komatsu Kan—three; Tsuru Tadahisa (Communist)—one.[31] Satō was even unable to get public support of his original mentor, Mayor Aragane Keiji. As Aragane remarked to the author,[32] support for Satō would have resulted in his being unable to function effectively as mayor. So much of the economic development of the city is dependent on grants and subsidies from the national government that good relations with the district's Diet members are a prerequisite for a mayor[33] and supporting Satō would have incurred the animosity of the district's incumbent L D P Diet members.

[31] Three other members of the Assembly belong to the Kōmeitō and did not support any of the Diet candidates. *Beppu Yukan,* January 17, 1967.

[32] Interview, August 10, 1967.

[33] "Local government . . . is supported by equalization tax rebates and subsidies from prefectural and central governments. Similarly, local government loans cannot be floated at will; permission is necessary and for the most part these loans depend on central government funds . . . The size of the grants or subsidies received determines the funds available for in-

In the discussion of Satō's organization in rural areas it was noted that, because of the geographic concentration of the support base of local politicians, there was a tendency for Diet support to cluster in narrow geographic areas of a particular town or village. A parallel tendency is evident in Beppu, where support for the Diet candidate often is restricted to only that element of the conservative sector in the neighborhood with which the neighborhood association leadership is closely associated. Satō's organization in the neighborhood of Ueno illustrates this point.

Ueno consists of 239 households and has a population of 815. Satō's *sewanin* in the neighborhood, Doi Takeshi, is one of the few men of the *sewanin* group not to have been a supporter of Satō when he was in the Prefectural Assembly. Thirty-six years old, Doi supported Satō for the first time in 1963, joined the L D P in 1964, and became Vice-President of its youth group in Ōita Prefecture. He acts as liaison between Satō's headquarters and a group of Ueno supporters that has campaigned for Satō through many elections. It includes the present neighborhood association president, his predecessor, the president of the elderly people's club and his wife, who was president of the women's club at the time of the 1967 election and both her predecessor and successor as women's club president. In short, Satō had the support of almost the entire leadership of Ueno's neighborhood association.

Ueno, as the rough sketch in Figure 4 shows, is divided into eleven *kumi*. Satō's supporters, indicated by the mark ✕, are concentrated in three connecting *kumi,* the second, sixth, and

---

dustrial and economic development. Without loan issues it is difficult to go ahead with the building of schools and municipal offices. For these reasons mayors and influential members of the Council must maintain close connections with members of the Prefectural Assembly and the latter's ultimate patrons, members of the national Diet. And it goes without saying that these Diet members have to be members of the government party if they are to have any influence." Fukutake Tadashi, *Japanese Rural Society,* trans. Ronald P. Dore (London, 1967), pp. 191–92.

Figure 4
Sketch of the Neighborhood of Ueno

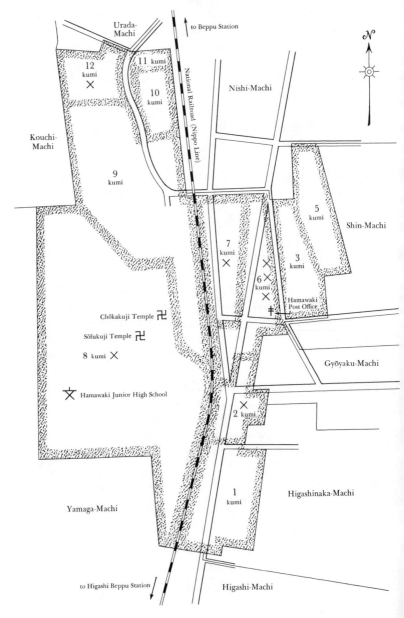

Table 12
Occupations of Household Heads in Ueno

Kumi	No. of houses	Public workers	Merchants	White collar	Laborers	Other
1	20	2	11	3	3	1
2	20	2	6	5	3	4
3	16	2	1	6	1	6
5	8	1	0	2	2	3
6	44	4	10	11	5	14
7	44	4	4	18	5	13
8	6	0	1	0	1	4
9	41	4	4	10	18	5
10	18	2	0	5	7	4
11	6	1	1	1	3	0
12	16	3	1	3	6	3
Total	239	25	39	64	54	57

Data obtained from house registers in possession of the neighborhood association president. These registers list the occupation only of the head of the house. There is no number four *kumi* because of the superstition that four, which in Japanese has the same pronunciation as the word for death (*shi*), is an unlucky number.

the seventh. There is one woman supporter in the eighth *kumi* and one in the twelfth. In the rest of the *kumi* Satō is unrepresented by any member of his Ueno organization. Others who took part in the campaign did so at the request of those mentioned above were from the same *kumi*.

The above table shows the number of houses in each *kumi* and divides the heads of houses according to very rough occupational categories.

Because the categories are very broad and the figures apply to heads of houses rather than working population, the data are of limited usefulness. What conclusions can be safely drawn are that, for one, the *kumi* in which Satō's support is mainly located, the sixth and seventh, are the most populous in terms of number of houses. They are in fact the commercial center of the neighborhood. What is also apparent is that the four *kumi* on the one side of the railroad tracks where Satō has his least support (9, 10, 11, 12) are the only ones in which the number of laborers outnumbers each of the other categories of workers. Particularly in the populous ninth *kumi,* where Satō has no acknowledged supporter, the heads of eighteen of the forty-one houses are laborers. This area is truly the other side of the tracks of Ueno. It is a poor section that houses many people who work on the railroads. These *kumi* are socially isolated as well as physically separated from the other part of the *chōnai,* which continually provides the leaders of the neighborhood association. Satō's organized support in Ueno is in effect limited to three of eleven *kumi* in which the *chōaikai* leadership is located. Whether this clustering of support means a similar clustering of votes is a moot question. At the least it means that people invited to hear Satō speak, the people that receive his greeting cards, newsletters, and invitations to political rallies; in short, the voters that are the object of the activities of Satō and his Ueno organization are concentrated in the few *kumi* where the leadership in his support is located.

One of the most important functions of this neighborhood leadership before the calling of elections was to arrange meetings between Satō and neighborhood residents. In the nine to ten months preceding the election, Satō spent about three days a week talking before groups in the city's 121 neighborhoods. These meetings were billed as Political Study Sessions, a free translation of *Seiji Kyōshitsu,* and a euphemism made necessary by the legal prohibition on all campaigning outside of a short specified period. By the time the House was dissolved and new elections called in December, 1966, Satō had succeeded in speaking at more than 100 of the city's 121 neighborhood associations.

In organizing his neighborhood speeches, Satō attempted to cover one school district at a time, systematically going through the several *chōnai* in a district and then moving on to the next area. The first step in preparing for these speeches was to hold a dinner party for the *sewanin* from one of the school districts. Two or three men from each neighborhood in the district would be invited to these parties, where Satō would express his gratitude for their support, outline the talk he would give in their neighborhoods, and share some interesting "inside" story of the campaign or of national politics to demonstrate the special position of confidence he wanted these men to feel they held in his organization. Attendance at the parties reaffirmed the *sewanin*'s involvement in Satō's campaign, and the responsibility placed upon them to arrange neighborhood meetings tested their enthusiasm and abilities. There is always a danger of atrophy in an organization that exists largely by virtue of personal relationships if these ties are not continuously reaffirmed and maintained. The dinner parties gave Satō an opportunity to reaffirm those ties and to identify and begin to reconstitute those parts of the organization that had become atrophied.

Within a few days of these parties, Satō's secretary would visit each of those in attendance to arrange a time and place for a meeting in the neighborhoods. These neighborhood speeches were informal affairs, lasting about two hours and with between twenty-five and forty people in attendance. Sometimes the meeting would be advertised in advance, but most often the *sewanin*, because of his knowledge of and involvement in neighborhood association affairs, would time the meeting to coincide with that of the women's club or elderly people's club or some other *chōnaikai* meeting. Satō's audiences were always at least half female and the average age over fifty-five.

Sitting in front of the thirty people or so who had come to listen to the *sensei*, Satō would talk for an hour or two. He would move from one anecdotal story to another, adeptly using the local dialect, interspersing his stories with humorous sidelights and entertaining his audiences with his intimate and engaging conversational style. His speeches centered around such topics as the spiritual malaise in postwar Japan, the need for rejuvenation of the L D P, the importance of Japanese tradition, and, his major theme, the need for renewed confidence in Japan's greatness.[34] With an accent on resurrection rather than reform and tradition rather than innovation, his speeches hardly reflected his self-proclaimed "new right" liberalism, but pleased his generally elderly and conservative audiences. As a conservative addressing conservatives, and hoping to take votes away from other conservative candidates, Satō found it difficult to discuss issues on which his position was at the same time different from the other L D P candidates and appealing to his audience. The only issue, if it could be called such, that set Satō apart from all the other candidates was the issue of getting younger conservatives into the Diet to rejuvenate the national party organization and the government. With the series of scandals that hit the LDP in the last months of 1966, this issue was given added relevance because of the call for "cleaning up" the conservative party. Satō, at forty-seven, was the youngest among the candidates, and he made the most of his appeal as an energetic, handsome, studious, and sufficiently tradition-minded conservative untainted by corruption.

The major issue Satō harped upon in appealing to his audience was not one of policy but of geography. In addressing his neighborhood audiences, he constantly emphasized that he was the only candidate from Beppu. He appealed to the sympathy and pride of the local residents to "get one of their own" into the Diet. He began every speech by thanking the

34 Political Study Session does not do justice to the Japanese term *Seiji Kyōshitsu*. *Kyōshitsu* literally translated is a classroom. The use of this term was to further the image of Satō as a teacher (*sensei*) who was holding a class in politics for the local residents. A speech Satō gave at another Political Study Session, one for a group of 500 women from the district, was representative of the speeches he gave in Beppu's neighborhoods. Sections of it are translated and discussed in Chapter VI.

[124]

people for the support they gave him in the previous Diet election and recollecting the "narrow margin" (*wazuka na sa*) by which he had lost. In addition to this attempt to pick up the "sympathy vote" (*dōjōhyō*), he also appealed to considerations of material interest, stressing the benefits eventually to be derived from having a Beppu man representing them at the highest level of government. As Satō invariably told his audiences, after twelve years in the Prefectural Assembly he had decided that "for the development of Beppu" he wanted to enter the "national political arena."

Through these neighborhood speeches Satō was able to speak to somewhat over 2,500 people. With their two-pronged purpose of activating and testing the leadership of the neighborhood organization and of bringing Satō into direct contact with the city's voters, the neighborhood speeches represent a connecting rod between a strategy of relying on a small organization of supporters to mobilize the vote and one that aims at directly organizing support among the general electorate. While Satō talked his secretary took down the names and addresses of everyone in attendance. These formed the crucial *meibo,* or name list, for the neighborhood; lists of people who would be sent New Year cards and copies of Satō's newsletter and who would be encouraged to become members of the *Fūsetsukai,* Satō's "supporters' organization," the subject of the following chapter.

V

The *Kōenkai*

WHEN JAPAN'S ADVENTURE in empire building ended on August 15, 1945, the country lay in a state of physical collapse and spiritual despair. Largely blaming their own leaders for Japan's precipitous descent into chaos, many people questioned not only the virtues of those who had led them into disaster but also the social and political system that had produced such leaders. With an Occupation philosophy that saw the sources of Japanese aggression in the nation's social structure and internal political system, *demokurashii* became the cherished ideal, and all that could fall under the rubric of "feudalism" became the disease to be eradicated. For the first time the primacy of the individual over the group was given legitimacy in the official ideology, and a new constitution that reflected Western concepts of the rights of man was adopted. The Occupation authorities undertook a program of directed social change that reached into nearly every nook and cranny of Japanese life. With a two-pronged objective of demilitarization and democratization, they pushed the adoption of various measures intended to shake the nation's rulers out of their seats of power and to provide a firm foundation for the development of democratic practices. Soon after the Occupation began, the voting age was lowered from twenty-five to twenty, and women were given the vote. A far-reaching purge of political leaders eliminated from public office many of those who had been in power on both the national and local levels, while reforms in the system of local government created more elected offices with a greater degree of local autonomy than had ever existed before. With the carrying out of a land reform that expropriated the landlords and virtually eliminated tenancy, the conservative politician's traditional base of support was all but destroyed. Candidates for public office could no longer rely on landlords to gather the vote; they had to deal with an enormously enlarged electorate, one that was to some extent disenchanted with politics as it had been conducted. And they had to pay at least lip service to the new ideology of democracy and individual rights. The consequence of all these developments for campaign strategy, as one author succinctly summed it up, was that "votes could no longer be gathered only with the support of the bosses."[1] It was this period and these new and unsettling developments in the political and social environment that saw the emergence of kōenkai.

There is general agreement, in the little scholarly work that has been done on the kōenkai, that it emerged in the postwar period as a response to new factors in the environment within which campaign strategies operate. One Japanese political scientist has referred in this connection to the kōenkai as a "modern" form of political organization:

the typical Liberal Democratic Party member's kōenkai is a Japanese form of a "modern" political organization. This is an organization that first appeared in the postwar period with the expansion of the electorate and the fall from grace of the local bosses. It is a substitute for a formal party organization. It is not at all feudalistic but, on the contrary, is a technique which inevitably arose as a response to the destruction of the feudalistic order.[2]

There is some disagreement, however, about what makes the kōenkai significantly "modern." Scholars such as Matsushita Keiichi maintain that the kōenkai is most importantly

[1] Fukutake Tadashi, " 'Jimoto Rieki' O Seiritsu Saseru Mono," Interview with Ishikawa Hideo, *Asahi Jānaru*, IX (February 26, 1967), 95.

[2] Matsushita Keiichi, *Sengo Minshu Shugi No Tenbō* (Tokyo, 1965), p. 231; Cf. Sōma Masao, *Nihon No Senkyo Seiji* (Tokyo, 1963), p. 121: "The building of individual candidate kōenkai is a phenomenon of the postwar period and is a reflection of changes that have occurred in community social structure."

the organization of the "new ruling class," the local elected officials who have replaced the dispossessed landlords as the support base for conservative politicians.[3] The thesis forwarded by Matsushita and others is that the demise of the landlords forced the Diet candidate to expand his campaign organization to include a whole array of local officials in order to have the organization successfully function in gathering the vote. Sociologist Fukutake Tadashi writes that "A Diet member builds his *kōenkai* around influential leaders and spreads its net to include men of lesser influence. . . . At election time these big bosses (*ōbosu*) and little bosses (*kobosu*) go to work on his behalf."[4]

Analyses such as these, which emphasize the role of community leaders, fail to give adequate attention to what is significantly modern about the *kōenkai*: the use of a mass-membership organization with the function of organizing large numbers of the general electorate on behalf of a particular Diet candidate.

The use of local elected officials to perform functions provided by landlords in the prewar period was, as has been discussed in an earlier chapter, part of the response of Diet candidates to changes that occurred following the war. This strategy, however, represented only a limited change in techniques of support mobilization insofar as the ability of local politicians to deliver the vote was predicated on the same assumptions of community consensus and traditional hierarchical modes of social intercourse as had made landlords effective supporters before the war. What is significant about the use of such a campaign strategy in the postwar period is the change in the composition of the local elite and the lack of change in the functions the organization of such leaders is expected to perform.

The *kōenkai*, contrary to what the analyses of many Japanese

[3] See Matsushita Keiichi, *Gendai Nihon No Seijiteki Kōsei* (Tokyo, 1964), chapters VI and VII, and his *Sengo Minshu Shugi No Tenbō*, p. 150.
[4] Fukutake Tadashi, *Nihon Nōson Shakai Ron* (Tokyo, 1966), pp. 222–23.

scholars imply, represents more than a mere change in ruling personnel. It represents an innovation in campaign strategies and is to be contrasted with a strategy of reliance on local politicians and other community leaders. The *kōenkai* emerged as politicians tried to compensate for an inability of such elites to adequately perform their intended function of gathering enough votes to insure election. While relying on local leaders to deliver the vote to the extent possible, Diet candidates have in addition created *kōenkai* for the purpose of organizing support directly among the electorate. In terms of their functions and historical development, organizations of local leaders and of the general electorate in the *kōenkai* represent distinct approaches to campaign strategy.

While no Japanese scholar has explicitly developed this thesis of the *kōenkai* being the organization of the general electorate as distinct from an organization of community leaders, some accept it implicitly. Thus, Tokyo professor Watanuki Jōji, indicating his own drawing of a distinction between the support of the "ruling class" and that of members of the *kōenkai*, reports that "In the case of [the 1967] Diet election, there was already talk of dissolution in the spring [of 1966] and a number of candidates, expending a great deal of money and energy, held meetings with the members of their *kōenkai* and with the local bosses. . . ."[5]

One reason for confusion about the nature of *kōenkai* is the quite common practice of Diet candidates to formally incorporate their supporters among local politicians within the *kōenkai* structure. The common pattern is for local politicians to be made "officers" of a *kōenkai*. One *kōenkai* in Ibaragi Prefecture, for instance, has thirty-eight branches spread over the district's three cities and six counties, and it counts among its leadership one-fifth of all prefectural assemblymen and half of the assemblymen in several towns in the district.[6] Having such members is not what makes the *kōenkai* a "modern" po-

5 Watanuki Jōji, *Nihon No Seiji Shakai* (Tokyo, 1967), p. 222.
6 *Asahi Shinbun*, January 4, 1967, p. 14.

litical organization, however. Having an estimated membership of 40,000 is. Nakasone Yasuhiro has divided his constituency into seven federations and has his supporters at the
Prefectural Assembly level serve as the "federation chiefs" of
his *kōenkai*. Local assemblymen are the presidents of the
kōenkai chapters in the several towns and villages.[7] While such
titles as "federation chief" may be impressive, more significant
is that there are somewhere around 50,000 members in Nakasone's *kōenkai*.

There are several reasons for incorporating local politicians
into the *kōenkai* structure. For one, there is a greater air of
"democracy" in a mass-membership supporters' organization
of which local community leaders are a part than in an organization purely of "bosses" who deliver the vote. By dis-
guising in a sense their support among the bosses in the robes
of the *kōenkai*, the Diet politician can to some extent avoid
the criticism of being an old style or "feudalistic" type politician. For another, institutionalizing the support of local
politicians in a *kōenkai*, with the feeling of self importance
that attaches to such titles as "federation chief," makes it somewhat more difficult for the local politician to switch to another
candidate. Third, the incorporation of local politicians into
the *kōenkai* in some cases reflects their changing functions in
the Diet campaign. Some Diet members see the function of
the local politician not to be the gathering of votes by techniques they consider effective in only the most rural communities but rather the more limited one of adding prestige,
providing opportunities for the candidate to meet with voters
and recruit members for his *kōenkai*, and influencing the
electorate in terms of explaining to his own constituents the
benefits to be gained from voting for the Diet candidate he
supports. Such a limited role is opposed by the local politicians themselves because they obviously have the most to
gain the more their support is believed to be crucial to the

[7] See Nathaniel Thayer, *How the Conservatives Rule Japan.* (Princeton,
1969), pp. 91-92.

candidate's success. In this sense the *kōenkai* stands as a serious challenge to the continuation of a dominant role for such leaders in Diet campaign strategy.

The *kōenkai* membership of LDP Diet members is in some cases of almost staggering proportions. One *kōenkai* in Ibaragi Prefecture has already been mentioned as having a membership of 40,000. Another in Osaka's Third District is reported to have over 30,000 members.[8] In one district in Gumma Prefecture, Fukuda Takeo is said to have 50,000 people in his *kōenkai* and Nakasone Yasuhiro another 50,000 in his. Perhaps the most mammoth was that of the late Ōno Bamboku, whose *Bokuyūkai* (the Friends of [Bam]boku Club) is alleged to have had a membership of as many as 150,000 people.[9] In all, it is estimated that *kōenkai* of LDP Diet members have a total membership of somewhere around ten million.[10]

Kōenkai usually consist of several divisions: a women's group, a youth group, and so on. One Diet member's *kōenkai* consists of a youth friendship club (*seinen dōshikai*), a women's club, a "blue cloud" club (*Seiunkai,* the term "blue cloud" being used to refer to those who harbor lofty ambitions), and a *Hōtokukai,* a term referring to Buddhist moral principles and used as a euphemism for an elderly people's club.[11] The *kōenkai* of Nakasone Yasuhiro, in addition to having groups similar to these, also has been trying to develop a separate division for young ladies.

Although the "supporters' organization" is in fact created and financed by the politician it is to support, the fiction is maintained that it is created by the will of the people to advance the political career of a particular person. The politician at the head of a *kōenkai* constantly endeavors to expand the organization's membership in order to foster an image of mass support which in turn is used to attract new support.

8 *Asahi Shinbun,* January 3, 1966, p. 14.
9 Ishida Takeshi, *Gendai Soshiki Ron* (Tokyo, 1965), p. 81.
10 Watanuki Jōji, *Seiji Shakai,* p. 67.
11 *Asahi Shinbun,* January 4, 1967, p. 14.

The members participate vicariously in the politician's political career and are encouraged to see themselves as the backbone of his support. The hoped for result is some stability in support and a group of enthusiastic campaigners.

Despite the emphasis that is placed on recruitment, *kōenkai* membership is generally of an informal sort. Politicians tend to avoid putting the voter in a situation where he must make a conscious choice between joining or not joining a support organization. Rather, through his *kōenkai*, the politician sponsors various activities which serve to give him publicity and contact with large numbers of the electorate. Through such activities and through the followup of greeting cards, *kōenkai* newspapers, and the like, the participants are gradually made to feel a sense of identification with the politician and a commitment to his political success. In many *kōenkai*, membership is largely the name lists of people who have participated in *kōenkai* activities. This is particularly true of nonincumbent or new members of the Diet who have not had sufficient time to build up their organizations.

Few *kōenkai* apparently collect membership dues, though many officially have a nominal membership fee, usually of one hundred yen or so per year. Even where dues are collected, the *kōenkai* member is more than reimbursed by the activities he enjoys at *kōenkai* expense. These activities have been the source for considerable strident criticism, particularly in the mass media. Just before the 1967 Diet election, several national newspapers ran series on the *kōenkai*. The title of the *Asahi Shinbun*[12] series is typical of the tone of the reporting: "The *Kōenkai*—Background to the Black Mist," the black mist being the term given to corruption exposed in the months preceding the election. These articles invariably stressed the party-like atmosphere of *kōenkai* meetings, the provision at ridiculously low cost or at no cost at all of trips to hot springs, sightseeing tours of the Diet building, records,

[12] See series "Kōenkai—Kuroi Kiri No Haikei," *Asahi Shinbun,* January 1–8, 1967.

fans, towels, and other souvenirs of the Diet member, and in general an emphasis upon entertaining the participants lest they start thinking about politics. The value of the meals, the souvenirs, and the other things the membership enjoys at *kōenkai* expense far exceed the amount of money they are requested to pay. As one scholar lamented: "In the United States a hundred-dollar-a-plate dinner is held, with the money remaining after the costs of the dinner being used for the politician's campaign. In Japan, the *kōenkai* method is to give the members a vacation at a hot springs for a hundred yen membership fee."[13]

Following the 1967 Diet elections, the Fair Elections Federation conducted the first nationwide poll to question voters about the *kōenkai*. Voters were asked the question, "Are you a member of a *kōenkai* that give support to a particular candidate?" For those who answered "No" or "Don't Know" the pollsters asked if the respondent had ever been asked to join a *kōenkai* or had been a member of one in the past two to three years. The responses are found in Table 13. Most striking is the small percentage of people who said they were members of a *kōenkai* (5.8 per cent), a much smaller percentage of the electorate than is estimated by both scholars and politicians to be *kōenkai* members. Over 80 per cent maintained they had never been a member nor had they ever been asked to join a *kōenkai*. Only 1.5 per cent of the respondents said they pay a *kōenkai* membership fee (see Table 14). *Kōenkai* membership is certainly somewhat greater than this response would indicate, but the low affirmative response perhaps reflects the informality of much *kōenkai* membership.

Looked at from a somewhat different perspective, even this small percentage of people who said they were members of a *kōenkai,* if projected to the entire electorate, represents a substantial number. In the 1967 Diet election 63 million people were eligible to vote. If the sample of the poll is representa-

13 Tsuji Kiyoaki, "Mūdo to Jitsueki No Tatakai," *Asahi Jānaru* IX (February 12, 1967), 14.

Table 13: Kōenkai Membership

"Are you a member of a *kōenkai* that gives support to a candidate?" For those who answer No or Don't Know: "Have you ever been asked in the past two or three years to join a *koenkai*?"

	Yes	Not a member; don't know		
		Have been asked	Am not now a member but have been a member in the past 2–3 years	Have not been asked; don't know
TOTAL (N = 2,484)	5.8	11.4	1.8	81.0
7 metropolitan cities	4.2	18.1	2.4	75.3
small & medium size cities	6.4	11.0	1.9	80.6
(medium size)	7.3	14.2	2.0	76.4
(small size)	5.3	6.9	1.8	85.9
towns and villages	5.8	8.0	1.3	84.9
AGE				
20–29	3.3	8.4	0.8	87.5
30–39	5.7	12.8	1.7	79.7
40–49	6.7	13.5	2.4	77.4
50–59	6.8	12.9	2.6	77.7
60–over	7.0	8.0	1.5	83.4
AGE: Male				
20–29	5.4	11.4	—	83.2
30–39	8.5	18.8	1.5	71.2
40–49	9.3	18.7	3.1	68.9
50–59	9.9	18.0	4.1	68.0
60–over	10.8	11.3	2.0	76.0
total	8.9	16.0	2.2	73.0
AGE: Female				
20–29	2.0	6.6	1.3	90.1
30–39	3.6	8.3	1.9	83.5
40–49	4.7	9.8	1.9	83.5
50–59	3.4	7.4	1.0	88.2
60–over	3.1	4.6	1.0	91.2
total	3.4	7.6	1.5	87.4
EDUCATION				
primary	3.9	5.2	1.0	89.8
old high primary; new junior high	5.9	11.0	1.9	81.2

Table 13 (continued)

	Yes	Not a member; don't know		
		Have been asked	Am not now a member but have been a member in the past 2–3 years	Have not been asked; don't know
old middle; new high school	6.2	13.6	2.3	77.9
old high & technical; new university	6.5	17.3	1.1	75.1
OCCUPATION				
self employed:				
agriculture; forestry; fishing	9.5	13.9	2.2	74.5
merchant, service trades	10.8	20.2	2.9	66.1
other self employment	17.1	5.7	8.6	68.6
employed:				
total	4.9	13.2	1.3	80.7
administrators, managers	9.5	38.1	—	52.4
technical; white collar	5.7	13.9	0.9	79.5
laborers	3.6	9.7	1.7	85.0
family workers:				
agriculture; forestry; fishing	2.9	2.9	1.4	92.8
merchant, service, other	8.1	10.1	1.0	80.8
housewives	3.9	9.6	2.1	84.4
others, unemployed	4.8	6.8	0.8	87.6
POLITICAL PARTY SUPPORTERS				
(in 1967 Diet election):	6.4	12.0	1.8	79.8
L D P	7.9	13.3	1.7	77.2
J S P–D S P–J C P–Kōmeitō	6.0	11.9	2.0	80.1
J S P	4.6	10.6	1.8	83.0
D S P	6.6	14.0	3.7	75.7
J C P	9.4	21.9	—	68.8
Kōmeitō	15.9	14.5	1.4	68.1
Independ. & Minor Parties	3.8	11.5	—	84.5
Others	—	—	—	100.0
Don't Know	1.0	5.5	1.5	92.0
Non-voters	6.8	10.9	1.6	80.8

Source: Kōmei Senkyo Renmei, *Shūgiin Giin Sōsenkyo No Jittai,* pp. 77–78.

Table 14

Kōenkai *Membership Fee*

"Do you pay a *kōenkai* membership fee?"

	Kōenkai Members	Pay	Do not pay	Don't know
Total (N = 2,484)	5.8	1.5	4.2	0.1
seven metropolitan cities	4.2	0.9	3.3	—
small and medium-size cities	6.4	1.3	5.0	0.2
towns and villages	5.8	2.2	3.6	0.1

Source: Kōmei Senkyo Renmei, *Shūgiin Giin Sōsenkyo No Jittai,* p. 81.

tive some 3.5 to 4 million voters considered themselves to be members of *kōenkai,* and a total of some 12 million had in one way or another had contact with these supporters' organizations.

Other data in the poll concerning the types of people who are *kōenkai* members suggest that *kōenkai* are more popular with older than younger voters and more with men than with women. *Kōenkai* have more members among the self-employed and management-level employees than among blue- and white-collar workers. This is because *kōenkai* are formed mainly by politicians within the LDP which has greater support among employer and management classes than among others. The poll's breakdown of *kōenkai* members in terms of party support, however, is inconclusive and reflects a general confusion and misunderstanding about the meaning of the term itself. The 30 per cent of those who voted for the Communist party who allegedly are members of *kōenkai* or have been asked to become members are probably referring to a request to join the party, not a personal support organization.

Kōenkai may have another important characteristic that is not reflected in the polls in figures statistically significant. They appear to be most prevalent in small and medium-sized cities and less so in both rural and metropolitan areas. In highly rural areas reliance on local leaders to mobilize support is the dominant campaign strategy and the *kōenkai* play only a secondary role. The politician is well aware that the small or medium-sized city, in contrast, is large enough that a breakdown in more traditional modes of social behavior makes reliance on community leaders irrational, while at the same time small enough that a strategy of organizing large numbers of voters is feasible. Heavily populated urban areas, on the other hand, may make unrealistic such an attempt at organizing the general voter since extremely large numbers of votes are needed for election. When I asked Kōno Yōhei,[14] a young Diet member from a district in Kanagawa Prefecture near Tokyo, about his *kōenkai,* he replied that he did not give it much attention because in his district, one of the areas referred to as Tokyo's "bedroom," a residential heavily populated area from which people commute to work in the nation's capital, there are *too many* floating votes. His belief is that it would be impossible to organize enough voters into a *kōenkai* to make the endeavor worthwhile. In his district he had no choice but to put major emphasis on a strategy that provided maximum personal exposure to the voters through speeches and whatever coverage could be obtained in the mass media. Thus further research into the *kōenkai* and future developments in Japanese campaign strategies may mark the *kōenkai* as being something of a midpoint on a rural-urban continuum.

What can be said about *kōenkai* on the basis of information presently available is that they are organizations of politicians created by them for the purpose of expanding and to some extent institutionalizing their support among the general electorate. They aim for mass membership in order to build a broad base of support among the average voters as an alternative or addition to a campaign strategy that gives local poli-

14 Interview, July 1967.

ticians and other community notables the responsibility of gathering and delivering a substantial vote.

The development of mass-membership organizations to support particular LDP politicians has been paralleled by a concerted effort on the part of the LDP to make more effective the party's regional organizations. As part of that effort, the LDP has attempted to incorporate the *kōenkai* into the party structure with a view to eventually dissolving these personal organizations and making election campaigning party-oriented and party-directed. This attempt has been notably unsuccessful and has exposed the fundamental conflict between the *kōenkai* and the party.

Yamanashi Prefecture has been a particular target for LDP organizational efforts, and a serious attempt has been made there to bring the *kōenkai* into the party's organizational structure. The inability of the party organization to gain any control over these personal organizations and the obstacle to the party's organizational development that the *kōenkai* present was given graphic expression in the February 16, 1960 report to the Secretary-General and Chairman of the Organization Committee from the Yamanashi Prefecture LDP Chapter.

In face of the Prefectural Chapter's firm determination to regenerate its organization, each LDP Diet member is trying to form with large financial investments, his personal *kōenkai* in each town and village in the prefecture to secure support for himself. . . . As a serious obstacle to [party] organization, [the *kōenkai*] is a source of constant despair. . . . The personal *kōenkai* disintegrates the party's basic organization in the prefecture. As long as stern measures are not taken against the personal *kōenkai,* all the splendid plans party headquarters may make for the consolidation of the party organization are similar to the hope that fish can be had from wood.[15]

The fundamental reason for this conflict between the *kōenkai* and the party is the fear of individual candidates that in the single entry ballot multimember districting system,

[15] Quoted in Matsushita, *Gendai Nihon No Seijiteki Kōsei*, p. 150.

party control would in fact work to the benefit of some candidates and to the disadvantage of others, depending on the degree of support commanded by these individuals among the Chapter's leaders. The authors of a study called *Senkyo* (*Elections*) have written in regard to this point that

In addition to the fact [that the organizational base of political parties is weak], when attempts are made to organize, they are blocked by the personal *kōenkai* . . . the reason being that if Diet members and candidates turned over to the party the *meibo* (name lists) of their own *kōenkai* there would be considerable likelihood that other candidates would use them to cut into their personal support. Politicians, therefore, oppose bringing their own supporters into the party organization.[16]

The same instinct for self-preservation that keeps local politicians from sharing the name lists of their supporters with the Diet candidate they support works on the Diet candidate to keep his supporters secret from possible opponents and, thus, secret from the party organization.

The LDP Chapter in Ōita Prefecture has also attempted to effect some kind of communication between the party organization and the *kōenkai* of the several Diet members in the Prefecture. In the Chapter's 1961 report on planned party activities, the Committee on Election Strategy indicated as one of the party's prime goals the "development of close communication and cooperation between the [party] organization and the *kōenkai*."[17] The Committee envisaged the creation of a group of liaison men which would establish ties between the Chapter organization and the individual *kōenkai* and which would provide information necessary for the party to coordinate the campaign activities of its candidates. In preparation for the Upper House election in 1962, the Chapter prepared a document entitled "The Establishment of a Cam-

16 Kobayashi Naoki, Shinohara Hajime and Sōma Masao, *Senkyo* (Tokyo, 1960), p. 91.
17 Jiyūminshutō Ōita Kenren, *Katsudō Hōshin* (Ōita, 1961), p. 28.

paign Organization Structure."[18] A major point of this document was that "Only those *kōenkai* . . . activities which are conducted within the framework of the Chapter organization's activities will be allowed. *Kōenkai* activities will be conducted in close cooperation with the Chapter and under the unified command of the Chapter's election strategy committee. . . ." It was expected that once the party Chapter, through the system of liaison men, had established some sort of direction over *kōenkai* activities, it would be possible to then dissolve the *kōenkai* by bringing their members into the party organization and having the party conduct the election campaigns of its candidates. The plan never got off the ground. The liaison men were regarded as spies by the *kōenkai* with which they were supposed to communicate, and the fear that any information given the party would serve the interests of a competing politician caused the entire project to collapse.

By 1966 the Chapter had given up any attempt to gain influence over the campaign activities of its candidates. The Chapter's new position was that as long as the present electoral system continued to exist, the Chapter could play no effective role in the election campaign beyond making recommendations for party endorsement. People who were primarily concerned with the fortunes of individual candidates should be encouraged to join *kōenkai* while the party's efforts should be concentrated on developing a group of dedicated party workers. Reversing itself completely from its position five years earlier, the Chapter decided that rather than try to regulate the campaigns of its endorsed candidates, it would be best to let the party's candidates fight each other freely. The fiercer the battle, the more the candidates would attempt to increase their votes and, in the aggregate, the greater the total number of votes the party would receive. One of the candidates who built up his *kōenkai* for such a battle in this Prefecture was Satō Bunsei.

18 Jiyūminshutō Ōita Kenren, *Senkyo Soshiki Taisei No Kakuritsu* (Ōita, 1962).

Organizations which are clearly for the purpose of support-ing a politician are defined as political groups (*seiji dantai*) in the Political Funds Regulation Law[19] and are required to register with the Autonomy Ministry or its local Election Man-agement Commission within seven days of formation.[20] Such political groups must submit annual accounts of all income and expenditures to the Ministry.[21] Few *kōenkai*, however, are registered. The common practice is for politicians to estab-lish the organization as a so-called "cultural club" (*bunka dantai*) that ostensibly has a broad range of interests and usu-ally consists of several divisions for women, youth, mountain climbers, music lovers and the like, but which in fact has the one function of mobilizing support for a particular politician. The use of such cultural clubs avoids the necessity of sub-mitting financial accounts and, because of its wide range of activities, allows for an appeal to a broad sector of the elec-torate without forcing a conscious decision on whether or not to join a political club. One of the few academics to analyze the *kōenkai* writes that there are "two major groups [of *kōenkai*]: those which are clearly for the purpose of support-ing and backing a particular Diet member or Diet candidate . . . and those which are ostensibly cultural clubs . . . with the Diet member or candidate as President and which serve as campaign organizations when the President is a candidate for office."[22] Even more common for incumbent Diet mem-bers is to have both types of organizations. One, duly regis-tered with the Local Autonomy Ministry, is usually located in Tokyo and is for the financial backers of the politician. The other "cultural club" is organized in the election district and is the politician's general membership organization among the electorate. In general use the term *kōenkai* refers to the organization among the voters in the politician's district.

[19] *Seiji Shikin Kisei Hō*, Article 3.
[20] *Ibid.*, Article 6.
[21] *Ibid.*, Article 12.
[22] Yoshimura Tadashi, *Nihon Seiji No Shindan* (Tokyo, 1965), p. 223.

"In 1957 the cultural club *Fūsetsukai,* was born as an organ of friendship bringing together our elders, friends, and juniors."[23] This "Wind and Snow Society" is Satō's *kōenkai.* The *Fūsetsukai* organization is fairly typical of the LDP *kōenkai.* It was modeled after the *Seiunkai* or Blue Cloud Society of Nakasone Yasuhiro, who was the guest speaker at the *Fūsetsukai's* gala inaugural meeting. The *Fūsetsukai* has several divisions. There is a reading club, a mountain climbing club, a club for traveling, a youth organization, a women's division, and a division "for the study of politics and economics." The *Fūsetsukai* has a headquarters, the *Fūsetsukaikan,* built as an annex to Satō's home in Beppu. Unlike the imposing structures that house the *kōenkai* of some incumbent Diet members, the *Fūsetsukaikan* is a small two-story building with an office downstairs and one large room on the second floor that can accommodate twenty to twenty-five people. It is here that Satō's staff, officially the *Fūsetsukai* staff, works. The permanent staff is small, consisting of a director, a secretary, and two clerical workers. Also on the staff is Saita Matato, forty-nine years old, the owner of a small inn in Beppu, and Satō's unofficial *sanbōchō,* a military term meaning the head of the general staff and used by politicians to refer to their campaign manager.[24]

After his defeat in the 1963 election, Satō, writing in his *kōenkai* newspaper, the *Fūsetsu Kaihō,* told his readers that "the flame of our ideals has not been extinguished," and appealed for new *Fūsetsukai* members to help carry that flame forward.[25] At the time of the January, 1967 election, the *Fūsetsukai* claimed a membership of about 8,000 people, almost all of whom lived in Beppu.

"Membership" in the *Fūsetsukai,* as in *kōenkai* generally, is largely informal. Particularly for a nonincumbent candi-

23 *Fūsetsu Kaihō,* March 1, 1964.

24 Like Americans, Japanese use a great deal of military terminology in regard to elections.

25 *Fūsetsu Kaihō,* March 1, 1964.

date like Satō, whose *kōenkai* is still in the formative stages, the membership is largely the name lists of people known to support him or people with whom he has come into direct contact, such as audiences at the neighborhood speeches, and those who have taken part in some *kōenkai* activity. Building *kōenkai* membership is largely a matter of meticulously building up these name lists, bombarding the people on them with a constant stream of correspondence, and inviting them to *Fūsetsukai* functions, all of course at the expense of the politician who is being supported by the *kōenkai*. Membership dues of one hundred yen a year are accepted if proffered by a voter but are not systematically collected. While there is a small percentage of members who acknowledge their membership, faithfully pay dues, and wear a *Fūsetsukai* badge in their lapel, membership for the great majority is informal.

The *Fūsetsukai* is organized almost exclusively in Beppu. Only here did Satō have an already established base of broad support as a result of his Prefectural Assembly elections, and only here could he appeal as the home town candidate to the voters to band together to get a native son into the Diet. In addition to these factors, the concentration of *kōenkai* activities in Beppu was the result of Satō's basic perception of the differences between floating and hard votes and their implications for strategy. The *kōenkai* is for the purpose of organizing the floating vote and accordingly it was a technique used mainly in those areas where floating votes were seen as most prevalent. In rural areas Satō's *kōenkai* activities were of a tentative, almost wary sort, as if he were hesitantly jabbing at the structure of his own perception of hard votes and the inaccessibility of the rural electorate. In the few places where he was urged by local politicians who supported him to meet with the electorate he established "Chapters" of the *Fūsetsukai*. Kunisaki town assemblyman Takami, as discussed in Chapter III, urged Satō to speak in his village. At one of these meetings the Kunisaki town, Kamikunisaki village Chapter of the *Fūsetsukai* was dedicated, with Assemblyman Takami being made Chapter president (*shibuchō*). Chapters were established in a few other places as well, but these represented a very limited attempt at introducing new strategies into the rural sectors of the district and were never considered as an alternative to a strategy of reliance on local politicians. Satō drew a clear distinction between his elitist supporters and the functions they were to perform and the *kōenkai*. Even when the former, as in the case of Takami, were given positions in the *kōenkai*, they were considered responsible for performing functions of gathering the vote distinctly separate from functions related to *kōenkai* membership.

Satō's perception of rural and nonrural voting behavior not only inhibited him from attempting to extensively use the *kōenkai* approach in rural areas but also led him to largely discount the impact of the rural voters that were brought into the *kōenkai* in areas such as Takami's village in Kunisaki. In Satō's strategy a member of the *Fūsetsukai* in Beppu is calculated to provide him with five votes. The presence of floating voters generally indifferent to the various candidates and not susceptible to the pressures of local community leaders means that any supporter should be able to obtain the votes of at least two or three people outside his own family. An energetic campaigner without any particular influence in his community should be able to obtain the support of ten or so voters for the candidate he supports. Thus 5,000 Beppu members of the *Fūsetsukai* should provide close to 25,000 votes. In rural areas, in contrast, such nonelite voters were calculated to provide no more than three votes apiece. Satō's view was that in rural areas there are few floating votes to whom the average voter can appeal. The support of a farmer in the district was expected to result in no more than the vote of his own immediate family. Consequently Satō's *kōenkai* activities were limited almost entirely to Beppu and the second largest city of Nakatsu.

Despite the various divisions of the *Fūsetsukai* and the large number of functions it ostensibly sponsors, the activities of this cultural club are directed exclusively at organizing support for Satō. The *Fūsetsukai* publishes at irregular intervals the *Fūsetsu Kaihō*, which gives accounts of Satō's activities and occasionally publishes pamphlets or books by or about Satō. Members are the objects of an almost unbroken stream of correspondence: copies of the *Fūsetsu Kaihō*, New Year and Mid-Summer cards, and other materials that keep them informed of the latest developments in Satō's political career. When Satō gives a speech it is "sponsored" by the *Fūsetsukai* and Satō appears at the guest *sensei*. Having the *kōenkai* sponsor a meeting is a useful technique not only for the image of grass roots support it gives the "invited" *sensei,* but also because it provides a convenient means for getting around the legal ban on pre-election campaigning. Satō in his speeches before the beginning of the official campaign period was merely discussing political matters with members of the club for the study of politics and economics that is one of the divisions of the *Fūsetsukai*.

Like many other politicians Satō uses his *kōenkai* as the ostensible sponsor for virtually all his activities. As a result, the *Fūsetsukai* operates very much like a small political party. People identify with it and turn to it for various favors and services much as Americans turned to the urban party machine in its heyday earlier in the century. It is this doing of a great variety of favors for the electorate that imposes the greatest demands on the *kōenkai* staff's time and the politician's purse.

The reasons for the considerable emphasis Satō places on the doing of favors can be analyzed in terms of political dynamics applicable to any system of representative democracy. The Japanese politician is not unique in seeing the benefits to be derived from doing favors for the people who go to the polls. It is important to note, however, that the doing of favors, for Satō and other LDP politicians, is not only for the purpose of obtaining the vote of the recipient of the favor in the relevant election, but is also a specific means for recruiting *kōenkai* members. Once in the *Fūsetsukai* the voter who had been the recipient of a favor from Satō would be the object of *Fūsetsukai* correspondence and would in the candidate's strategy be expected to campaign for other votes on his behalf. Doing favors is intended to produce a sense of indebtedness to and a feeling of identification not with a political party but with a particular politician and his *kōenkai*.

A visit to the *Fūsetsukai* headquarters on almost any day reveals the central role the doing of favors plays in the daily activities of Satō and his staff. A culling of entries from a diary I kept while living in Satō's home gives an idea of the atmosphere in the headquarters:

At 9:00 this morning when I went down to the office there was already a man waiting for Satō's secretary to arrive. When he did the visitor said that he was from Nishi school district and was told by Satō's *sewanin* in a neighborhood in the district that the *Fūsetsukai* could help him find a job for his son in one of Beppu's hotels. The secretary immediately got on the phone to arrange for an interview for the son at a nearby hotel. Just as he was leaving, the octogenarian President of the elderly people's club in Satō's own neighborhood came in to ask if Satō would contribute a couple of bottles of sake for the meeting the club was holding that evening. . . . Satō's secretary spent the afternoon today driving around Hasuda school district inviting the *sewanin* to a dinner party in preparation for the neighborhood speeches Satō wants to begin there next month. While he was out several people dropped by to have a cup of tea and pass on the latest gossip about so-and-so switching support from Nishimura to Ayabe and some former supporter of Noyori who has "at least a hundred votes he'll give to Satō if Satō pays him a personal courtesy call." One very diffident woman whose son had failed a high school entrance exam came in to ask if there was anything Satō could do to have him admitted to the school anyway. . . . Satō spent the afternoon at a wedding in which he was acting as official middleman. This is the third wedding he has had to officiate at this week. . . .

There is an almost unceasing stream of visitors to the *Fūsetsukai* office that gives it the atmosphere of being a combination employment agency, school placement service, marriage counseling center, and a kind of social club where people may drop in, have a cup of tea, and talk of elections and politics.[26] From early in the morning to late at night Satō worked to do favors for the voters. The "agony of the three *kai*" (*sankai no kurushimi*) is the expression Satō has coined to describe his daily life: interviews (*menkai*), introductions (*shōkai*), and dinner parties (*enkai*).

The combination of being a nonincumbent candidate and a locality-oriented politician lent a highly local color to Satō's activities and the nature of the favors and services he could provide the constituents. Heading the list of favors Satō does for the voters is help in getting jobs and in school placement. In 1966 the *Fūsetsukai* was asked to help nearly 100 people to get into high school. In 1967 seventy-three such requests were received. Satō has close ties with several high school principals in Beppu who are strong supporters of the LDP, in contrast to the teachers on their staffs who are members of the Japan Teachers Union (*Nikkyōso*), which supports the Socialist Party. He prevails upon these friends to admit borderline cases, and his staff is in constant contact with the child's parents, keeping them informed of Satō's efforts. Where unsuccessful, Satō tries to get the student into a less difficult high school. In March and April, graduation time in Japan, school entrance is practically the sole concern of the *Fūsetsukai* staff. There are also attempts to help students get into college, but here Satō cannot exert the influence he has with the high school principals. Similarly, there are 100 to 150 requests yearly for aid in finding desired employment. There is one hotel in Beppu in which virtually the entire staff was hired through Satō and Murakami Isamu, his faction boss.

---

[26] This atmosphere is reminiscent of that of political clubs in the fabled heyday of the urban party machine in the United States: "[It] offered . . . a range of services that made it, in contemporary terms, a combination of employment agency, legal aid society, social worker, domestic relations counselor, and community social center." See Frank J. Sorauf, *Political Parties in the American System* (Boston, 1964), p. 4.

In the case of incumbent Diet members, the number of requests such as these goes much higher.[27] In Satō's case these activities were limited almost entirely to Beppu.

A considerable portion of Satō's time and daily expenses are involved in the favors he does in connection with what is called in Japanese *kankonsōsai*, literally the occasions of coming of age, marriage, and death, a term used to refer generally to all ceremonious occasions. In the *Fūsetsukai* office there is, for example, a large file of *miai shashin*, pictures of eligible young ladies whose parents have asked Satō's help in finding a suitable suitor. In addition to this matchmaking role, Satō and his wife act as the official matchmaker (that is, for the ceremony only) at weddings on the average of once or twice a month. In the marriage seasons of the fall and spring, attending weddings becomes an almost daily activity.

One of the *kankonsōsai* activities which entails a constant and considerable expense is the sending of wreaths to funerals in the district. In Beppu alone Satō send an average of fifteen each month, large round wreaths of artificial flowers with the donor's name in big characters in the center. He sends an additional ten a month to funerals in areas outside of the city. His *sewanin* in the neighborhoods inform his office of any deaths in the area and whether the occasion necessitates a wreath, the presence of Satō or a staff member, or merely a telegram of condolence.

The Japanese year is dotted with an almost continuous series of religious and social celebrations that the politician utilizes for sending greetings and presents to constituents. At

27 Newspapers, particularly around election time, provide a wealth of information on the services Diet men provide their constituents. See, for examples, *Asahi Shinbun*, January 4, 1967, p. 14, and *Mainichi Shinbun*, January 3, 1967, p. 1. Though activities of the Diet politicians in their home districts are generally neglected in academic writings, there are brief discussions in Fujiwara Hirotatsu and Tomita Nobuo, *Seijiaku E No Chōsen* (Tokyo, 1967), pp. 31ff., Yomiuri Shinbun Seijibu Hen, *Seitō* (Tokyo, 1966), pp. 21ff., and Ishii Kinichirō and Yamada Hiroshi, *Gendai Nihon No Seiji* (Tokyo, 1967), pp. 79–88.

the beginning of the year Satō sends New Year cards and in the middle of the year midsummer greeting cards to approximately 20,000 voters in the district. He also occasionally sends early summer or later summer cards. At the time of the *Bon* festival in honor of the spirits of the deceased, presents and greetings are sent for *hatsubon,* for people who have lost a relative within the year since the previous *Bon* festival. In 1967, for instance, Satō's wife and three members of Satō's staff traveled over the whole district personally delivering 300 packages of incense to those observing the *hatsubon.* Sympathy cards were sent to many others.

Through these types of activities and an innumerable variety of others, the politician expresses his interest in and his concern for the people of his constituency, and strives for the reputation most sought by politicians, that of *sewazuki*—a person who likes to do favors.[28]

Contributions (*kifu*) require a special note because of the great expense they entail for the politician in his home district. From a couple of bottles of sake for an elderly people's club party to several thousand yen for the building of a bridge or a public hall or for a religious group, the politician, particularly a Diet member or Diet candidate, is called upon to make contributions for a variety of groups and purposes. The *goshūgi,* the gratuity or congratulatory gift that Satō brings to functions he is invited to as a guest or, when he cannot attend, delivers through the local liquor store in the form of sake, is a small but constant expense. In addition to these are large contributions, ones that hit hard at the politician's pocketbook but which show that he is "looking after" his district. In the six

[28] The reputation sought by the Diet member or candidate received fitting expression in the following statement by a supporter of an incumbent member of the Diet: "Thanks to the *sensei,* bridges were built, roads were made wider. Whenever there was a fire he always kindly sent a condolence gift. He was generous whenever asked to make a contribution and he invited us to take trips at very little expense. In finding jobs or helping out with school entrance he was always there, a man with a heart and a proper sense of obligation." See Mainichi Shinbun, January 3, 1967, p. 1.

months preceding the election in January 1967, Satō made contributions of considerable sums for the building of a new roof for a Buddhist temple in Usa county, for the building of two public halls in Beppu, for the building of a bridge in Kitsuki, for the erection of a statue in honor of a famous Meiji period dentist in Nakatsu, and a sizeable donation to a religious group in Beppu that was supporting him. The financial burden such contributions place on Diet politicians has become a matter of national concern, and the Fifth Electoral System Study Council has recommended that they be prohibited by law.[29] The giving of such contributions is, however, so much a part of social custom that the politician is in constant fear of getting a reputation for being stingy or disdainful of the customs of the common people if he refuses to make them.

The cost of various greeting cards and presents alone is well over one million yen annually. In addition there is a minimum expense of 600,000 to 700,000 yen a month. This does not include campaign expenses or the cost of special projects, nor does it include personal family expenses. In one typical month, for example, Satō spent 680,000 yen. This included 250,000 yen in office expenses and 280,000 in contributions. The latter were for the construction of three public halls, the refurbishing of a shrine, donations for two shrine festivals, and another toward the building of a bridge. During the month Satō sent twenty funeral wreaths and spent 30,000 yen in telegrams of condolence. Another 100,000 yen was spent for dinner parties and entertainment.[30]

The supporters' organization, as mentioned earlier, does

29 See *Yomiuri News,* April 4, 1967, p. 1.

30 Satō's expenses are apparently much less than those of incumbent Diet men. One million yen is generally reported to be the minimum monthly expense for any member of the Diet. One source sets the minimum at one-and-a-half million yen (*Yomiuri Shinbun,* January 7, 1967, p. 15) and another contends that two million yen is the figure for the average monthly expenditures of Diet members (*Asahi Shinbun,* October 4, 1966), p. 1.

not, despite its name, provide financial support. For his daily expenses Satō relied on three sources of income.[31] The most important was the salary he received as Board Chairman (*kaichō*) of an electrical engineering company with offices in Ōita City. The position of Board Chairman is an honorary one, the real control of the firm being in the hands of its President (*shacho*). A second source of funds is the stipend received from serving as advisor (*komon*) to several business firms in the Prefecture. Satō is officially advisor to four firms and unofficially receives a monthly stipend from three others. The most important source of support in this group is one of Ōita's largest construction companies. The Vice-President of that company (the son of the President) and the owner of the electrical supply company are both closely associated with Satō's third source of funds, the local LDP Chapter, or more accurately, Satō's political benefactors, Iwasaki and Murakami. Satō receives mid-year (*chūgen*) and year-end (*seibo*) presents of considerable sums from these two LDP leaders, and it is they who play the central role in collecting contributions from businessmen for the campaign at election time. Together these three sources provided the *Fūsetsukai* with an average of between six and seven hundred thousand yen a month, just enough to meet minimum expenses.

In addition to these minimum monthly expenses were the costs involved in special *Fūsetsukai* activities and the costs of the actual campaign itself. The *Fūsetsukai* was the sponor of periodic meetings, rallies, and parties. The conduct of these activities has certain peculiar characteristics that result from the nature of the *kōenkai* organization and the provision of the election law prohibiting pre-election campaigning. This provision has resulted in what may be called the strategy of the "noncampaign." This strategy and the role of the *kōenkai* in it are the subject of the following chapter.

---

[31] These are not to be confused with the sources that financed the official campaign, a question to be discussed in Chapter VIII.

A Sidewalk Speech in Beppu
Courtesy of Ōita Gōdō Shinbun

VI

The *Kōenkai* and the "Noncampaign"

IN THE 1934 REVISION of the Lower House Election Law an entirely new provision, inserted as Article 7, paragraph 4, stated that "Election campaigning . . . may be engaged in only after the registration of candidacy is completed."[1] Before that time there was no official campaign period in law, though campaigning before the registration of candidacy was restricted by the police on the basis of "campaigning without qualifications" (*mushikaku undō*).[2] With the new provision, *jizen undō* or pre-election campaigning, was explicitly made illegal. In the Public Offices Election Law of 1950 the "prohibition of pre-election campaigning," as the above provision came to be known, was incorporated in almost identical language as Article 129. As yet unamended, the article reads: "Election campaigning for each election shall be engaged in only during the period from the day candidacy is registered to the day preceding the date of the election concerned."[3] Registration of candidacy begins on the day the elections are officially announced (*kōji*), which is at least twenty days before Election Day. Elections must be held within forty days of the dissolution of the Lower House.

While Article 129 prohibits pre-election campaigning, there is no article in any law which defines election campaigning; in other words, which defines what is to be prohibited.[4] Con-

---

[1] Senkyo Seido Nanajyūnen Kinenkai, *Senkyohō No Enkaku* (Tokyo, 1959), p. 14.

[2] Hayashida Kazuhiro, *Senkyohō, in Hōritsugaku Zenshū,* v (Tokyo, 1958), p. 168.

[3] *Election Law,* Article 129.

[4] Jichishō Senkyo Kyokuhen, *Sōsenkyo No Tebiki* (Tokyo, 1967), p. 4.

[153]

sequently, the question of what actions constitute *jizen undō* has become a matter of legal interpretation.

A history of court decisions and a consensus of scholarly opinion have resulted in a definition of election campaigning as being "those activities that are for the purpose of influencing voters to vote for a particular candidate in a particular election."[5] The three parts of the definition have resulted in what is called the "three essentials of election campaigning": (1) the action has to be for the purpose of soliciting votes. This includes what is called direct action, meaning action to obtain votes for a particular candidate, and indirect action, meaning activities to prevent votes from going to a particular candidate;[6] (2) the action has to concern a particular candidate. This includes not only people who have declared their candidacy but also anyone who may be planning to become a candidate in the future.[7] Political activities that are not for the purpose of electing a particular candidate are, consequently, not election campaigning, even if such action is in relation to a particular election. Thus, a speech by an official of the Liberal Democratic Party explaining the policies of the party and asking support for the party rather than for any particular candidate is not election campaigning;[8] (3) the action has to concern a particular election. As Lower and Supreme Court decisions have made clear, this provision does not mean that the action has to be at the time of the election but that it merely has to be in relation to a particular election. Conceivably, activities as much as a year or two before an election could be election campaigning if they were intended to obtain votes for a particular candidate in that particular election.[9] Conversely, activities by candidates are not con-

---

[5] *Ibid.*, p. 5; Court decisions and scholarly opinions are cited in Hayashida, pp. 167 ff.

[6] Hayashida, p. 167.

[7] *Ibid.*, p. 167.

[8] Gakuyō Shobo Henshūbu, *Senkyo Undō* (Tokyo, 1967), p. 8; Jichishō p. 5.

[9] Gakuyō Shobō Henshūbu, p. 7; Hayashida, p. 167.

sidered election campaigning if they are not intended to get votes in a particular election.[10]

In law and in practice a distinction is made between election campaigning (*senkyo undō*) and political activities (*seiji katsudō*), the latter being defined as "activities of political parties and other political groups for the purpose of publicizing their policies, developing the party, or increasing political education. They are not activities that are directly intended to elect a particular candidate in a particular election."[11] Accordingly, no politician ever engages in pre-election campaigning but all are very busy with "political activities." As Diet dissolution appears to get closer such political activities increase at a frantic tempo.

Besides the opportunities this distinction between "political activities" and "election campaigning" provides for getting around Article 129, there are two types of activities that lie outside the scope of the pre-election campaigning ban. One is composed of activities necessary to prepare for the campaign. This covers mainly routine matters such as printing posters, renting a campaign office, obtaining a transcript of the family register, arranging for a campaign car, loudspeakers, and halls for speeches, and making the deposit of 100,000 yen required of all candidates. Also included, however, are activities such as obtaining the endorsement of a political party, procuring campaign funds, requesting recommendations of people to be included on campaign postcards, and arranging for an accountant and for campaigners.[12] The other type of activity permitted is that called *sebumi kōi*. *Sebumi* means wading into water to test its depth and is figuratively used to mean a trial balloon or a feeler. *Kōi* means "action," or "activities." Such "trial balloon activities" are intended to let the candidate "learn the views of the electo-

10 Jichishō, pp. 1–2, 5.

11 Hayashida, p. 168.

12 Jichishō, p. 15; Naikaku Hōseikyoku Daisanbu, *Senkyo Jitsumu Roppō* (Tokyo, 1966), p. 324.

rate for the purpose of deciding whether to run or not. . . ."[13] He can make speeches, hold discussion meetings with voters, and in general try to "feel out" the voters "without violating the election law so long as the purpose of such activities is not to obtain votes."[14]

The various legal interpretations of Article 129 have obviously done little to remove its ambiguity. If the ambiguity had made the article a dead letter, it would obviously be of little interest. But the government does attempt, however unsuccessfully, to enforce the prohibition on pre-election campaigning, so candidates plan and organize their campaigns with Article 129 in mind.

For the candidate who hopes to discover the permissible scope of activities allowed outside the official election campaign period, the government is of very little help. In its official guide for candidates in Lower House elections, the Local Autonomy Ministry suggests that, in common-sense terms, it is natural to consider all of a politician's activities as being intended to obtain votes. Lest the candidate feel he can therefore do virtually nothing until the official campaign begins, the Ministry goes on to suggest that activities such as reporting to constituents on the work of the current Diet session or the holding of discussion meetings, *kōenkai* meetings, and the like are not, in themselves, violations of Article 129.[15] But, adds the Ministry ominously, "even these types of activities are in many cases adjudged to be election campaigning. . . ."[16] "The line separating election campaigning and political activity is a very vague one. One wrong step can result in a violation."[17]

13 Jichishō, p. 1.
14 *Ibid.*, p. 2.
15 *Ibid.*, p. 6 ff.; Gakuyō Shobō Henshūbu, p. 14.
16 Jichishō, p. 5.
17 *Ibid.*, p. 6; The government also publishes a handbook that discusses in considerable detail permissible political activities for political parties and other political groups in connection with Lower House elections. See Jichishō Senkyokyoku, *Shūgiin Senkyo Ni Okeru Seitō, Seiji Dantai No Seiji Katsudō No Tebiki* (Tokyo, 1967).

According to the Election Law, the maximum penalty for pre-election campaigning is one year in jail or a fine of 15,000 yen.[18] In fact, though, almost all cases of violations of the ban result in nothing more than a warning *(keikoku)* from the police. The great majority of warnings issued deal with the distribution and posting of written materials, that is, postcards, newspaper advertisements, posters, handbills, and so forth. In the months preceding the calling of elections for January 1967, numbers of such warnings were made throughout the country. One warning, for example, was issued to a Diet hopeful who sent out a large number of postcards in his constituency announcing his retirement from the bureaucracy; another to a Diet member who sent out calendars with his picture engraved on the cover; and one to a conscientious owner of an electrical appliance firm who thought he had an ingenious way to get around the prohibition by putting an ad in a local newspaper saying that "I request your understanding if I do not have the time to provide repair service during the campaign period because I have decided to run in the coming general elections."[19]

By December 27, 1966, the day before the House was dissolved, the police had issued 348 warnings for violations of Article 129, 102 more than had been issued in the comparable period preceding the previous Lower House election in 1963.[20] From the day of dissolution to January 7, the day on which candidates could register and campaigning for registered candidates could officially begin, the number of warnings rose at an ever increasing rate. By January 4, 999 warnings had been issued throughout the country, and two days later the number had doubled to 1,939, of which 1,685 were for distribution of written materials.[21] For the entire period preceding *kōji*, the official start of the campaign, 2,504 warnings, the National Police Agency disclosed, had been issued. Ninety

18 *Election Law,* Article 239.
19 *Yomiuri Shinbun,* December 6, 1966.
20 *Ibid.,* December 27, 1966, p. 13.
21 *Nishi Nihon Shinbun,* January 6, 1967, p. 12.

per cent of these were for distribution of written materials. The fight against pre-election campaigning concluded without any arrests being made.[22]

The prohibition of pre-election campaigning, though ambiguous in what it actually prohibits and largely unenforced, nonetheless creates an important element of the framework within which Diet candidates formulate campaign strategies. It may be said with a certain degree of truth that "the routinization and generalization of . . . pre-election campaign activities have made complete nonsense out of the election law's restricted campaign period provision."[23] Obviously candidates do not allow the prohibition to prevent them from engaging in activities intended to mobilize support. Importantly, however, the "routinization" of pre-election campaign activities has been influenced by considerations for getting around the Article's prohibition. Because of the legal ban, candidates are careful to cover up their campaign activities in such a way as to qualify them for classification as "political activity" rather than election campaigning. The Diet candidate cannot allow that any of his activities prior to the calling of the official campaign are intended to garner him votes in a particular election. In their speeches candidates avoid mention of their intention to run in the coming election. They tend to talk in terms general if not vague, particularly since they cannot say that if elected they will do this or that. For one unaware of the art of the "noncampaign," listening to speeches of politicians more than three weeks before election day would fail to indicate that there might be any candidates.

The need to work around Article 129 is one reason politicians use *kōenkai*. Within a *kōenkai* the discussion of political matters is simply one of the organization's many activities, and to have the politician who heads the supporters' organization address the membership simply means to keep

22 *Asahi Evening News,* January 13, 1967, p. 3.
23 Fujiwara Hirotatsu and Tomita Nobuo, *Seijiaku E No Chōsen* (Tokyo, 1967), p. 31.

the members informed on political developments. So long as the politician uses a minimum of subtlety in making "recruitment of members" and *kōenkai* meetings opportunities for campaigning for votes, the *kōenkai* can function quite smoothly as a front for campaign activities.

As part of his "noncampaign" Satō held several large *kōenkai* meetings. The most elaborate of these was a two-day meeting of women from the entire district held in Beppu three months before the election. The meeting illustrates several important aspects of Satō's campaign: the different characteristics of his supporting groups in Beppu and in rural areas; the relationship between LDP party organs and the individual candidate; the techniques for building up *kōenkai* membership; the way in which a *kōenkai* meeting is conducted; and the type of appeal Satō made to the voters in his noncampaign speeches.

In Ōita's Second District there are 156,017 female and 122,567 male voters. Women outnumber men in both the cities (83,928 female voters to 63,636 male) and the counties (72,089 women and 58,931 male voters).[24] In Beppu, with its hotels, bars, and tourist industry, the 45,100 female voters account for 58 per cent of the city's voting population. In the Prefecture as a whole women make up 54 per cent of the electorate.

Satō placed particular emphasis on attracting the support of women. One way to solicit such support was simply to get public exposure in the hope that the female "floating vote" would find him the most attractive of the candidates in terms of age and looks as much as in terms of policy. This effort, concentrated mainly in Beppu, involved little active participation in the campaign on the part of women voters. Another aspect of the appeal to the women was the creation of an organization of female supporters throughout the district that would bring a large number of women into active partici-

[24] Data taken from Senkyo Kanri Iinkai, *Senkyo No Kiroku, Shūgiin Giin Sōsenkyo,* January 29, 1967 election (Ōita, 1967).

pation in Satō's campaign. Satō's efforts in this direction culminated in the holding of "The First Satō Bunsei Women's Political Study Session" *(Dai Ikkai Satō Bunsei Seiji Kyō-shitsu Fujin No Tsudoi),* a two-day affair held on August 24 and 25, 1966, at one of Beppu's largest hotels.

Throughout the first six months of 1966 Satō was considering the idea of holding a large meeting of women in an attempt to give some direction and organization to his support among the district's numerous women voters. In July, with House dissolution appearing ever closer, Satō and his staff began to make plans for the meeting. Without any previous experience to build upon, everything from means of recruitment to writing of the program for the meeting presented new problems.

The first problem was one of timing. In order to capitalize on the participants' enthusiasm, Satō wanted to hold the meeting as close to dissolution as possible but was afraid of trouble arising from the prohibition of pre-election campaigning if held too close to the calling of elections. It was finally decided to hold the meeting at the end of August. Postponing it further would increase the dangers of being caught by a sudden dissolution of the House and, since the autumn months are both the tourist season in Beppu and the rice harvesting season in the rest of the district, recruitment of participants would become difficult if held later in the year.

The greatest problem facing Satō was that of choosing the women to be invited. In Beppu recruitment was based, as all other Satō activities in the city, on the city's eleven school districts and 121 neighborhoods. A figure of 150 participants from Beppu was established, with the idea that one woman from each neighborhood and two or three from a few neighborhoods would be invited. Originally it was planned to have the *sewanin* in each neighborhood recommend a neighborhood representative to attend the meeting. The method for recruiting the participants from Beppu quickly changed, however, because of the new support given Satō by the executives of the LDP women's group in Beppu.

There are two women's organizations in Beppu that became involved in Satō's campaign. One is the organization of neighborhood women's clubs. The city-wide organization is known as the Federation of Beppu Women's Clubs *(Beppu-shi Fujin Dantai Rengōkai)*, and it is associated with one of the largest nationwide organizations, the *Chifuren (Zenkoku Chiiki Fujin Dantai Renraku Kyōgikai)*.[25] Women's clubs in Beppu are organized in 102 of the 121 neighborhoods and the association has a total membership of 4,850. Membership in the organization requires the payment of dues in the amount of thirty yen annually. These neighborhood women's clubs are overwhelmingly conservative party supporting[26] and there is a considerable overlap in membership between them and the second group of women to play a role in Satō's campaign, the LDP women's division in Beppu.[27] The executives of the latter are all active in the local clubs. The President of the Beppu association of local women's club, Ikezaki Chiyo, has served in that position for the past six years and is concurrently Vice-President of the Beppu Branch of the LDP Women's Division. Preceding her as president of the neighborhood club association was Mrs. Kawamura Muga, the present President of the L D P Women's Division in Beppu.

The LDP Women's Division in Beppu *(Beppu-shi Jimintō Fujinbu)* was first formed in 1964[28] and had a membership of 100 in that year. In 1965 its membership increased to 860, and is said to have passed the 1,000 mark in 1966. The

[25] For a discussion of *Chifuren*, see Asahi Jānaru Hen, *Nihon No Kyodai Soshiki* (Tokyo, 1966), pp. 36–52.

[26] *Ibid.*, pp. 47–48; other authors assert that these local women's groups serve as "an essential element in the building of the conservative base of support." See Kobayashi Naoki, Shinohara Hajime, and Sōma Masao, *Senkyo* (Tokyo, 1960), p. 82; another author maintains further that "they are used by the L D P as local branches of the party organization." See Matsushita Keiichi, *Sengo Minshu Shugi No Tenbō* (Tokyo, 1965), p. 173.

[27] Information concerning neighborhood women's clubs based on an interview with Mrs. Ikezaki Chiyo, August 9, 1967.

[28] Information concerning the L D P women's division based on an interview with Mrs. Kawamura on December 8, 1966.

women's division in Beppu is organized on three levels. Basic
is the neighborhood organization, with a section leader in
each of the neighborhoods. These neighborhood groups, following a familiar pattern, are organized into eleven school
district organizations, with a Chairman and Vice-Chairman
in each. At the top of the structure is the President of the
city's division. From its inception, the organization's President
has been Mrs. Kawamura, sixty-five years old, a former teacher,
and a person long active in conservative party politics in
Beppu. The Vice-President of the division, as has been mentioned, is the President of the Beppu association of local
women's clubs, Mrs. Ikezaki.

Satō did not have the support of Mrs. Kawamura in the
1963 election, and her support in 1967 was considered a considerable boon by the Satō camp. In Prefectural Assembly
elections Mrs. Kawamura has long been an active supporter
of Utsunomiya Hidetsuna who, it is to be remembered from
the discussion of party endorsement, is Ayabe's leading supporter in Beppu. In line with her support for Utsunomiya,
Mrs. Kawamura has campaigned for Ayabe in Diet elections.
In the 1963 election there was some talk of the women's group
supporting Satō, but Mrs. Kawamura and the other executives
of the LDP organization continued to back Ayabe. The reason for their failure to support Satō in 1963 was, in Mrs.
Kawamura's explanation of the situation, due to a belief that
Satō would not receive the party's endorsement. It is to be
remembered that in that election Satō obtained LDP endorsement only in the last issuance of names of endorsed candidates,
which was but a few days before the start of the official campaign. By this time Mrs. Kawamura and the other leaders of
the organization were already committed to Ayabe. It was
also felt that Satō did not stand a chance of winning and that
the race was a trial run for him, one in which he would build
up his support for the next election. The result of the 1963
election, accordingly, came as a great shock to Mrs. Kawamura.
If she and her organization had supported Satō, she believes,

he would have received the 1,600 votes by which he lost to the Socialist and the LDP would have taken all three seats in the district. In 1967 Mrs. Kawamura's position was clear. As she told a meeting of the leadership of the Beppu women's division: "Kunisaki is Nishimura's and Ayabe has a base of support running from Kitsuki to Usa county. Therefore, Satō's home town, Beppu, has to make a special effort to get him elected."[29]

In organizing the women's meeting, Mrs. Kawamura played the leading role. With her leadership, responsibility for recruiting participants from Beppu was taken by the executives of the LDP women's division in Beppu. Mrs. Kawamura suggested that rather than try to directly invite women from each of the neighborhoods, Satō should meet with a group of women representing each of the eleven school districts and delegate to them the responsibility for inviting women from the neighborhoods within their respective district. Mrs. Kawamura took the responsibility for inviting the school district representatives to a meeting with Satō and his wife held on August fifth. These women became the core group of activists among Satō women campaigners in Beppu. They are all elderly and active in various organizations in the city. All are executives of the LDP women's division and are active in their local neighborhood women's clubs. Of the twenty-two school district chairmen and vice-chairmen, only one, according to Mrs. Kawamura, did not go along with her in supporting Satō. This was due to long and close relations between her family and Nishimura. In other words, Satō managed to enlist the Beppu women's division of the LDP organization in support of his campaign and his alone.

The major problem in recruiting participants from Beppu was the impossibility of keeping the number of invitees down to the originally planned number of 150. There was no neighborhood in which inviting only one woman would not have

[29] In a meeting with Satō and the executives of the L D P women's division on December 8, 1966.

had the effect of insulting others to the point where some basically friendly to Satō would consider the lack of an invitation sufficient reason to refuse to campaign for him in the election. As a result the guest list rose daily. In the end 248 women were invited, of which 239 attended the meeting.

Outside of Beppu, recruiting participants was the responsibility of Satō's *sekininsha*. During the last week of July, letters were sent to these campaign managers informing them of the planned meeting. They were told that they had sole responsibility for selecting participants and were requested to inform the *Fūsetsukai* office by August fifth of the names and addresses of those who would attend. Each *sekininsha* was given a quota to fill. In general, the quota provided for fifteen participants from Nakatsu, ten from the other two cities, Kitsuki and Bungo Takada, six to seven from the seventeen towns, and five each from the two villages of Ōta and Sanko, providing a total of approximately 150 participants, the thought being that an equal number would be invited from Beppu and from the rest of the district.

The question of who within the quota should be invited proved to be a problem of major proportions in most of the areas. As in Beppu, inviting one group of women inevitably resulted in the dissatisfaction of others. None of the *sekininsha* was able to comply with the August fifth deadline, and in the first week of August a second letter was sent out giving the *sekininsha* further guidelines on how to choose the participants. They were in this letter given the authority to select one to two women from each of the amalgamated villages in their areas. Inviting representatives from each of these subdivisions meant, of course, that the quota of 150 could no more be maintained in the countryside than it could in Beppu. Other problems, the consequence of the nature of the support organization, also arose in regard to recruitment. For one thing, the wives of the *sekininsha* and the former village-level campaign managers were invited to the conference. From the wives' point of view they should attend because they were important supporters of Satō. From the candidate's perspective, the expense of such a conference could hardly be justified if participants were women whose support was already assured.

Another problem was that in those places where Satō had several top-level supporters each had to be allowed to invite one or two people. In one small town, for instance, this problem resulted in the original quota of six participants being increased to thirteen. In Nakatsu the original quota of fifteen was almost immediately realized to be inadequate. Satō's several top-level supporters in the city each wanted to invite a sizeable number of women, and it was decided to allow each a quota of ten. In addition to these, Mrs. Satō personally invited seven women, and a total of forty-eight attended the conference from the city.

Finally, the problem of the most severe proportions resulted from what has been referred to as the inward-looking nature of the support organization. The *sekininsha* naturally tended to invite women with whom they were friendly and whom they knew to support Sato and not others who could play an important role in Satō's campaign if approached. This is why the question of refusals to attend the meeting did not arise. Women who might refuse were not the women who were issued invitations.

Day by day the number of invitees rose past the original figure of 300, and on the eve of the conference 514 people had indicated their intention to attend. At this point Satō, worried about seating, feeding, and sleeping all these women, was almost hoping that the typhoon then threatening Kyūshū would make it to Beppu in time to keep some of the guests away.

On the morning of August 24, women began arriving at the Hakuunsansō hotel for the meeting. The choice of the Hakuunsansō, one of Beppu's most luxurious hotels, as the site for the meeting was not based solely on its ability to host a meeting of 500 people. The hotel is owned by Murakami Haruzō, member of the Upper House of the Diet and younger brother of Satō's faction leader, Murakami Isamu. For Satō this meant that the facilities of the hotel were offered him at a minimum cost.

Though the meeting was scheduled to begin at 2:00 in the afternoon, the first women participants began arriving at the hotel at nine in the morning. As they entered the lobby they were directed along a line of tables where they were registered by Satō's staff. At the first reception desk they were asked to write their names and addresses and indicate whether they were staying overnight, the meeting being planned to end after breakfast the following day. With this document duly stamped they moved on to the next table to pay the conference fee. For those who planned to stay the day only the cost of participating in the study session, including the cost of lunch and dinner, was 300 yen. For those who stayed overnight the fee was 500 yen, including breakfast the following morning. It was expected that while participants from the countryside would spend the night, the women from Beppu would mostly return home after dinner. Not many women, however, passed up the opportunity to spend a night at one of Beppu's largest hotels for what amounted to 200 yen (about fifty-five cents). Of the 486 women that registered, 403 paid the 500-yen fee. At the following table the participants got back most and in some cases more money than they had just paid out in conference fees. Each participant was reimbursed for the round-trip transportation cost entailed in attending the meeting. For participants from Shimoge country, this came to over 1,000 yen. Approximately 230,000 yen was taken in in conference fees and 350,000 yen paid out in transportation costs. After receiving her transportation expenses, the registrant moved on to the next table to receive a name badge and lunch ticket. Finally, at the last table in the line, the participant received a souvenir of the meeting, a *Fūsetsukai* towel engraved with Satō's calligraphy, and an envelope containing the following: a copy of Satō's book, published in

1963 by the *Fūsetsukai, Ōita Ken O Kangaeru (Thinking About Ōita Prefecture)*; a four-page pamphlet entitled *"Satō Bunsei No Subete"* (All about Satō Bunsei") outlining his career; the jacket for the record *"Bunchan No Uta"* ("The Bunchan Song") with a large picture of Satō on a yacht on the front, pictures of Satō with theatrical and political luminaries on the back, and the words and music for the song on the inside; a copy of the latest *Fūsetsukai* newspaper made up especially for the occasion; a two-page mimeographed sheet explaining the types of activities on behalf of a candidate that could be engaged in without violating the legal prohibition against pre-election campaigning and the types of activities the voter could engage in during the official campaign period; a program of the evening's entertainment, including a map explaining how to get to a nearby hotel where there was to be a show of Okinawan dancing free for the participants in the meeting; and a printed program of the meeting and a notebook and pencil so that the women could take notes at the study session.

At two o'clock the nearly 500 women, dressed for the most part in the hotel-provided *yukata*, began assembling in the large straw-matted conference room that was to be the scene for the study session. At first glance the conference looked like one of the LDP women's division. Chairing the meeting was Mrs. Kawamura and sitting next to Satō at the guests' table was the Chairman of the Ōita Prefecture LDP women's division. Also at the table with Satō were Mrs. Ikezaki, Vice-President of the Beppu chapter and four other executives of the L D P organization. Though the meeting was ostensibly a study session, "studying," which meant listening to speeches by Satō and two guest speakers, was scheduled to last no more than two hours.

The printed program for this first general meeting of the *Fūsetsukai's* women's club defined its purpose to be to "make clear the difference between conservatism and progressivism" and, because most of the participants were mothers, "to give particularly deep thought to the problem of the wholesome education of the young."

In these twenty postwar years, through our diligence, we have certainly made great economic progress. The recent consumer boom and leisure boom are certainly remarkable. But, on the other hand, what is the situation in regard to our spiritual recuperation? Right before our eyes can be seen an overflow of inferior culture, satanic crimes and a frightening increase in traffic accidents. As mothers we must give particularly deep thought to the problem of the wholesome education of the young. It must be the work of us mothers to awaken in our children in the correct way a sense of racial pride.

The program went on to suggest that

For the organization and advancement of women it is important to have mutually close relations. For this purpose everyone will strive to become core activists in building mutual friendship and trust in community life under the leadership of Satō Bunsei.

With its theme thus set, the meeting was opened by Mrs. Kawamura, who, after thanking everyone for attending, introduced Satō as the first speaker. Satō's speech, which lasted for about forty-five minutes, was virtually identical with those he had been giving all year in his tour of the neighborhood associations in Beppu. The main difference was more emphasis on light talk intended to amuse the women and on the unique "spiritual" aspects of Japanese culture, including a fifteen-minute discourse on the tea ceremony, flower arrangement, the Japanese dance, and such concepts as *wabi, sabi* and *mono no aware.*

As you all can see, I'm quite well. Today meeting the chairman of the LDP women's division of Ōita Prefecture, Satō Tei *sensei,* for the first time in a long while, I was asked why I had had my head shaved like a priest.[30] "Your grey hair shows up and with a head like that, Bunchan, you're sure to lose votes." [laughter] But I explained to her that I'm President of the Ōita yacht club which is going to participate in the national athletic meet next month and I'll be

30 Satō had some days earlier had a "crewcut."

serving as guide for the Crown Prince and the Princess. Now, I want to see our yacht team come in first in this meet which is only held in Ōita once in fifty years and I've been down to the harbor every day with the high school students who will be racing. Long hair just doesn't fit that situation. Indeed, though, it looks pretty bad and I think that more than a politician I look like a third rate actor in some old *samurai* movie you see on television. [laughter]

When I asked Professors Tada and Omata to address this group today I told them not to make their speeches too difficult but to talk in such a way that difficult things would be easy to understand. "If you get too complicated," I said to them, "everyone's head will begin to ache and they'll start wondering what they came to Hakuunsansō for. [laughter] So just lower the aim of the speech so that it hits around the belly button rather than the head. Then it should be just right." [laughter]

As in his speeches throughout the period preceding the calling of the elections, Satō devoted several minutes to reviewing his career in local politics and his defeat "by a narrow margin" in the 1963 Diet election. In his neighborhood speeches in Beppu he attributed his entering the Diet race to his desire to work for the "development of Beppu." Now, in front of ladies from the entire district, the expanded his concerns to cover the Prefecture.

In 1951 the present mayor of Beppu, Mayor Aragane, resigned from the Prefectural Assembly. He chose me as his successor and I was elected to the Assembly. Thereafter, for twelve consecutive years, three terms in office, I was under continual indebtedness to the people of Beppu whose support permitted me to lead a life in politics. In 1963, three years ago, with twelve years of political experience in the Prefectural Assembly behind me, I decided that I wanted to participate in some way in national politics; that I wanted to create a more affluent Ōita Prefecture—an Ōita Prefecture which would provide a good environment for a good life; an Ōita Prefecture in which children would have a good education; an environment in which to create a splendid Ōita Prefecture. With these thoughts in mind and with twelve years experience in the Prefectural Assembly, I declared my candidacy in the 1963 election for the Lower House. At that time

I became greatly indebted not only to the people of Beppu but to everyone from the entire district. However, because of just a narrow margin, I have spent these past years in political study outside of the [political] arena.

Satō continued this theme of his defeat by a narrow margin in 1963 and the need for him to get inside the political arena with a few of his favorite stories:

In a zoo you can see a young monkey lose his balance and fall down from a tree. No matter how many times he falls he still remains a monkey. However, for the person who devotes his life to politics—who participates in national politics, who tries to have politics realize the aspiration of all of you, who tries to create a finer society for everyone to live in—being outside the political arena for a long time or falling [i.e. losing] in an election threatens him with the loss of what it is to be a politician. That is why I must exert all my energies to getting into the political arena—this is what I am constantly told by my elders.[31] In the last election I was unable, due to a narrow margin, to get into the political arena. But over these past years I have studied well. A week after the last election, together with the President of this hotel, Upper House member Murakami Haruzō, I went to Tokyo to pay a visit on Ōno Bamboku, who was then still in good health. Murakami, in introducing me to Bamboku *sensei*, said "I am very sorry. We let Satō lose by a narrow margin." I don't know what got into Bamboku *sensei* that day—he must have been in a bad mood—but he turned on Upper House member Murakami saying "You're a fool." Now of course, Ōno Bamboku *sensei* calling Upper House member Murakami *sensei* a fool really shocked me. I just lowered my head but Ōno continued. "A narrow margin! What do you mean by that? Elections are something you lose by only one vote. From here on value highly each single person." That was all he said and I learned a good lesson, a very good lesson. Highly valuing each person in politics is what democratic politics means. Wartime

31 This story is based on a popular expression attributed by some to Ōno Bamboku and others to Miki Bukichi. It is a play on the word *ochiru*, which can mean to fall or to lose. "*Saru ga ki kara ochite mo saru da ga daigishi ga ochitara daigishi de nakunaru.*" ("If a monkey falls from a tree it is still a monkey but if a Diet man falls [i.e. loses an election] he is no longer a Diet man.")

fascist politics dealt with large numbers of people, making the individuals only victims—that is fascist politics. Since I, like others, have had the bitter experience of that period, I was deeply struck with the meaning of Ōno *sensei's* blunt command to highly value every single person.

In my own experience I have known the importance of what Ōno *sensei* was talking about. In 1963, before the election, I went to Ekisen [in Usa county] to give a speech. For a week we had posters up announcing the talk, which was held in the Ekisen middle school. When we got there nobody was at the meeting place. So we waited. Still nobody came. We waited some more. Finally an old man came in. We waited for other people to come but nobody did and I was afraid the old man would leave. So I just sat myself down in front of that old farmer, the head of a local agricultural cooperative, and for two hours talked just to him—just the two of us in that large hall for two hours. He fidgeted around a little and I thought he might walk out on me but he sat through right to the end of my speech. As a result, the people of Ekisen gave me 480 votes. Talking to one person resulted in the support of 480 people. Recollecting these experiences I have been constantly thinking, in three years of study outside the arena, of how democracy means highly valuing each person.

One of the major themes of Satō's speeches and one that came increasingly to dominate his talks as the election drew nearer was the question of reforming the LDP, of establishing "pure" politics. Satō usually broached this topic, as he did at the women's meeting, with a story of meeting a young policeman from the prefecture in Tokyo.

I know a young fellow from Hayami county named Kudō who is in Tokyo. His elder brother is a high school teacher in Ōita. The younger Kudō decided that when he graduated high school he would not go to college but would become a policeman. The reason he decided to do that was that the demonstrations you see on television of *zengakuren* just struck him as being all wrong. Those students take money from their mothers and fathers, go to Tokyo and then, instead of studying, spend their time taking part in demonstrations. Because of that Kudō decided he would go to Tokyo, become a policeman and fight against the *zengakuren* demonstrators. Being a good student he passed the exams right away and entered the police department's mobile force. Then, last year, for the first time in five years, I met Kudō in Tokyo. I had not seen him in a long time. He looked tired. He was pale. When I asked him what was wrong he said, "Satō *sensei*, please, I have to talk to you." [Satō took him to a restaurant and] . . . after eating, he looked at me and asked, "Mr. Satō, are you a member of the L D P?" I immediatley replied, "Yes, I am" and he then said that he was disillusioned with the L D P. Ladies! Do you know the only force that could overthrow the Japanese government? The Socialists could not do it. The Communists, even if they attempted a revolution could not do it. The only way the government can be overthrown is for the police and the self-defence forces who have the military power to join together to do it. If people like Kudō become disillusioned with the ruling L D P what may happen? I was terribly worried and asked Kudō why he was saying bad things about the L D P.

[Satō then described at length Kudō's shock at the revelation of corruption within the L D P.]

Seeing all this, Kudō who had given up going to college to enter the police department, decided to quit his job and go back to Ōita.

When I listened to how this policeman was disenchanted with the L D P I was shocked. Because the L D P has held the reins of power for so long all kinds of problems have arisen, all kinds of unfortunate things have happened. In order to build a really fine conservative party it is necessary to create a political movement in which the women, in which the young men join together to build a really fine Japan, a truly fine Oita Prefecture. When I listened to that policeman's story I realized that what was most essential for Japan's politics was pure politics. The need for pure politics is something I have really come to think about this past year or so. If that movement for pure politics is not undertaken, political power at some point may pass into the hands of the progressives. The conservative party is the best party because it is dedicated to preserving Japan's traditions but I think we must have a movement within the conservative party for pure politics. Pure politics, correct politics—the need for a movement to achieve these goals was something that impressed me very deeply when I talked with Kudō.

This theme led into the major theme of Satō's talk before the assembled ladies: the spiritual malaise of postwar Japan and

[172]

a failure to recognize the glory of Japan's history and tradition, a history of Japanese uniqueness. This part of the speech went on for almost twenty minutes and only a few excerpts are given here.

In Beppu's high schools in the past few years there has been a tremendous increase of delinquents—an increase in students who take drugs, students who smoke cigarettes. The number of arrests of students that I personally know of exceeds twenty. Why indeed has this happened? Why? There's going to be no good served by covering up its real cause. Those people born within the last twenty years, those postwar babies, have suffered from the confusion of the postwar years. They suffered because you, because I, because all of us had no confidence. What should the family teach the children? How should young people be led in society? I believe it's this loss of confidence that is the cause for the delinquency among young people today. . . . Young people—what do they want? They want strong leadership. In the home the mother's strong leadership; at school, the teacher's strong leadership; in society they want the strong leadership of their elders, the leadership of us, the prewar and wartime groups. They want to ask their mothers what is the pride and glory of their people— that's what children want to ask. Those things, though, the mothers of our generation forgot with the end of the war. That is why children became perplexed.

The tradition of fighting against all adversity is Japanese history; that strength which was born in our people is Japanese history. That strength of our people is not something developed in the postwar period. That strength is Japanese history from the Emperor Jimmu and it is that history that I wish everyone to seriously think about today. . . . The first bequest of our ancestors, one we should clearly acknowledge here today, is the pride of our race developed through the long years which we passed under a line of Emperors unbroken for ages eternal. Like the history of no other country in the world, Japan through three thousand years was under the guidance of the Emperor and with that guidance its course of development became defined. The only people in the world who have led a life under such guidance are the Japanese. . . .

What is the second bequest of our ancestors? When you think about that question, everyone, you think about that wonderful culture seen in the dance, in the tea ceremony, in flower arranging, in

[173]

Noh. Things like the tea ceremony or flower arranging are things that neither Americans nor Englishmen nor anyone else have. They are things born out of the extraordinary, unique spiritual culture of Japan. Words like *mono no aware, sabi, wabi* exist in the language of no other people in the world. They are unique to Japan. . . .

To have confidence built on the history of this wonderful Japan—strong politics, strong family education, strong leadership—the realization that these things are necessary in present day Japan is the broad objective of today's political study session.

By this point in his speech Satō had been talking for more than forty minutes. He concluded with some comments about Ōita Prefecture.

Finally I want to make a few remarks about Ōita Prefecture which is at present in a very bad state.[32] I have been given the opportunity to study Ōita Prefecture's politics for more than a decade. You may all believe that your lives are somewhat better now than during the war. However, this Ōita Prefecture of ours, this Beppu City of ours, this Shimoge County of ours—this Prefecture of Ōita that belongs to all of us is in a state of decline. In 1955 Ōita Prefecture ranked number 32 in per capita income. Today we are number 41. In the country as a whole an average of thirty children in a thousand die at birth; in Ōita 36. . . . That's an indication of Ōita's backwardness. In all ways Ōita is falling behind as other prefectures make economic progress and I, in some way, want to work to stop this decline in Ōita's prosperity. Since this cannot be done by one alone, I want to join with all of you here today in discussing how to build a more prosperous Ōita Prefecture; an Ōita Prefecture few in crimes, an Ōita Prefecture in which children don't die at birth; an Ōita Prefecture in which old people live long. The discussion of the means by which these goals can be achieved is a major objective of today's political study session. Please, to the end, listen to the speeches of the *sensei*, ask questions and return home from this political study session with the dedicaton and confidence necessary for creating clean, just politics in Japan.

Following Satō's speech was a reading of congratulatory

[32] It is to be remembered that the Governor of the prefecture is an Independent who defeated Ōita L D P chairman Iwasaki.

telegrams from several Diet members of the Murakami faction, Nakasone Yasuhiro and Iwasaki. This was followed by a short speech by the chairman of the prefecture's LDP women's division, Satō Tei. The main theme of Mrs. Satō's speech was expressed in the following concluding remarks which included perhaps one of the most ingenious ways to ask the women to campaign for Satō without once mentioning the election or his candidacy.

We have heard from Satō Bunsei *sensei* a talk dealing with many things. Satō is a truly rare person. Politics, sports, Buddhism, the tea ceremony, so many interests, so many things he's studied. It is almost too much for the average person to really appreciate. As an egg of a politician this is a golden egg. . . . We would wish that this kind of political study session could be held very often but, of course since it cannot, please, today, study a lot; yes, study a lot and then, lastly, I have one favor to ask of you—Help hatch this golden egg.

A short recess followed and then the two guest speakers addressed the assemblage. Tada Shinsuke is a professor of politics at Keiō University. He gave a talk entitled "What Is Conservatism?" In his exposition of the view that the conservatives are really the progressives because they adopt new policies in line with the changing times while preserving what is good in tradition, the professor seemed to be doing his best to heed Satō's request to aim at the belly button rather than the head. The second speaker was Omata Hideaki, a lecturer at Ōita University and a well-known political commentator in Ōita Prefecture. Omata is perhaps known not as much for the nature of his political comments as for the words he chooses to express them—a humorous and, to many residents of the Prefecture, a now exotic use of the local dialect. Omata is from Kitsuki and was a classmate of Satō in middle school. His speech, which dealt in a humorous way with the progress of women's rights in the postwar years, proved the hit of the day because it kept most of the women laughing for the entire half hour he spoke. While neither Tada nor Omata mentioned Satō's intention to run in the

[175]

coming Diet election, they both praised Satō as one of the young, forward-looking conservatives who should be given a chance to help modernize the conservative party. As Omata put it, "In the world at large and in Japan almost everything is changing at a rapid pace. The only thing that doesn't change in Japan is the faces of the men elected to the Diet."

The speeches were to be followed by an extended discussion period but the lack of time forced this part of the program to be kept down to ten minutes. In its entirety the study part of the political study session took a little over two and a half hours and at five o'clock the meeting was recessed so the ladies could enjoy a hot springs bath before dinner.

With the closing of the afternoon meeting, the study session came to an end and the vacation began. The evening saw a program of singing and dancing led by local entertainers who were friends of Satō. Everyone joined in the show by singing the "Bunchan Song"[33] and the fun went on until ten o'clock uninterrupted by any talk of politics. The next morning Satō briefly addressed the participants at breakfast, thanked them for coming, and closed the First Satō Bunsei Women's Political Study Session.

The women's meeting was conceived of as a step in the process of organizing the women voters, not the achievement of that goal. Therefore, the follow-up to the meeting was of the utmost importance. A few weeks after the meeting, a new issue of the *Fūsetsukai* newspaper was printed and sent to each of the women who attended the meeting. With the newspaper went a self-addressed stamped envelope with a letter asking the women to submit the names of ten women from their locality for membership in the *Fūsetsukai*. Through this proc-

---

33 It has become popular for politicians to have songs written for them, some of which are recorded by leading vocalists. See Ishii Kenichiro and Yamada Hiroshi, *Gendai Nihon No Seiji* (Tokyo, 1967), pp. 84–85. Satō commissioned a writer to compose a song but then felt he could not afford to have it recorded. The end result was that he had the record jackets without the records printed.

ess, the "women's division" of the *Fūsetsukai* jumped within a month to over 2,500 members. The intention was then to repeat the process vis-à-vis the women whose names were submitted, asking each of them to submit ten more names. By this time, however, the end of September, it was considered too dangerous, in light of the prohibition against pre-election campaigning and a seemingly impending dissolution, to send so many newspapers through the mails. Furthermore, the mailing costs were becoming prohibitive. In a few areas the newspapers without the stamped envelopes were given to the local *sekininsha* for distribution to the women whose names had been submitted by the participants. In all, by the time of the dissolution of the House the women's meeting had resulted in somewhat over 3,500 names being added to Satō's mailing list.

In December, 1966, pressure on the Satō (Eisaku) government for a new election rose to such a high pitch that Satō (Bunsei) decided he would gamble on a late December or early January dissolution of the House, and arranged to hold on December 17 a final city-wide rally. One purpose of the rally was to bring Satō into contact with more of the voters. But this was a minor purpose. The major aim of the rally was to get the entire Beppu organization activated to provide a kind of final dress rehearsal before the official campaign began. To be successful, Satō felt the rally had to draw at least 1,300 people, and to achieve that number he set a goal of 3,000 participants for his organization to recruit. Recruitment was conducted through four main groups: the 235 neighborhood *sewanin* were responsible for recruiting 1,800 participants; the 260 women who had attended the women's conference from Beppu were to bring two women each to the meeting for a total of somewhat over 700; thirty-three voluntary organizations within which Satō had support were to supply a total of 300 participants; and Satō's successor to the Prefectural Assembly, Shutō Kenji, was to recruit 200 voters. To help the machine work efficiently funds were supplied sufficient enough to pay the transportation costs for everyone attending.

A couple of days before the speech, 1,000 posters announcing the rally were posted around the city and a large sign hung outside the hall in which the session was to be held. On the day preceding and the morning of the speech, Satō had members of his staff drive around the city in a loudspeaker-equipped car publicizing the speech.

On December 17 what was to be Satō's last political study session before the dissolution of the House opened with an estimated 1,500 people in attendance. Once the hall was nearly full and the session begun, the rest was somewhat anticlimactic. Speeches were made by Satō and by the President of the *Kenseikai,* a conservative youth organization. The guests enjoyed box lunches compliments of the *Fūsetsukai* and each received a *Fūsetsukai* towel as a souvenir of the meeting. But the major objective of the meeting was achieved when the session was called to order. The organization had proved fairly efficient in providing what was allegedly the largest audience ever assembled in Beppu for a political speech; the organizers had the name lists of all those in attendance; and Satō was now ready to move from the "noncampaign" into the hectic three weeks of official campaigning.

VII

The "Organizational Strategy"

THE APPROACHES TO CAMPAIGN STRATEGY discussed in the previous chapters represent a so-called vertical approach to mobilizing support. The campaign is organized separately in the several administrative divisions of the district—the cities and the towns and their subdivisions. The strategy is vertical in that the campaign conducted in each town or city is isolated from neighboring areas. Each area forms a distinct compartment. Such a vertical organization of support in separate *chiiki* or geographical areas is typical of conservative party politician campaign strategies. In contrast to this, Socialist Party candidates depend heavily on the support of labor unions and consequently rely primarily on a so-called horizontal strategy. With the support of a labor union such as the Public School Teachers' Union, for instance, the Socialist candidate's campaign organization spreads out over the district, cutting across *chiiki* lines.

The efforts made by LDP politicians to utilize various voluntary associations in their campaigns represent an attempt to create their own horizontal strategy for reaching the voter. Tokyo Professor Ishida Takeshi quotes a young prefectural assemblyman as saying that "from now on the conservative party is finished if the only method it uses in vote getting is reliance on the gentlemen in *haori*, the local bosses. In [the LDP's] case too, without organization. . . ."[1] As Ishida points out, by "organization" this assemblyman was not referring to his own personal campaign organization but to the utilization of established organizations. Similarly, when Satō refers

---

[1] Ishida Takeshi, *Sengo Nihon No Seiji Taisei* (Tokyo, 1961), p. 166.

to an "organizational strategy" he means a strategy for gaining the support of various existing voluntary associations.

While never clearly articulated, Satō's "organizational strategy" was premised on the assumption that a significant number of voters feel a geater identity with the interests voiced by the leaders of organizations to which they belong than with the interests expressed by traditional leaders in their local communities. In most rural areas Satō had been unable, as discussed in previous chapters, to obtain the support of any but the weakest elements among the community leadership. By hanging on to the coattails of a great variety of voluntary associations he hoped to get into these areas through the back door of group interest, so to speak, rather than, or more accurately as a supplement to, the more traditionally used front door of an organization of local politicians. In places like Beppu and Nakatsu, organizations were to play a somewhat different but no less important role than in rural areas. Here, where the electorate was "floating," the support of various organizations would help the candidate reach down to individual voters largely indifferent to the desires of such people as the neighborhood association leaders but often very conscious of an identity of interest with particular associations to which they belong.

The extent to which Satō relied on an "organizational strategy" was very limited, however. He was convinced that the vertical approach was the best technique for mobilizing the support of the conservative party supporting sector of the electorate. The support of voluntary associations was never perceived as a substitute for such an approach but rather as a subsidiary strategy of limited usefulness. Satō was also aware of one of the most important effects of the Election Law on the role of voluntary associations in Diet campaigns: that, as a rule, the greater the identification of an association with the LDP, the less able it is to give effective support to LDP candidates in Lower House elections. Because of the multimember district single-entry balloting system, unless a district has only one LDP candidate, support for one man means that an organization's efforts will incur the animosity of the other candidates of the party. Support for all LDP candidates means nothing to any one of them because it does not affect the ability of one to get votes that might otherwise go to another candidate of the party. To maintain good relations with all LDP candidates the usual policy, at least in Ōita Prefecture, is for organizations to give official endorsement to all the LDP candidates or to none and to avoid becoming involved in the campaign on any one candidate's behalf. Exceptions to this pattern are discussed within the following survey of voluntary associations that figured in Satō's organizational strategy.

Economic organizations in Ōita provide a typical example of how important LDP-supporting organizations eschew commitment to the campaign of any one candidate. Six economic associations were approached by Satō in a search for electoral support. With one exception he failed to receive the effective support of any. They either gave a *pro forma* endorsement to all the LDP candidates or to none. The six organizations are (1) the Association of Local Merchants and Manufacturers; (2) the Chamber of Commerce; (3) the Merchant Block Association (4) the Federation of Business Managers; (5) the Association of Small and Medium-Size Enterprises; and (6) the Junior Chamber of Commerce.

The Ōita Prefecture Federation of Local Merchants and Manufacturers Associations *(Ōita Ken Shōkōkai Rengōkai)* was founded in 1957. The *Shōkōkai,* as it is called, is organized in the forty-eight towns and villages of Ōita Prefecture and in the city of Kitsuki. There are an estimated 17,024 merchants and manufacturers in the areas organized by the *Shōkōkai,* and 9,102 of these are members of the Association. In the Second District there are 8,738 people who qualify for membership in the organization, of which number 4,738 are members.[2]

The officers of the prefectural *Shōkōkai* organization have

[2] Ōita Ken Shōkō Rengōkai, *Ōita Ken Shōkō Yōran* (Ōita, 1965).

the responsibility to determine the Association's recommendation for candidates in prefectural and national elections. The Prefectural Association usually recommends candidates in national elections, but except in cases where one of its own officers or one of a similar organization like the Chamber of Commerce stands for election (as in the national constituency of the Upper House), it generally supports all LDP-endorsed candidates.[3] In the 1967 Diet election, official recommendations were given to the six LDP candidates in the Prefecture, and the members were asked to campaign for any of these candidates. The *Shōkōkai* gives no money to recommended candidates. To the extent that the organization actively supported candidates, it apparently divided along the lines of indigenous candidate strength in particular areas; that is, Nishimura receiving support in his stronghold of Higashi Kunisaki County and Ayabe being supported by the members in Kitsuki.

In the cities of the Prefecture, the functions of the *Shōkōkai* are largely assumed by the Chamber of Commerce. Chambers of Commerce are organized in Ōita Prefecture's ten major cities, with Chamber organizations in the Second District in Beppu, Bungo Takada, and Nakatsu. The ten Chambers of Commerce are associated in the Ōita Prefecture Federation of Chambers of Commerce. The prefectural organization formally gives recommendations to candidates in the Lower House elections. In the Second District recommendations of the organization in the 1967 election went to all official LDP candidates.[4] Aside from giving its formal recommendation, the Chamber played no active part as an organization in the campaign. According to its Vice-President,[5]

3 This discussion of the Ōita Prefecture *Shōkōkai's* election policy is based on an interview with the organization's business manager, Miyanaga Tamahiki, May 24, 1967.

4 Interview with business manager of the organization, Satō Shōzō, May 24, 1967.

5 Interview with Vice-President Ichimaru Gohei, May 24, 1967.

it took a hands-off position, not giving active support or financial assistance to any of the candidates. Individual members of course played a significant role in the election, largely on behalf of incumbent candidates. In Beppu, for example, Construction Minister Nishimura had the support of the former president of the Beppu organization.[6] For Satō, the Chamber's recommendation meant little if anything in terms of real support.

The Ōita Prefecture Association of Small and Medium-Size Enterprises (*Ōita Ken Chūshō Kigyō Dantai*) consists of 500 cooperative unions *(kyōdō kumiai)* organized on an industry basis.[7] At the time of the Lower House election, 340 of these unions were active. The Prefectural Association as a rule plays an active role in an election only when an association representative is running. The individual cooperative unions are free to give recommendations to candidates but it is not a common practice. Usually, if any action is taken at all in regard to Lower House elections it is to endorse all LDP candidates and leave the choice of which candidate to support up to each individual member. In the 1967 election no recommendations were given.[8]

The Ōita Prefecture Federation of Business Managers *(Ōita Ken Keieisha Kyōkai)* is the Ōita branch of a mammoth national organization, the *Nihon Keieisha Dantai Renmei*, or *Nikkeiren* for short, founded in 1948 for the purpose of consolidating management's power in the face of organized labor's increased strength.[9] The Ōita association consists of the managers of 172 business enterprises in the Prefecture and represents the most powerful elements in Ōita's economic world.

6 *Mainichi Shinbun*, January 18, 1967, p. 14.

7 Ōita Ken Chūshō Kigyō Dantai Chūōkai, *Ōita Ken Chūshō Kigyō Dantai Meibo* (Ōita, June 1965).

8 Interviews with Kondō Takayuki and Teshima Tsugio, May 25, 1967.

9 For a discussion of the national *Nikkeiren* organization see Asahi Jānaru Hen, *Nihon No Kyodai Soshiki* (Tokyo, 1966), pp. 70–89. For the membership of the Ōita branch see Ōita Ken Keieisha Kyōkai, *Ōita Ken Keieisha Kyōkai Yōran* (Ōita, 1966).

The Prefectural Organization plays no active role in the Lower House election. It gave no recommendations or financial contributions to any of the candidates.[10] Satō attempted to get the support of individual members of the association but was largely unsuccessful. Satō's own background, his lack of office and political power on the national level, and the prevalence of small merchants in the Beppu economy combined to make him the least attractive of the three conservative candidates to the big businessmen of the district, and inclined him toward championing the cause of the small entrepreneur rather than that of the wealthy capitalist.

The type of businessmen to which Satō aimed his appeal was represented by such organizations as the Ōita Prefecture Federation of Merchant Block Associations (*Ōita Ken Shōtengai Rengōkai*). The merchant block associations are organized in the same ten cities as the Chamber of Commerce. These associations are concerned with the blocks in which small merchant stores are congregated. Each block association has a President, the *kumiaichō*. All the block associations in a city are organized into a city federation, and the city federations compose the prefectural organization. While informal merchant block associations have long been in existence, the national association was first formed in 1953 and the Ōita Prefecture Federation in 1960.[11] It is a weak organization, and in Ōita Prefecture less than half of the stores in the various merchant blocks are enrolled in the association.

The Prefectural Federation often makes recommendations for Prefectural Assembly elections but takes no official action in regard to Lower House elections. In the popular folklore of Japanese election practices, however, the merchant block associations, particularly the *kumiaichō* of the separate associations, are alleged to play an important role in campaigns. With the support of the *kumiaichō*, so the story goes, the candidate can corner the votes of, literally, blocks of voters.

10 Interview with Taguchi Akira, May 25, 1967.
11 Interview with Miyanari Yoshimi, May 25, 1967.

There is no evidence that such practices actually prevail. In Beppu there was only one case known to the Satō staff of a block association giving him its recommendation, and this was not one of merchants but of bar owners in one of Beppu's popular nighttime sections.

Satō tried to project an image of being the representative of the small businessman and conversely to imply that the other conservative candidates represented only the interests of big business. He was unable, however, to obtain support from any association representing these lower strata of the business community. And whatever support he did receive from such businessmen was achieved through means other than the backing of economic organizations in the district to which they belong.

The role of the economic associations so far discussed may be summarized as general support for all LDP candidates with no specific, active support for any particular candidate. The only economic association that did give Satō significant support was the Junior Chamber of Commerce.

In Ōita Prefecture's Second District there are two Junior Chamber of Commerce organizations, one for Beppu-Ōita and the other in Nakatsu. The Beppu-Ōita chapter has seventy-four members, of which thirty-four are from Beppu.[12] Of this number, fifteen or sixteen are said to have worked actively and openly for Satō, three or four were supporters of other candidates, and the rest refrained from openly supporting any of the candidates. There is also an organization of senior members of the Junior Chamber—Jaycee members who have passed the age of forty. In the Beppu-Ōita chapter this group has twenty-four members. Fifteen of these men were active supporters of Satō both in campaigning for the vote and making a joint financial contribution of 250,000 yen to his campaign.[13]

[12] Beppu-Ōita Seinenkaigisho, *Beppu-Ōita Seinenkaigisho Meibo* (Beppu, 1967).

[13] This discussion is based on an interview with the president of the Beppu-Ōita Junior Chamber of Commerce, Kanda Yasugi, in May, 1967.

Like much of the story of the sources of Satō's support, his intimate relationship with the members of the Junior Chamber of Commerce dates from his days in the Prefectural Assembly. Satō was one of the first members of the Junior Chamber when it formed in 1953 in Beppu and Ōita. He played an active role in the organization and was responsible for establishing a sister relationship with the Hong Kong Jaycees. Satō became active in the international Junior Chamber and on reaching the age of forty became a senator of the international organization and a senior member of the Beppu-Ōita group.

The most active support Satō received was from the group of senior members of the Jaycees, men who were active in the organization with Satō during its early years and, as his peer group, form a close circle of personal friends. These senior members are all prosperous businessmen and many are engaged in the hotel business. It is also part of the folklore surrounding election campaigns that someone like a hotel owner acts as *parentis in loco* to the young people from the countryside who make up his staff and can "order" his workers to vote a certain way. The workers, out of gratitude to, respect for, and fear of their employer will do as commanded. Though a stereotype of dubious accuracy there is no doubt such supporters were perceived as possessing very significant influence over considerable numbers of voters and as such were highly valued by Satō and his staff.

The present regular members of the Jaycees entered the organization after Satō became a senior member and thus do not have the same ties with him as do the senior members. Satō, however, was the youngest of the candidates, the only one from Beppu, and the sole candidate in the Prefecture to have been a member of the Junior Chamber of Commerce. Though some members of the organization refused to take part in the campaign, the entire leadership and the majority of members did campaign on Satō's behalf. Both organizationally, in giving its recommendation to only one candidate, and

[186]

individually in giving active support, the members and senior members of the Jaycees formed an effective and significant campaign group.[14]

The Junior Chamber of Commerce in Beppu was the only one of the several economic interest groups active in the Prefecture to give significant support to Satō, but economic groups were only a small portion of the associations involved in Satō's organizational strategy. Medical associations, agricultural groups, religious organizations, sports clubs, and a variety of other voluntary associations were also approached.

The Ōita Prefecture Medical Association (Ōita Ken Ishikai) is made up of seventeen city and county branches with 1,083 members. In the Second Electoral District there were 455 doctors in the Association.[15] The recommendation of the Prefectural Association for candidates for the Lower House is decided by a conference of the Chairmen of the seventeen city and county organizations.[16] In the 1967 election this recommendation went to all the LDP candidates in both districts plus an independent conservative candidate in the First District. The recommendation for all the conservative candidates represented a significant change in the organization's election policy from the previous campaign.

The Medical Association in Ōita has long looked to two of the Prefecture's politicians to promote its goals on the national level. These two are Murakami Isamu in the First District and Nishimura Eiichi in the Second. The Associa-

---

[14] The importance that Satō's close personal ties with the membership of the Beppu-Ōita Junior Chamber and his status as the only candidate from Beppu played in getting the backing of that organization was emphasized by the failure of the other Jaycee organization in the Second District, that of Nakatsu, to give Satō its recommendation. Nakatsu's Junior Chamber of Commerce has forty members, of whom only eight are known to have actively worked on Satō's behalf. Because of differences among the members, no recommendation was given to any of the candidates.

[15] Ōita Ken Ishikai, *Kaiin Meibo* (Ōita, July 1966).

[16] This discussion of the election policies of the Medical Association is based on an interview with its President, Katō Shin, on May 27, 1967.

tion's ties with Nishimura were particularly strong because of Nishimura's former position as Welfare Minister. In 1963, because of this cabinet position, Nishimura received the sole recommendation of the Association in the Second District and the Association's members carried out a systematic campaign effort on his behalf. In 1967, however, Nishimura was no longer Welfare Minister and he could not command the united support of the Association. Though he continued to have much support among the members, there was now enough support for other candidates to render a recommendation for only one candidate unobtainable. Thus in this election, according to the Association's President, the group adopted a neutral policy, providing neither financial backing nor coordinated campaigning for any of the candidates.

Satō had little hope of getting much support from the doctors outside of Beppu, and little effort was made to solicit such support. In Beppu Satō's staff approached a select number of doctors on an individual basis (rather than trying to work through the city Medical Association). Similarly, in Nakatsu approaches were made to a few medical men whom it was thought might be favorable to Satō. For Satō, the Medical Association was valuable precisely because it did not limit its recommendation to only one candidate as it had in 1963. In light of its close relationship with Nishimura, the Association was regarded as a hostile organization by the Satō forces. Its endorsement of all the conservative candidates was considered a defeat for Nishimura because it formally freed the members to vote for whichever conservative candidate they wished, and Satō felt sure that in Beppu at least this would redound to his benefit.

In direct contrast to the neutral policy adopted by the Medical Association was the Prefecture's Dental Association's policy of support for only one candidate in each district. The Ōita Prefecture Dental Association (Ōita Ken Shikaishikai) provided the only truly organized support and coordinated campaigning among all the groups that nominally gave Satō their support in the form of official recommendations.

Satō serves in an advisory position to many organizations in the Prefecture. Positions as adviser (*komon*) are sought by the politician because they give him an inside track to the membership of the organization that would otherwise not be available. Because of his long career in the Prefectural Assembly and his close relationship with the Prefecture LDP leadership, Satō has been able to obtain the position of adviser to several groups, one of the most important of which was the position of "political adviser" (*seiji komon*) to the Prefecture's Dental Association.

The Dental Association has a policy of giving support to its advisers when they run for public office, and in both the Diet elections of 1963 and 1967 Satō has been the only candidate in the Second District to receive the recommendation and active support of the organization.[17]

Dentists, like teachers and doctors, hold a respected position in local society. Because of their sparse number and the nature of their profession they are regarded as being less inhibited by local pressures and more conscious of their organizational interests than people in many other occupations. In rural areas in particular, Satō eagerly sought the support of dentists because of their high status and their familiarity with the people in their communities. Of the 195 dentists in the Second District, 102 are in Beppu and Nakatsu.[18] With only 93 dentists to take care of the population of the other two cities and all the towns and villages of the district, it is not surprising that they have considerable status in local society. In many rural areas where local political pressures have prohibited Satō from obtaining support among local politicians, support was often limited to the area's dentists. His organiza-

[17] Information on the role of the Dental Association was obtained from many sources. Most important was an interview in May 1967 with Baba Takashi.

[18] Ōita Ken Shikaishikai, *Kaiin Meibo* (Ōita, 1966).

tion in Aki Town in Nishimura's stronghold of Higashi Kunisaki County was largely centered around three dentists, one the President of the county Dental Association. In Kunisaki Town, one of the four men on the *sekininsha* level of his organization is Vice-President of the prefectural Dental Association.[19] Particularly in areas such as Higashi Kunisaki County which are so strongly the domain of other conservative Diet politicians, members of the Dental Association provided support that could not be obtained through the more traditional method of relying on local politicians.

The Ōita Prefecture Dental Association has city and county subdivisions and, with the calling of the general elections, these groups set up election strategy committees to coordinate campaign activities on behalf of the recommended candidates. The election activities of the Beppu Association were organized by a committee headed by two of Satō's most enthusiastic supporters, Baba Takashi and Nonaka Toshihide. Under their leadership were eleven district leaders responsible for the campaign in each of Beppu's eleven school districts. The members of the Association were divided into the eleven groups according to the area where they practiced.

Considerable pressure was put on all the members of the Association to campaign for Satō. Those who would not take part in the campaign had to explain their reasons for not supporting Satō to the election committee and receive the committee's approval to abstain. No one was allowed to campaign for any other candidate. Of the sixty-three dentists in the Beppu Association, two were permitted to refrain from campaigning for Satō. One was a relative of Ayabe and the other a relation of Komatsu. Three dentists were sick at the time of the campaign and five others, being brothers or husband and wife teams, were considered as one unit, thus bringing the number of Satō campaigners in the Association to fifty-three. In addition, fifteen laboratory workers and eight

19 See above, p. 72.

dealers in dental supplies were brought into the campaign organization.

The Beppu Association set a goal of 20,000 votes to be obtained for Satō by the dentists of the city. Each school district was to provide a certain number of votes in accord with its population and its number of dentists. The eleven school district campaign managers divided the quota for their area among the dentists in their particular group. Campaign headquarters were established in the home of Association President Nonaka, and one entire wall of the house was covered with a graph showing the number of votes each dentist had obtained.

Between January 15 and January 28 the Association's election committee met six times. At each meeting the school district managers would announce the number of promised votes obtained for Satō by each dentist in their district. This would be recorded on the chart over the name of the particular dentist concerned and then recorded in the column that gave the particular district's total. Vote getting was made into a competitive sport with both the individual dentists vying for the tallest line on the graph and with the district leaders fighting to obtain the highest district total. Those dentists who were failing to maintain the pace were subjected to minute questioning on why they could not obtain more votes and were encouraged to try harder. The district chiefs were given the responsibility of making sure all the dentists in their areas actively campaigned, and they had to give detailed explanations of the reasons for the poor performance of any dentists within their districts.

The election committee met[20] for the first time on January 15, at which time quotas were established for each district and questions of campaign techniques were discussed. The dentists were urged to stress two slogans in asking for support for Satō: "elect the home town candidate" and "re-

[20] I attended two of these meetings. Information on the others was obtained from Baba Takashi.

juvenate the conservative party." In the following weeks several meetings were held to tally the votes obtained by the dentists and to discuss the progress of the campaign. At the first such meeting on January 20, a total of 3,800 votes toward the 20,000 vote goal were recorded on the graph. At the next meeting on January 24, the total had risen to 8,558 votes. On January 26 and 27 the dentists started a "human wave tactic" (*jinkai sakusen*). These two days were to be the final push with each dentist required to campaign for a minimum of two and a half hours each of the two days and with their wives campaigning during office hours. Dentists were urged to take a day off from work if possible to campaign for Satō. On January 28th, election eve, the Dental Association's election committee met in its final session. The number of promised votes was tallied for each district and for Beppu as a whole, with the grand total coming to 15,688 votes.

Throughout the cities and counties of the district, members of the Dental Association campaigned for Satō though the organizational effort was on a much smaller scale and without the coordination and unanimity that characterized the Beppu effort. The total number of votes for all the areas outside of Beppu was 8,799.

The Dental Association's role in Satō's campaign came closest to the ideal type of organizational support sought by Lower House candidates. Its effectiveness was due to its recommendation of only one candidate and the pressures placed on the membership to actively support the recommended candidate.

The support of the Dental Association for Satō resulted from no rational consideration of the organization's interests. When Satō was in the Prefectural Assembly his position as "political adviser" had real meaning for the Association because of his influence within the prefectural government. Support for him in the Diet election was a consequence of his holding this position and not a consequence of any role he was expected to be able to perform on the national level on behalf of the Association's interests. On the contrary, by supporting only Satō, the Association alienated the other LDP candidates in the District, incumbents of considerable tenure in the Diet who might be expected to be less than anxious to do favors for the Association.

In prefectures with large rural populations like Ōita, agricultural cooperative unions (nōgyō kyōdō kumiai) are large and powerful organizations. The 106 cooperative unions in Ōita prefecture have 103,000 members.[21] Because the membership of these cooperatives is so large, the support of cooperative union leaders can be of significant value to a candidate in providing a channel to the rural voter. It is an indication of his urban orientation that Satō had the support of no cooperative union leaders except for one from the Nakatsu area.

All the local unions are organized into a prefectural organization which can make recommendations for candidates in Prefectural Assembly, Lower and Upper House Diet elections. In the 1967 election the prefectural association itself did not make any recommendations for candidates but its conference of union chiefs (kumiaichōkai) sent "telegrams of encouragement" (gekirei) to two LDP incumbents in the first district and to Ayabe and Nishimura in the second.[22] The telegrams of encouragement were indicative of two points. First they reflected the support that Ayabe and Nishimura, with their rural orientations, commanded among the local union chiefs (the members of the conference of union chiefs), and second, they reflected the inability of the prefectural organization to officially back any one candidate.

Like many interest groups, the agricultural cooperative union organization functions most effectively in support of Upper House candidates in the national constituency elections who run with the backing of the national organization and in support of candidates to local Assemblies. In the April 1967

[21] Ōita Ken Nōgyō Kyōdō Kumiai Chūōkai, (Ōita Ken Nōgyō Kyōdō Kumiai Tōkeihyō (Ōita, 1967).

[22] Interview with Yoshitake Masayoshi, May 22, 1967.

local elections, twelve Prefectural Assembly candidates received the recommendation of the prefectural organization. The Assembly has an "agricultural cooperative group" (*Kengikai Nōkyō Giin Dan*) which had nine members following the April election. All are officers of agricultural cooperative unions. Four are independent conservatives, members of an informal group known as the *Nōsei Kurabu*, three are members of the LDP, and two belong to the Socialist Party.[23] No such close ties between candidates and the agricultural cooperative unions existed on the Lower House level. Individual cooperative union leaders were brought into campaign organizations, and apparently provided many of the active campaigners for Ayabe and Nishimura, but none of the candidates was able to convince the union that its interests would best be served by uniting its support behind only one candidate.

There were a variety of other agricultural associations Satō approached for support but with no significant success. These organizations included the association of livestock owners (*chikusangyō rengōkai*), the union of tobacco growers (*tabako kosaku kumiai*), and the association of veterinarians (*jūishikai*).

The island of Kyūshū produces the greater part of Japan's bamboo. Ōita, with its 18,046 hectares of bamboo forests and its skilled artisans in Beppu and other areas, has the largest income of all prefectures in the country from the combined sale of bamboo and bamboo products.[24] To the people involved in Ōita's bamboo industry, Satō is the *take daigishi*, the "bamboo Diet man."

Satō has long taken an active part in attempts to improve the industry in the Prefecture. In trips abroad he wore bamboo hats and gave presents of bamboo products to publicize the Prefecture's industry. Following his election to the Diet he furnished his office in the Diet building with bamboo products from the Prefecture and even listed the stores that provided them and the prices so people could order similar items

23 *Ōita Gōdō Shinbun*, May 17, 1967, p. 1.
24 Ōita Ken, *Ōita Ken Tōkei Nenpan* (Ōita, 1966).

through Satō's office. Most importantly, he helped create in 1959 the Ōita Prefecture Federation of Bamboo Industries (*Ōita Ken Take Sangyō Rengōkai*) and has served as the organization's President since its inception.

The organization of the producers of bamboo and bamboo products was created in an attempt to revitalize the then sagging bamboo industry in the Prefecture. The Federation's 429 members represent only a fraction of the people involved in the industry but they are the people who own the largest bamboo forests and the largest factories that process bamboo. Seventy-five per cent of the members are owners of cultivated (as distinguished from wild) bamboo forests. The remainder are owners of factories that cut and glaze the bamboo, and a few are owners of firms that produce finished products. Two hundred fifty-three of the Federation's members are in the Second Electoral District.[25]

Satō's relationship with the members of the Bamboo Federation was similar to that with the members of the Dental Association. He had intimate personal friendships with the leaders of the group and his position as President provided many opportunities to personally meet the general membership. The Bamboo Industries Federation decided at a general meeting of its membership before the 1967 election to endorse its President for election to the Lower House. No other candidates in the district were endorsed.[26] Unlike the Dental Association, most of the members of the Bamboo Federation live outside of Beppu and felt more keenly the pressures to support the local candidate. There was no coordinated campaigning among the membership on behalf of Satō and there were apparently only a small number of members who actively and openly campaigned for him.[27] The main significance of

[25] Ōita Ken Take Sangyō Rengōkai, *Kaiin Meibo* (Ōita, 1966).

[26] Interview with Federation business manager Ishikawa on May 23, 1967.

[27] One was the owner of a large bamboo processing plant in Bungo Takada who is an opponent of Satō's main supporter there, Kiyohara. His is the only case Satō's headquarters knows about of support coming from that

Satō's support by the Federation appears to have been to inhibit members from campaigning for other candidates. Like the Dental Association, the Bamboo Federation demanded of its members that they give support to Satō or explain to the Federation why they could not do so. Several members, pressured to campaign for another candidate, used the organization's recommendation for Satō as an excuse for abstaining from the campaign. Active support for any candidate but Satō, they argued, would threaten their membership in the organization. To the Federation, on the other hand, they argued that active support for Satō would threaten their position in local society. With a few important exceptions, local community pressures apparently were sufficient to prevent open campaigning on Satō's behalf. The support of the organization created pressures of its own sufficient enough, however, to keep members from campaigning for other candidates and to encourage some to quietly support, if not openly campaign for Satō. Furthermore, the activities of the top leadership of the organization were important in gaining Satō support among the several thousand unorganized owners of bamboo forests and producers of bamboo products.[28] The appeal to people in the industry to elect a "bamboo Diet man" was aided by newspaper articles which pictured Satō as the representative and promoter of Ōita bamboo.[29]

Among the organizations discussed so far, the Junior Cham-

---

city that was not organized by the Kiyohara machine. Kiyohara readily admits that Satō would not have gotten the support of this plant owner were it not for Satō's relation with the bamboo organization. "He's opposed to Mizunoe [the man Kiyohara "made" mayor] in Takada politics," Kiyohara once remarked to me, "so I never would have approached him to support Satō." Cf. above, chapter III.

[28] There are no figures on the total number of people involved in the bamboo industry in Ōita Prefecture. The estimate of the Federation's business manager is that there are nearly 20,000 people involved in the industry full and part time. Interview May 23, 1967.

[29] See, for instance, *Asahi Shinbun*, January 18, 1967, p. 14; *Nishi Nihon Shinbun*, January 11, 1967, p. 9.

ber of Commerce, the Dental Association, and the Bamboo Industry Federation alone limited their recommendations for candidates in the Second District to Satō. There are two other organizations, as diverse in their interests as the above three, that endorsed only Satō. One is an organization of fruit and vegetable dealers and, the other one of Japan's "new religions."

In 1963 the President of the Ōita Prefecture Chapter of the LDP, Iwasaki, resigned his position as President of the Ōita Prefecture Federation of Green Goods Retailers' Unions (*Ōita Ken Seika Kouri Kumiai Rengōkai*). Iwasaki's resignation followed immediately upon the Diet election of that year, and the LDP chief recommended defeated Diet candidate Satō as the new President for the Union. Thus in late 1963 Satō became the President of an organization that includes both the retail and wholesale fruit and vegetable dealers in Ōita Prefecture, an organization that has approximately 350 members in Beppu and 700 in the Second District as a whole.[30]

The position of President of the vegetable dealers' union entails few duties and the actual running of the organization is in the hands of the business manager, a position held by the same man since the union's inception in 1957. Business manager Mieno, in the months preceding the election, arranged for Satō to address several meetings of local unions in the Second District. The exposure these meetings provided Satō

[30] Though the union is called one of retail dealers it includes the wholesalers (*nakagainin*) as well. Unions of wholesalers exist only in areas that have central markets. Such central markets, built with public money, are in cities with populations over 150,000. Ōita city with a population of 170,000 has been allocated funds for the building of a central market that is expected to be completed in 1970. At that time a wholesale dealers union will be formed. For the present all dealers are in the retailers' union. The unions are organized at the several markets where the dealers buy their merchandise. In the Second District there are thirteen such markets: three in Beppu, five in Nakatsu, two in Bungo Takada, two in the town of Nagasu, and one in the town of Usa.

was one of the most important aspects of the union's support. Mieno would inform Satō of the date of the meeting of one of the local unions and Satō would drop in unannounced to "say hello" to the group. When elections were called, the Federation, which is made up of the union chiefs of the several local unions, formally recommended its President for election to the Lower House. No other candidates in either district received the Federation's recommendation. Mieno and three other officers of the Federation formed the nucleus of the group's campaign effort, soliciting support for Satō throughout the district and calling on members in the First District to ask relatives and friends in the Second to vote for him. According to Mieno's estimates the most extensive support for Satō was in the cities of Nakatsu, Bungo Takada, and Beppu. In those areas which were the strongholds of Nishimura and Ayabe support was minimal. Mieno conservatively estimates the union vote for Satō at 900 to 1,000: half of the membership plus their families.[31]

The rapid growth of *Sōka Gakkai* and the electoral successes of its political arm, the *Kōmeitō*, have perhaps obscured the fact that direct political activity, in the sense of putting forth or recommending candidates for office, is a practice engaged in by many religious groups in Japan. Many of the so-called new religions play an active role in politics and elections, recommending candidates for various offices and often putting forth their own candidates for election to the Upper House in the national constituency.

The social landscape of Ōita Prefecture is dotted with a large number of religious organizations, and Satō approached nearly all in his search for group support. While unable to obtain the official recommendation or complete support of any but one such organization, Satō made a concerted effort to get supporters in each of the following large religious organizations and a score of small religious groups in Beppu:

31 Interview, May 23, 1967.

Risshō Kōseikai, PL Kyōdan, Tenrikyō, Shingonshū, Kon-kōkyō, and *Sōka Gakkai.* While Satō did manage to gain support from some people who were active in these groups, he was unable to get significant group support. The *Sōka Gakkai* officially decided to give no support to any of the candidates and to give complete freedom to its members in deciding whom to support. The attention of the organization was focused on the April local elections and in helping Kōmeitō Diet candidates in neighboring Fukuoka Prefecture.[32]

Satō did get the official recommendation and active support of one of the new religions that takes an active part in politics, mainly on behalf of right-wing causes, *Seichō No Ie* (the House of Growth).[33] While a "new right" conservative when talking with certain groups, Satō more often than not turned to an old-right concern with Japan's spiritual health and the decadence plaguing the postwar generation when speaking before audiences in his district—particularly if they were old. His talk of the Emperor, the family system, and the *wabi* and *sabi* uniqueness of Japan had considerable appeal for the members of *Seichō No Ie* if the thinking of the President of the Beppu branch of that Association is at all representative.[34]

Seichō No Ie has been active in Ōita Prefecture for nearly twenty years but its membership is quite small. The organization claims 400 members in Beppu and 900 to 1,000 in the

[32] *Ōita Gōdō Shinbun,* January 6, 1967, p. 1.

[33] For a description of *Seichō No Ie* and a brief discussion of its advocacy of a "religious political movement" see Harry Thomsen, *The New Religions of Japan* (Tokyo, 1963), pp. 153–72.

[34] President Koguchi Hiroshi describes the group's political goals as revision of the Constitution to return sovereignty to the Emperor, recognition of the central role of the family (rather than the individual) in Japanese life, and, in general, sweeping measures to eliminate most of the postwar reforms and supposedly put the country on a road of progress directed by its own traditions rather than by the alien ideas of Westerners. While Satō has never come out in favor of any of the measures the group supports, he has not come out in opposition to any of them either.

Second District as a whole. Even this figure appears somewhat inflated. Satō believes the support of the organization may have helped in obtaining a few hundred votes in Beppu and had no effect anywhere else. Koguchi, with true missionary confidence in the benefits to be derived from joining the organization, claimed the membership gave Satō 5,000 votes.

In a highly polarized political party system like Japan's, candidates tend to concentrate their activities on mobilizing the support of voters within their own camp. The chasm between the conservative and the progressive camps is too wide to allow swing voting to the degree that prevails in more consensus-oriented party systems. All the associations discussed above are identified with the LDP and brought Satō into conflict with his fellow LDP candidates rather than with the opposition. Even within the moderate opposition Democratic Socialist Party, which had no candidate in the election, Satō appealed for and received no organized support. Both the DSP and its supporting *Dōmei* affiliated unions avoided direct involvement in the campaign and left their members free to decide for themselves among the candidates.[35] Similarly, Satō made little effort to gain the support of Socialist Party supporting groups. Among the more than a score of groups involved in Satō's organizational strategy, only one became a battleground for a confrontation between Satō and Socialist candidate Komatsu in the fight for group support. The organization at issue is the Ōita Prefecture Public High School Teachers' Union (*Ōita Ken Kōtōgakkō Kyōshokuin Kumiai;* known as *Kōkyōso*).

Seventy-eight per cent of Japan's 180,784 high school teachers are organized in labor unions. Of this number *Nikkyōso* (*Nihon Kyōshokuin Kumiai*) accounts for 38.6 per cent, or 69,688 teachers, and *Nikkōso* (*Nihon Kōtōgakkō Kyōshokuin Kumiai*) for 34.2 per cent, or 61,918 members. Twenty-two per cent are unorganized and the remaining 5.2 per cent are

[35] *Ōita Gōdō Shinbun*, January 6, 1967, p. 1.

in a variety of small unions.[36] In Ōita Prefecture virtually all public high school teachers (98 per cent) are members of the Ōita Prefecture Public High School Teachers' Union (*Kōkyōso*), which is affiliated with *Nikkōso*. While *Nikkyōso* is an important supporter of the Socialist Party, *Nikkōso* is split into right- and left-wing factions. According to figures published by the Education Ministry, the unions in fifteen prefectures are controlled by the right-wing faction and account for 23,900 of the organization's 61,918 members. Ōita's *Nikkōso* affiliated union is listed among these right-wing factions, a position confirmed by the leaders of the Ōita union.[37]

Labor unions, like the other organizations discussed in this chapter, often make recommendations for candidates in public elections. In 1967 the national headquarters of *Nikkōso*, however, did not issue a list of endorsed candidates and left the decision on which candidates to be recommended up to the prefectural unions. The leadership of Ōita's union is conservative in orientation. It supported Satō but the union is officially on record as having recommended only Socialist Komatsu Kan for election to the Lower House. Part of the reason for this anomoly is *Kōkyōso's* affiliation with the *Ōita Ken Rōdō Kumiai Hyōgikai (Kenrōhyō)*.

Ōita Prefecture is estimated to have 240,000 laborers, of whom 86,430 are organized in 688 labor unions. The majority of union members are in the First Electoral District. The Second District has 188 unions with a membership of 23,249.[38]

As on the national level, labor unions in the Prefecture are divided into several federations. Some are affiliated with

[36] As of June 1, 1966, according to Ministry of Education figures. A copy of the Ministry's document was provided the author by the President of *Kōkyōso*, Asada Hiroaki.

[37] *Ibid.;* Interview with Asada Hiroaki, May 1967.

[38] Information on Ōita labor unions based on an interview with Murai Hisao, Ōita Prefecture's Division of Commerce, Industry and Labor, Labor Affairs Section Chief in May 1967, and on the detailed materials in Ōita Ken Shōkō Rōdōbu Rōseika, *Rōdō Kumiai Meikan* (Ōita, 1966).

Sōhyō, the General Council of Trade Unions of Japan, the largest national labor federation and the most important backer of the Socialist Party. Others are associated with *Dōmei,* the smaller federation that backs the Democratic Socialist Party. Many others are affiliated with no prefectural or national organization. On the prefectural level there are three associations of labor unions, the largest being *Kenrōhyō,* with a membership of 56,245 people in eighty-two unions. *Kenrōhyō's* membership consists largely of workers in publicly owned enterprises and public servants,[39] and it is affiliated with *Sōhyō* on the national level. The other two are *Ōita Dōmei (Zen Nihon Rōdō Sōdōmei Ōita Chichō Dōmei),* with 10,966 members, and a small federation of 4,544 workers in small enterprises (*Ōita Ken Chūshō Kigyō Rōdō Kumiai Rengōkai*). These three prefectural organizations account for 68,755 of the 86,430 organized workers. The remainder are in the many small unions existing in the various cities and counties of the prefecture. These local unions (*chikurō*) are also for the most part affiliated with *Sōhyō* or *Dōmei* through the *Chikurōdō Kumiai Sogikai (Sōhyō)* and the *Chiku Dōmei* (*Dōmei*).

Though as a general rule unions in the Prefecture affiliated with *Kenrohyō* are also affiliated with *Sōhyō,* and vice-versa, the realities of union development in the Prefecture are much more complicated than the organizational charts would indicate. There are, for instance, some unions which are members of *Sōhyō* but are not in *Kenrōhyō,* and some, like the High School Teachers' Union, which are in *Kenrōhyō* but are not affiliated with *Sōhyō.*

Kenrōhyō recommends candidates for Diet and local elections. The member unions vote on the candidates to be recommended, and the endorsed candidates then become the recommended candidates of all *Kenrōhyō* affiliated unions. In the 1967 Diet election *Kenrōhyō* endorsed Socialist Komatsu

[39] With 37,780 such workers, as compared to 18,465 workers in private industry.

Kan. Though the top-level leadership of the High School Teachers' Union is opposed to Komatsu, the need to maintain their position in *Kenrōhyō* and to avoid a serious split among the membership of their own union led the leaders to acquiesce in the *Kenrōhyō* endorsement and covertly campaign for Satō.

In the immediate postwar period all public school teachers were in one union in Ōita (*Kenkyōso*) which was affiliated with the national *Nikkyōso* organization. In the mid-1950s a dispute led the high school teachers to break away from *Kenkyōso* and form their own union. The present president of the High School Teachers' Union, Asada Hiroaki, asserts that Komatsu was involved in the fight that led to the split and that, consequently, "Among teachers over forty-five those opposed to Komatsu are in the overwhelming majority and their support has gone to [Satō] Bunsei."[40] Komatsu relates that he was an officer of *Kenkyōso* at the time of the split and attempted to mediate between the opposing factions. When his efforts failed and the high school teachers' group decided to leave the union, Komatsu, who was a junior high school teacher at the time, could do nothing more than accept the high school teachers decision and remain in his executive position in *Kenkyōso*. He agrees that this earned him the animosity of the leaders of the high school teachers group at the time, and that those people (those Asada refers to as being over forty-five) have kept tight grip on the union's executive positions.[41]

Satō was able to capitalize on opposition to Komatsu largely because of his position as Chairman of the Prefectural Assembly's Education Committee. In this position, Satō had been able to do favors for many people. A request to a friend in the prefectural bureaucracy could get a desired transfer for a teacher; a call from Satō to a high school principal might help obtain a position for the son of a constituent just out of college. Many of Satō's friends are bureaucrats in the educa-

[40] In a letter to the author of June 21, 1967. All quotes attributed to Mr. Asada are taken from this letter.

[41] Interview with Komatsu Kan, July 7, 1967.

tional section of the prefectural government and principals of high schools, particularly those in Beppu. His position on the Education Committee allowed Satō to develop personal friendships with the high school teachers, and after leaving the Assembly he continued to maintain these ties.

There are several other reasons alleged to account for leadership support for Satō. One is their political conservatism. The leaders of Ōita's High School Teachers' Union take marked exception to being labeled laborers. The President of the union believes that "The character of the High School Teachers' Union is unlike that of labor unions and teachers unlike laborers. This causes opposition to labor unions and consequently to the Socialist Party. The union maintains a posture of nonalignment in regard to political parties." President Asada and his group consider themselves political moderates and "Satō's modern sense appeals to the high school teachers. The contents of his speeches stand above conservatism or progressivism and offers a new approach. His liberalism is an important reason for his appeal among the high school teachers."

The Elementary and Junior High School Teachers' Union (*Kenkyōso*), with its approximately 2,700 members in the Second District,[42] provides the core campaign organization for Komatsu. One important reason for the failure of any candidate to get the united support of the high school teachers, in addition to those cited above, is indicated by President Asada in his statement that

the majority of the members of Komatsu's major supporter, *Kenkyōso,* are alumni of Oita University and possess a strong sense of familial (*dōzoku*) consciousness. In the case of the high school teachers, the colleges graduated from are diverse. Furthermore many have become teachers only after the War. It is impossible to match the unanimity of *Kenkyōso* in deciding on support for a candidate in the general election.

[42] Ōita Ken Shōkō Rōdōbu Rōseika, *Rōdō Kumiai Meikan,* pp. 17–19.

The High School Teachers' Union in Ōita has 2,856 members. Of these, 1,215 are in the Second District. With the union officially supporting Komatsu and the union leadership supporting Satō, estimates as to the degree of support for the candidates vary greatly with the person being asked. The union leadership implies in discussing the matter that support for Satō is limited pretty much to the old guard, the over forty-five group of teachers who have memories of the fight that led to the split with *Kenkyōso*. Satō talks of commanding the support not only of the union's leaders but of the majority of the general membership as well, and he considers himself unique among conservative politicians in having broad support among a "progressive" group like the High School Teachers' Union. Komatsu naturally deprecates Satō's support among the teachers. He argues that even though the union's leadership is conservative, the politics of the union and of *Kenrōhyō* force the leadership to keep their campaign activities for Satō circumspect while the union endorses Komatsu publicly. Komatsu believes he gets 70 per cent of the union support, Satō gets 20 per cent, and the remaining members support other candidates.[43]

More important than the question of how many of the teachers' votes Satō receives is the fact that the support given him by the union leadership effectively prevented a coordinated campaign effort by the union on behalf of an opposing candidate. Individual teachers may vote for and even campaign for Komatsu but he was unable to incorporate the union itself into his campaign organization. With the support of the leadership, union campaign activities, like those of the Elementary and Middle School Teachers' Union, can be rationally organized. The organizational structure of the union with its capacity for coordinating a joint effort can be mobilized; enthusiasm for the campaign effort can be instilled through the sense of participation and commitment to the

[43] Interview, July 7, 1967.

group effort; and through the union's hierarchy of influence and power pressure can be applied to insure a certain minimum of membership participation. Without such leadership support, the efforts of the union members, even if they are generally in favor of one particular candidate become, in a favorite word of Japanese politicians, *barabara*—"scattered." Coordination becomes difficult. The union, as a campaign organization, is rendered impotent. For Satō this is the major beneficial consequence of the support of the teacher union's leadership. In an exaggeration both of the extent of his support among the union membership and of the facts of politics in other prefectures, Satō talked of himself as being the "only man" running for election as a conservative to have the support of the "progressive" High School Teachers' Union. This union did represent the sole battlefield on which conservative met progressive in a search for organized support. That Satō tended to exaggerate his support among this group was largely the result of the heady effect created by the rarefied atmosphere of an interparty battle.

In addition to the groups discussed above, more than a score of organizations were approached by Satō. A listing of some of these indicates the broad range of groups that came within his "organizational strategy."

One group was composed of associations of former teachers and public officials, including the Association of Former High School Principals (*taishoku kōchōkai*) and the Federation of Former Public Officials (*taishoku kōmuin rengōkai*). Another category was that of veterans' associations, the large *gunon-renmei* and smaller local groups. A related group is the large *Izokukai*, the organization of bereaved families of the war dead. Satō was unable to get support from the organization but had his son make courtesy calls on several members from Beppu during the campaign in the hope that a few members might offer to campaign for him.

Another category was that of sports clubs. Satō serves as President or advisor to no less than six sports organizations. He is also a member of the Prefecture's Association for Physical Education and makes more speeches at sporting events than at political rallies. Through these activities he tried to promote an image of the sportsman-politician—young, healthy, vigorous, handsome, and interested in young people.

Also approached were the Barbers' Union, the Beauticians' Union, the Association of Hotel Owners, the Bartenders' Association, the Association of Midwives, the Association of Masseurs, and, in Beppu, an intriguing group called the *Bunchōkai*.

The *Bunchōkai* (the *Bun* is taken from Satō's name, Bunsei) is an organization of cooks in hotels in Beppu created for the purpose of supporting Satō's campaign. The *Bunchōkai* is interesting, if not of demonstrable importance, because it brings Satō's campaign into Beppu's underworld of gangsters, prostitutes, and other unheralded voters. The advisor (*komon*) to the Hotel Chefs' Union (*itaba kumiai*) is an ex-convict and a former cook. Beppu was at one time notorious for its criminal gangs, and the advisor to the Union was active in one of these. He currently works for one of Beppu's local newspapers, and it was through the editor of the paper that he met Satō. He became a devoted supporter of Satō and, establishing the *Bunchōkai,* organized most of the 450 men in the Cooks' Union (many of whom have similar histories in Beppu's underworld) on Satō's behalf. These men were urged to spread the word for Satō to all the waitresses in the places they worked and to use their influence with friends and acquaintances in Beppu's less respectable bars and other varied places of entertainment.

Virtually every group with a title was at least approached by Satō in the search for organization support. The Ōita Prefecture Abacus Association, of which Satō serves as advisor, the Beppu *Minyō Kenkyūkai* (folksong club), and the Beppu *Sangakukai* (the mountain-climbing club) were all included within Satō's "organizational strategy."

Of all the groups involved in one way or another in Satō's campaign, only one, the Prefectural Dental Association, provided full and effective support. Only four others, the bamboo growers, the Beppu Junior Chamber of Commerce, the vegetable dealers' union, and the Beppu branch of *Seichō No Ie* gave Satō their sole endorsement. The general pattern for voluntary associations that are supporters of the LDP was to make no recommendations for candidates in the election or to officially endorse all the LDP candidates. By not urging their membership to vote for a particular candidate, LDP supporting associations left the endorsed LDP candidate with precisely the same problem he had before endorsement: how to convince voters to vote for him rather than for another of the party's candidates. Association activities to provide meaningful support to a particular LDP candidate were, however, certain to incur the opposition of the other candidates of the party in the district. Thus an LDP supporting organization is in the unhappy predicament of being effective by supporting only one candidate and inviting the hostility of unsupported LDP candidates or being ineffective by endorsing all LDP candidates and earning the gratitude of none.

From the candidate's perspective, the support of an organization is valuable when it provides a horizontal cover to his campaign strategy; when it fans out across the district, providing support his area-based organization cannot recruit. Whether the candidate receives the sole recommendation of the organization or whether he is only one of several endorsed candidates, the crucial issue is the extent to which his support permeates down through the organization's membership across the district. As a consequence, the organizational strategy of LDP candidates is often a strategy for obtaining the support of particular subleaders within the organizations. This results in the phenomenon of the candidate paying, in effect, the interest group for its support rather than the interest group paying the candidate for his support of the group's policies. An LDP candidate who has received the recommendation along with the other candidates of the party of a particular organization will try to find out which subleaders (such as the Chairmen of the town or county organization) are favorable to him, and then give campaign funds to these leaders to distribute to members of the organization within their particular area of influence. This sometimes amounts to little else than bribery. Since all LDP candidates have received the organization's endorsement, the issue of which one is to be supported may be determined by a contest to see which one offers the largest amount of so-called campaign funds to the largest number of organization leaders. Even where one candidate has received the sole recommendation of an organization, the tendency is for him to distribute campaign funds to subleaders of the group in order to insure their support and avoid what one writer (for somewhat different reasons) has termed "executive campaigns," support that does not reach beyond the top level of the organization leadership.[44]

The amount of campaign funds offered by candidates is not, however, the sole or even major factor in determining which subleaders will support which candidates. More often than not such decisions are determined by geography. There is a strong tendency for organizations that have endorsed all party candidates to break up in effective support along the lines of indigenous candidate strength. Thus one finds many organizations giving Satō support in Beppu, Ayabe support in Kitsuki, and Nishimura support in Higashi Kunisaki. LDP supporting organizations show a tendency in supporting LDP candidates to back the native son candidate where there is no specific organizational policy to do otherwise.

Such dynamics of the political process on the local level suggest that a sharp distinction should be drawn between the relationship of powerful national interest groups with the LDP and with particular party leaders and the relationship of local branches of such groups with the larger number of backbenchers and new candidates. While the national organizations of various interest groups have an intimate relationship with the LDP in providing financial support and influencing policy, the component organizations on the prefectural level are for the most part infinitely weaker and have only the most tenuous ties with the LDP. It is the prefectural organization, however, that is mainly concerned with Lower House election cam-

[44] Matsushita Keiichi, *Gendai Nihon No Seijiteki Kōsei* (Tokyo, 1964), p. 137.

paigns.[45] In isolated cases a national interest group will give meaningful support to individual Diet candidates, such as the Medical Association did for Nishimura in the 1963 election, but such action is the exception rather than the rule. In Satō's case there was no instance of support from the national organization of any interest group, and even on the local level, as has been seen, meaningful organizational support was minimal. Where such direct support occurred it was the consequence of purely local and largely personal factors (his long-held position as advisor to the Dental Association for instance) rather than the result of the organization's conscious consideration of the benefits support for him would provide. There is a great difference in the role interest groups play in providing financial support for top LDP leaders and a body of voters who will vote for LDP candidates and their role in providing effective support for individual candidates. Glossing over this difference can lead to unrealistically inflated estimates of the role such groups play in Diet campaigns and the degree of influence they have over individual Diet members. For the large number of LDP Diet members, ties with various interest groups would appear to be generally indirect, through faction leaders and the party leadership.

Perhaps the major importance of Satō's efforts to gain the support of various groups was, as one reporter observed, its largely intangible effect of building the "Satō mood":

For three years, since losing in the last election by a narrow margin, Satō has been engaged in a minute organization of various groups: the bamboo growers, the vegetable dealers, hotel cooks, hotel owners and even masseurs. At barber shops, beauty parlors and *sushi* counters "Bunsei" is an often-heard word. As the word passes back and forth from the lips of waitresses and housewives the Satō mood is building up. . . .[46]

[45] On the predominant role of local chapters of national associations in Lower House election campaigns, see Taguchi Fukuji, *Nihon Seiji No Dōkō To Tenbō* (Tokyo, 1966), p. 174.

[46] *Asahi Shinbun*, January 8, 1967, p. 14.

VIII

The Official Campaign

⟁ ON DECEMBER 27, 1966, the Prime Minister, under the pressures of a Socialist boycott of the Diet and an incessant public demand for new elections, dissolved the Lower House and set January 29th as the day the nation's voters would elect a new House of 486 members. Under the law, candidacy must be registered within four days of the day of the official notification of the election (kōji).[1] This was set for January 8th. Since campaigning is allowed only during the period that extends from the day candidacy is registered to the day preceding the election,[2] the official campaign period for candidates who registered on January 8th was twenty-one days, January 8th through the 28th.

The candidate for public office in Japan is not only limited in time in conducting his official campaign but also must operate within the framework of an election law that sets extraordinary limitations on the types of campaign activities allowed.

Before 1950 separate laws governed elections for various offices in Japan. In the early Lower House Election Laws, those of 1889, 1890, 1900, and 1919, there were no restrictions on campaign activities except for a prohibition of campaigning in the polling places themselves. There was no limitation on the amount of money that might be spent on the campaign.[3] Revisions of the Election Law after 1919 have imposed increasingly severe limitations on permissible campaign prac-

[1] *Election Law*, Article 86.

[2] *Ibid.*, Article 129.

[3] Hayashida Kazuhiro, "Development of Election Law in Japan," *Hōsei Kenkyū*, xxxiv (July, 1967), 38; For the laws, see Senkyo Seido Nanajyūnen Kinenkai, *Senkyohō No Enkaku* (Tokyo, 1959).

The Moment of Victory on Election Night

tices and have provided for a very considerable degree of government management of campaign activities. This trend has continued in the postwar period, having been interrupted only temporarily in the early period of the American Occupation.

In 1925 a full-scale revision of the Lower House Election Law imposed for the first time a great number of restrictions on campaign practices. These included prohibition of house-to-house calls (*kobetsu hōmon*), restrictions on the distribution of campaign literature, and a limitation on the amount of money that could be spent in the campaign. The revised Law also included strict disciplinary provisions providing punishments for violators.

The articles of the 1925 Law dealing with campaign practices were largely modeled after the British Corrupt and Illegal Practices Prevention Act of 1883,[4] and to some extent reflected a desire to eradicate corrupt election practices. In the year 1925 Japan also adopted universal manhood suffrage. Fears on the part of the government of the possible consequences of the new suffrage resulted in the adoption in the same year of the repressive Peace Preservation Law which gave the government broad powers to control political activities. The legal restrictions on campaign practices were more in accord with the spirit of this Law than with the democratic implications of universal manhood suffrage. They are said to have been so complicated and severe that they allowed the government in power to effectively intimidate candidates, campaigners, and electors, and provided a serious "obstacle to a free and unrestricted expression of the popular will."[5]

As the government became more repressive, restrictions on campaign activities were expanded. In the revision of the Election Law in 1934, the prohibition of pre-election campaigning was introduced for the first time. Other restrictions on campaign practices were also incorporated and penalties for violations made more severe. This revision also introduced

[4] Hayashida, "Development of Election Law," p. 38.
[5] *Ibid.*, p. 39.

a greatly expanded government involvement in elections, providing for government management of campaign speech meetings, government printing of campaign brochures, and government control over various other aspects of the campaign.

Almost all of the provisions regarding campaign practices adopted in the prewar laws are in effect at the present time. Only in the election of 1946 were candidates, campaigning under a new House of Representatives Election Law adopted in 1945 under U.S. Occupation auspices, free of many of the earlier restrictions on campaign activities. From 1947 on restrictions were steadily reimposed. The Public Offices Election Law of 1950 incorporated many of the prewar restrictions on campaign practices, and revision of that Law in 1952 marked a return to the 1934 Law in terms of the limitations it places on campaign activities.[6] A candidate for the Lower House campaigns within a legal strait jacket. His every campaign activity, from the number of speeches he may make to the size of the one-paper lantern he may hang outside his campaign headquarters, is regulated by law.

Certain campaign practices familiar in other countries are prohibited in Japan. Canvassing from house to house for votes, whether done by the candidate, his staff, or people acting on their own volition in support of a candidate, is prohibited (138[1]).[7] Signature campaigns are similarly prohibited (138[2]), and no one is allowed to publish popularity polls (138[3]). The serving of food and refreshments as part of the campaign is forbidden (139), and no activities are allowed which are intended to "raise ardor" (140), "such as running a procession of cars, marching a large group of people, using a siren, employing a band or making a clamor for the purpose of attracting the attention of voters."[8]

In addition to such outright prohibitions are a multitude

---

[6] Kobayashi Naoki, Shinohara Hajime, and Sōma Masao, *Senkyo* (Tokyo, 1960), p. 57; cf. Sōma Masao, *Nihon No Senkyo Seiji* (Tokyo, 1963), p. 30.

[7] Numbers in parentheses refer to the relevant article in the Election Law.

[8] Jichishō Senkyo Kyokuhen, *Sōsenkyo No Tebiki* (Tokyo, 1967), p. 75.

of restrictions. Sidewalk speeches cannot be made later than nine in the evening (164[6]) and "repeated calling activities" (*renkokōi*, "the constant repetition of a fixed phrase in a short period of time"[9]) are prohibited except at a hall where the candidate is giving a private speech, while he is giving a sidewalk speech or from the campaign car, and are restricted to between the hours of seven in the morning and eight in the evening (140[2]).

Each candidate's campaign is permitted only one campaign car, which has to fit certain specifications and must be registered with the government. Its number of occupants and the size and number of signs that may be placed upon it are defined in the law (141).

Each candidate may have only one campaign headquarters in the district (131[1]), and the number and size of posters and signboards used in the headquarters are circumscribed (143). If the candidate wants to move the headquarters to another location he must file a formal request to do so with the government's Election Management Office. When the headquarters is moved all activity in the former headquarters must cease and all signboards visible from outside the former headquarters must be removed (130[2]).

The Election Law also places extensive restrictions on the types and quantity of written materials that may be displayed and distributed. All written campaign materials except those expressly permitted by the Law are prohibited. The only materials the Law allows displayed are signs, restricted in number and size, at the campaign headquarters, on the campaign car, and at a hall during the course of a candidate's private speech meeting, and campaign posters displayed along with those of the other candidates on official poster boards at specified locations throughout the district. The only material the candidate may distribute to the electorate are 25,000 campaign postcards. The government's Election Management Commit-

9 *Ibid.,* p. 67.

tee in addition distributes to all voters an election brochure (*senkyo kōhō*) that contains statements of 2,000 characters each by the candidates along with their pictures. Candidates and their supporters are prohibited from displaying or distributing any other written campaign materials to the constituents. Not only does this include posters, signs, handbills, buttons, and all the other paraphernalia familiar to American political campaigns but it extends also to noncampaign materials that might have the effect of influencing a voter's choice at the polls. Thus, "during the period of election campaigning, the distribution of greeting cards, New Year cards, winter greetings, summer greetings, and the like by a candidate or by supporters using the candidate's name is a violation of the law regardless of whether such distribution is for the purpose of campaigning or not. . . ."[10]

The speech-making activities the candidate may engage in are also defined by the Election Law. Candidate speeches during the official campaign period are restricted to three kinds: sidewalk speeches, joint speech meetings, and private speech meetings.

The candidate may give sidewalk speeches but he "must be stationary. He cannot give speeches while walking or while riding on top of a car."[11] Of course he cannot use any posters or signs or distribute any materials while giving such a speech. He cannot have more than fifteen campaigners with him and each must wear an armband distributed by the Election Management Committee.

The major speech-making activity of the Diet candidate is participation in the joint speech meetings (*tachiai enzetsukai*) conducted by the Election Management Committee of the Local Autonomy Ministry. Most districts have an average of thirty-five such meetings, participated in by six to seven candidates with speeches lasting twenty minutes.[12] In Ōita's Sec-

10 *Ibid.*, p. 80.
11 *Ibid.*, p. 104.
12 *Ibid.*, p. 104.

ond District in the 1967 election campaign there were twenty-five meetings, participated in by five candidates with speeches lasting thirty minutes.[13] Participation in these meetings is not compulsory in law but in fact it is rare for a candidate not to take part. For one thing the Law prohibits him from doing anything else while a joint speech meeting is in session. The large number of joint speech meetings means in effect that for most of the official campaign period the candidates' itineraries are determined by the Election Management Committee. The usual pattern is for a candidate to arrive in the morning in the part of the district where the joint speech meeting is to be held, spend the day riding around in a campaign car, getting out occasionally to give sidewalk speeches, and appearing at the joint speech meeting to give his twenty- or thirty-minute speech.[14]

The candidate can also hold private speech meetings (*kojin enzetsukai*). Each candidate is allowed sixty such speeches, which must be registered in advance with the Election Management Committee. Such speeches may not be scheduled during the hours when a joint speech meeting is in process, and they are subject to several other legal restrictions (161–64). It is not permissible, for instance, to display signs outside the hall in which a private speech meeting is being held or in any way advertise it in advance. In Ōita's Second District none of the candidates held private speech meetings.

The advent of television and the general expansion and sophistication of communication media have affected political communication in Japan as elsewhere. But because of the restrictions the Election Law places on candidate use of the media, campaign strategies have as yet been little affected by Japan's highly developed communications network. No candidate for public office in Japan is allowed to buy time on tele-

[13] Ōita Ken Senkyo Kanri Iinkai, *Senkyo No Kiroku, Shūgiin Giin Sōsenkyo*, January 29, 1967 election (Ōita, 1967), p. 29.

[14] A revision of the Election law following the 1967 election reduced the number of joint speech meetings by about one-third.

vision or radio or buy space for advertisements in newspapers. Candidates for the Lower House are allowed to make, free of charge, three radio broadcasts of five minutes each. No provision is made for the use of television.[15] The candidate may also submit a short biographical statement for broadcast by station personnel three times on television and ten times on the radio. He can also place five newspaper advertisements of determined length. The costs for all candidate advertising in the mass media are assumed by the government (149–51). This is the total extent to which candidates can use the mass media in their campaigns. Obviously the problems of strategy and finance relating to the use of communication media that face the American candidate are nonexistent in Japan.

Over and above these and many other restrictions and prohibitions too numerous to discuss, the candidate in his campaign is allowed to spend only a limited amount of money and must account for all expenditures to the Election Management Committee. Japanese law does not provide the loophole present in United States laws that limitations on campaign expenditures do not apply to expenditures of committees independent of the candidate. In Japan the candidate is responsible for all expenses on behalf of his campaign. There is no way to create a "Citizens For Satō" committee to get around the law.

The formula used for determining the amount of money a candidate may legally spend is to multiply the number of registered voters in the district by 10.5 yen, divide the total by the number of candidates, and add 1,200,000 yen. A consequence of this formula is that the amount of money each candidate may spend decreases as the number of candidates increases. In Ōita's Second District the formula resulted in a maximum legal expenditure of 2,182,400 yen per candidate, which is a little more than 6,000 dollars in U.S. currency. The

15 Another revision of the Law after the 1967 election provided each candidate three television appearances during the official campaign of four and a half minutes each.

highest figure was in Tokyo's Seventh District with 4,022,700 yen and the lowest was in Hyogo's Fifth District with 2,003,500 yen. The nationwide average was 2,573,800 yen, approximately 7,200 dollars.[16]

The purpose of the restrictions on campaign practices incorporated in the Public Offices Election Law is ostensibly to insure inexpensive and fair elections where no candidate because of political power or economic wealth has an advantage over another in appealing to the electorate for support. Defenders of the Law also maintain that restrictions on campaign practices are necessary because of the presence of modes of behavior in Japan antithetical to democratic practice. Prohibitions of house-to-house calls, the serving of refreshments, and even the prohibition of calling on supporters after the election to thank them for their help are necessary, so the argument goes, to insure a minimum interference of "feudalistic" customs and mores in the electoral process.

In fact the Law does little to realize such goals and has other undesirable effects.[17] The various restrictions have not made elections inexpensive. They have simply made most expenses illegal. The Japanese politician, as is discussed later in this chapter, expends considerable amounts of money on his campaign but, because of the Law, has developed ways to keep such expenditures hidden from public view. Furthermore, the restrictions on the use of the mass media, on the distribution of written materials, and on speech making have forced the politician to use other means of support mobilization less in accord with democratic ideals than the expensive but public appeal to the electorate utilization of communications media provides.

The most important consequence of the Election Law's provisions is to greatly enhance the strength of incumbents in

[16] *Yomiuri Shinbun,* January 6, 1967, p. 2.

[17] I have discussed some of these effects and other aspects of campaigning in "Nihon No Kyōikumamateki Senkyo," *Bungei Shunjū,* xv (June, 1967), 174–80.

elections. The Law "works to the benefit of those already elected, incumbents and former Diet members, whose names are known to the electorate. . . . [T]he law is clearly to the disadvantage of new men."[18] The various restrictions on campaign activities function largely to keep new candidates away from the public eye. The prohibition of pre-election campaigning, restrictions on the distribution of written materials and on the use of the mass media, and other seemingly minor things such as the prohibition of the use of convertibles or other open cars work their greatest hardship against the new and unknown candidate. The incumbent, who receives constant publicity in his constituency through his activities in the Diet, has all to gain by maintaining a law that effectively prevents new candidates from gaining public exposure. It is for this reason that efforts to substantially revise the Election Law have been doomed. Once a man becomes a member of the Diet he has all to gain by maintaining and extending the restrictions on campaign practices.

The Law has another important and deplorable effect. It makes the general voter a mere observer of the campaign. By effectively preventing popular participation in campaigns it inhibits if not actually works counter to the political socialization of the electorate that should be a major function of election campaigns. The Election Law's ideal campaign is much like a beauty contest. When the official campaign period begins the contestants, supposedly having had no pre-contest opportunity for influencing the judges, walk out on the stage and go through a rigorously supervised series of performances that gives each an exactly equal opportunity to demonstrate his attributes to the judges. They then all leave the stage for the judges to make their decision. The voters are in the position of passive judges. They can read posters and listen to speeches but can take almost no direct part in the contest. Not only does this make an election campaign unbearably

18 Kajiyama Toshiyuki, "Kane to Kōyaku No Matsuri Sōsenkyo," *Hōseki* (February, 1967), p. 54; cf. Sōma Masao, *Senkyo Seiji*, p. 35.

dull for the average voter. It makes a fundamental function of systems of representative government frightening to the politically concerned electorate because of the fear that efforts in support of a candidate may result in a violation of the Election Law. It is only in very recent years that political parties have come out with pamphlets explaining the activities "third parties" *(daisansha)* may engage in in support of candidates for public office.[19] The Law itself is mainly an exhaustive listing of the things voters may not do. In restricting the activities of the general electorate in the electoral process, the present-day Election Law is a direct descendent of the Law of 1925 which first introduced these provisions in an attempt to prevent universal suffrage from leading to mass movements which would threaten the continuation of conservative dominance.[20] A nonincumbent candidate such as Satō must attempt to gain support within the framework of an Election Law that limits to an extraordinary degree the campaign activities he may engage in and the activities that his supporters may undertake on his behalf. Inhibited by these restraints, Satō entered into the official campaign and the final three weeks of his struggle for election to the Lower House.

The three weeks of Satō's official campaign divide into three periods. The first encompassed the opening five days of the campaign. The second was the period of joint speech meetings that ran from January 13th to the 26th. The final two days of the campaign mark the third period.

As the discussion in the previous pages has indicated, the Election Law so restricts campaign practices that there is little opportunity for a candidate to employ imaginative or innovative campaign techniques. In Ōita's Second District all the candidates went through the same uninspired routine of driv-

---

[19] See, for example, Jiyūminshutō, *Dare Demo Dekiru Senkyo Undō* (Tokyo, 1967).

[20] For an excellent analysis of the effects on political participation of the Election Law's campaign practices provisions see Matsushita Keiichi, *Sengo Minshu Shugi No Tenbō* (Tokyo, 1965), pp. 195–202, 231.

ing around in a campaign car with a loudspeaker constantly repeating the candidate's name, stopping occasionally for short sidewalk speeches, and taking part in the joint speech sessions.

Satō spent the first two days of the campaign in Beppu. Taking one school district at a time, his official campaign car weaved in and out of the city streets, its loudspeaker droning out over and over again the monotonous phrase, "*Satō Bunsei de gozaimasu. Jimintō kōnin Satō Bunsei de gozaimasu. Dōzo yoroshiku onegai shimasu.*" ("This is Satō Bunsei. This is L D P-endorsed Satō Bunsei. I ask for your support".) A schedule giving the times he planned to pass through each neighborhood was issued to the neighborhood *sewanin,* who tried to round up groups of people to greet Satō as he came by. Whenever a group appeared the car stopped and Satō made a short sidewalk speech. Throughout Beppu these five-minute speeches all emphasized the same points. Satō is the native son candidate, the only candidate from Beppu. The L D P old guard is corrupt and the party must be reformed from within. Only young politicians like Satō, the youngest candidate in the district, could rejuvenate the party. Then back in the car and again the monotonous repeating: "*Satō Bunsei de gozaimasu. Jimintō kōnin Satō Bunsei. . . .*" Toward dusk Satō returned to the center of town and walked through its arcades with a megaphone, speaking to small circles of people and hitting at the same points: elect the native son candidate, rejuvenate the L D P and create a conservative party that is "loved by young people and women." At nine o'clock in the evening campaigning for the day came to an end.

This same procedure was followed throughout the first week of the campaign, that is, until the beginning of the joint speech sessions. On the third day of the campaign Satō moved north to Nakatsu and Shimoge county, then cut down through the central part of the district the next day, and spent the fifth day campaigning on the Kunisaki Peninsula.

In Beppu Satō appealed to local pride and constituent self-interest in getting "one of their own" into the Diet. He pre-

sented himself as Beppu's candidate, with the strong suggestion that it was both proper and in the voters interest to support the native son rather than some "outsider." Throughout
the district, Satō's strategy as it evolved in these first days of
the campaign was to take the offensive in attacking corruption in the LDP and stress the importance of getting young
uncorrupted conservatives into the Diet. In other words, in his
official campaign as in his activities in the period preceding
the campaign, Satō's major efforts were directed at maximizing support within the conservative party supporting sector
of the electorate. In the short sidewalk speeches Satō was able
to completely avoid dealing with political issues other than
the issue of political corruption. The only aspect of his appeal
that was aimed at obtaining votes that might go to Socialist
Komatsu was his argument that regardless of how poorly the
LDP did in the election, it would still be the majority party
in the new Diet. Therefore voters who were disgusted with
the LDP should not "throw away" their vote by voting for an
opposition party candidate but should vote for Satō so he
could work from within the party to reform it.

In this first period of the official campaign, newspaper estimates of candidate strength pointed to a close contest between
Satō and Komatsu for the third spot on the winners' ticket.
Komatsu was generally pictured as the underdog because the
votes of conservative independent Noyori Hideichi were expected to go to the other conservative candidates in this first
election following Noyori's retirement. As one reporter wrote,
"the votes the conservatives will pick up from Noyori supporters make it look like a bitter battle for Komatsu."[21]

The appointments of Nishimura as Construction Minister
in Prime Minister Satō's third cabinet reshuffle immediately

[21] *Nishi Nihon Shinbun,* December 6, 1967, p. 10. The same view was
expressed in articles in *Ōita Gōdō Shinbun,* January 1, 1967, p. 3; *Ōita
Nichinichi Shinbun,* January 13, 1967; *Higashi Kyūshū Shinbun,* January
11, 1967; *Mainichi Shinbun,* December 25, 1966, p. 14; and *Ōita Shinbun,*
December 28, 1966, p. 1.

preceding the election and of Ayabe as Speaker of the Lower House were seen as insuring the re-election of the incumbents. Both received a great deal of valuable publicity in the local papers[22] and the generally assumed implication of their appointments was indicated by a *Mainichi* newspaper reporter when he wrote that "Ayabe and Nishimura were facing a bitter fight because of the candidacy of Satō but with their appointments as Speaker and Construction Minister they have breathed a sigh of relief."[23] Their appointments, echoed another newspaper, meant that "their election victory can be considered a certainty."[24]

The incumbents themselves exhibited a new confidence. As Nishimura remarked in a television appearance with Ayabe following their appointments, "it would have been a difficult election if only one of us had received an appointment but, well, it has turned out very well."[25]

Though Komatsu was expected to suffer from Noyori's retirement, newspaper analyses recognized that he had overcome comparable odds in previous elections and that he could expect a significant number of votes from people upset with the "black mist" that enveloped the LDP. Thus the mass media was unanimous in its analysis. "Common sense," concluded one reporter, "shows that it is a fight between Komatsu and Satō for the third seat."[26]

Opinion among Satō's staff in the first days of the campaign was much the same as that expressed in the newspapers. The appointment of Ayabe came as a particularly heavy blow.

22 Typical of the coverage were articles in *Ōita Gōdō Shinbun*, December 4, 1966, p. 2, December 5, p. 1, December 24, p. 3, December 28, p. 8; *Asahi Shinbun*, December 3, p. 1; and *Ōita Shinbun*, December 4, p. 1.

23 *Mainichi Shinbun*, December 23, 1966, p. 14.

24 *Beppu Yūkan*, December 27, 1966.

25 *Ōita Gōdō Shinbun*, December 25, 1966, p. 1.

26 *Beppu Yūkan*, December 27, 1966. Other articles making similar predictions may be found in *Ōita Shinbun*, December 28, 1968, p. 1; *Nishi Nihon Shinbun*, December 30, 1966, p. 5 and January 11, 1967, p. 3; *Mainichi Shinbun*, December 25, 1966, p. 14.

First reactions were that the appointment indeed gave new life to Ayabe's campaign and meant that Satō could only hope for a narrow victory over Komatsu. As the campaign continued, opinion within the Satō camp began to turn more optimistic. The Speakership, it appeared to Satō's supporters, may well have doomed Ayabe. It is a post without power easily translatable to the constituents in terms of benefits and there seemed to be a growing mood that his appointment was the climax to a long career and that Ayabe should now step aside, or be pushed aside, for a new generation. With the beginning of the joint speech meetings Satō's campaign began to gain new momentum.

Between January 13th and January 26th the candidates took part in a series of twenty-six government-sponsored joint speech meetings (*tachiai enzetsukai*). During this period there were two speeches a day, one at one o'clock in the afternoon and another at 6:30 in the evening on all but two days, when the candidates had to give only one speech. Of the district's twenty-three cities, towns, and villages all but the island of Himeshima hosted one joint speech session each, with the two largest cities of the district, Beppu and Nakatsu, each being host to two sessions.

Because of the demands of the joint speech meetings, all the candidates followed almost exactly the same route in the standardized routine of constantly repeating the candidate's name over the car loudspeaker, making sidewalk speeches, and speaking at the joint speech meetings. The strategy of concentrating support in restricted geographical areas, though crucial to the campaigns of all the conservative candidates, was reflected to only a very limited degree in the official campaign period because of the demands of the joint speech meetings. Only in the opening five and closing two days of the campaign could the candidates spend the entire day in the areas they considered most important for their election.

The joint speech meetings, along with the officially distributed election brochure, the sidewalk speeches, and the limited advertisement allowed in the mass media, represented the sole methods by which the candidates publicly expressed their views to the electorate during the period of the official campaign.

In the joint speech meetings Satō was faced with the problem of convincing voters who generally vote conservative to vote for him rather than for one of the other two LDP candidates. In terms of policy all three LDP candidates were committed to supporting the party platform. An analysis of the statements of the three in the joint speech meetings and in the election brochure reveals no significant differences in policy. All advocated lower taxes, increased productivity, better housing, stabilized prices, better education, and increased welfare state legislation. There was no policy that one of the LDP candidates supported that another opposed. The differences between the candidates, where they existed, were largely differences of emphasis. Nishimura, for instance, emphasized the need for improving roads and reducing the high number of traffic accidents. As Minister of Construction he would be in a position, he modestly suggested, to do something about such problems. Ayabe was particularly concerned with the need to quickly settle the question of compensation for victims of World War II (bereaved families, wounded soldiers, repatriates) and establish government aid for the Yasukuni shrine. Satō, to the extent that his policy pronouncements differed in emphasis from those of his conservative opponents, stressed the LDP's concern with the "little man," with increased welfare legislation to protect "the young, the elderly and the mute," and with legislation that would improve the position of the worker and the small businessman. On foreign policy he stressed the need for Japan to increase its own defense capabilities and for the Self Defense Forces to gradually replace U.S. forces as defenders of the nation. In making this point in his speeches, Satō was able to give play to his concern that Japan exhibit greater "pride" in itself. It was an insult to the nation's history, he told the voters, that Japan had to rely on foreigners for its security.

Important questions of policy, either domestic or foreign, were not of major concern in the election of January, 1967. The House was dissolved because of a public outcry over incidents of corruption by Diet members and the campaign, both in Ōita's Second District and nationally, was dominated by the issue of corruption and reform.

In their platforms all the political parties had a plank dealing with "political morality." In Ōita's Second District all the candidates dealt at great length with the question. It was given more attention in their speeches in the joint speech meetings than any other issue and accounted for more space in their statements in the official election brochure than any other single issue.

The LDP incumbents were at the greatest disadvantage in dealing with the issue of corruption. They both argued that only a few politicians were corrupt and that it was wrong to condemn the entire LDP. They maintained that they themselves were righteous politicians and were as concerned with eliminating corruption in the party as anyone else.

Ayabe was the most defensive. He argued that he had faithfully represented the people of the district and that the LDP had faithfully served the people of the nation. A few isolated incidents of corruption should not be allowed to blacken the name of the party and its great majority of members. Ayabe almost pleaded with his listeners: "I am an honest politician, a politician that does not tell lies. There has been a lot of talk of a black mist but I have been clean and honest. Please, re-elect an honest politician."[27]

Nishimura also made it a point to disassociate himself from corruption in the LDP in his speeches, and tried to take the offensive by attacking the Socialists for "undemocratic" actions, particularly their boycott of the Diet just before disso-

[27] Joint speech meeting in Beppu, January 26, 1967.

lution. He told his audiences that such action was threatening the development of parliamentary democracy and "the future of parliamentary democracy is at stake in this coming election."[28] "Insure parliamentary democracy" was the official slogan of the LDP in the election. Nishimura turned the black mist controversy into a call for support for the revision of the Election Law to provide for single member constituencies. This would allegedly allow for inexpensive elections and thus remove the major source of corruption.

Only for Satō among the LDP candidates could the political morality issue be used to advantage. He was able to almost entirely avoid discussion of specific policy issues by concentrating on the issue of LDP corruption and the need for a "rejuvenation" and "cleansing" of the party. While Nishimura and Ayabe stressed their history of service in the Diet and the powers they had to do favors for the constituents, Satō emphasized his purity. He tried to turn being a new candidate to advantage by presenting himself as the somewhat virginial alternative to the incumbents. He wrote in his election brochure statement that his basic desire was "to become a virtuous politician, to keep my associations with others honorable, to effect a rejuvenation and reform of the political world, to clearly separate public and private matters. . . ." He added that "within the LDP corruption and errors have arisen. It is essential for the nation that well-intentioned representatives be elected who will be pioneers in cleaning up and reforming the LDP. As one of the progressives of the LDP I will reform the political world and effect a rejuvenation of the nation." In his speeches Satō hit at the same point. "In the next Diet the LDP will still have power and that makes it essential to change the old politics and create a new LDP."[29]

Satō's remarks on political morality were echoed by new LDP candidates all over the country. As one nationwide newspaper put it, " 'When scandals occur, new candidates profit'

[28] Quoted in *Nishi Nihon Shinbun,* January 13, 1967, p. 10.
[29] Joint speech meeting in Nakatsu, January 23, 1967.

is election common sense. . . . Formerly candidates used to
criticize the policies of the other parties but now the case is
entirely different. First to be attacked is the new candidate's
own party. . . . The new candidate stands forward as the
young politician who will conduct 'undirtied' politics."[30]
While incumbent conservatives could appeal for support on
the basis of deeds done, the new candidates, through a for-
tuitous turn of circumstances, could appeal for votes because
of deeds not done. Satō, in emphasizing his purity, was to repeat time and time again to his audiences "I was born in the
year of the sheep. This is also the year of the sheep and it is
only the white sheep that can clear away the black mist."[31]

On January 26 the last joint speech meeting was held in
Beppu. The size of the audience testified to the heightened
interest in the campaign as it came to a close. While an estimated 1,500 people had attended the first meeting in Beppu
on January 13th, an overflow crowd of 2,700 tried to cram
into Beppu's largest auditorium on the evening of this last
day of the joint speech sessions.[32] Satō once again asked for
the support of "everyone of my home town." The other candidates made their pleas for support, and with the closing of
the meeting by the Chairman of the Election Management
Committee the middle phase of the campaign came to an end.

During the period of the joint speech meetings, newspaper
estimates of candidate strength changed dramatically from
earlier predictions of a battle between Satō and Komatsu for
the third spot. The re-election of the incumbent conservatives was no longer seen as being a foregone conclusion and
Satō appeared to demonstrate increasing strength. On January

[30] *Yomiuri Shinbun,* December 11, 1966, p. 1.
[31] Quoted in *Asahi Shinbun,* January 9, 1967, p. 14.
[32] This was 1,200 more than had attended the closing meeting in Beppu
in the same hall in the previous election. In the district as a whole, by
contrast, attendance in 1967 (16,326 people) was less than in 1963 (20,613).
Greater interest in Satō's 1967 campaign than in his 1963 race was probably
responsible for the large turnout in his hometown.

18th the *Mainichi* newspaper summed up the changed estimate with its statement that "At the present moment Nishimura has a small lead. Satō is second and Ayabe and Komatsu appear to be heading for the goal line neck and neck."[33] No candidate, however, was seen as commanding overwhelming support, and in the final week of the joint speech meetings all the newspapers forecast an extremely close race. Newspapers are prohibited by Article 138(3) of the Election Law from publishing the data of polls taken to judge the popularity of the candidates. The prohibition applies only to the publication of the data, not to the conduct of polls or the use of their results in articles. During this middle period of the campaign the Japan Broadcasting Company took a poll of 800 voters in the district which resulted in an estimate that, though Satō and Nishimura were apparently strongest, differences in projected votes for the four candidates were not significant enough to allow any predictions.[34] At the same time (January 21–22) the *Ōita Gōdō* newspaper ran a survey of its own, interviewing 1,598 voters. To the astonishment of the entire editorial staff the results showed the highest vote going to Satō and the second highest to Socialist Komatsu, while Ayabe and Nishimura were fighting for the third spot. In the poll, in fact, Nishimura received 800 votes less than third-placed Ayabe.[35] Two other newspapers ran public opinion polls and the results of all of these led the editors to the same conclusion. "It is," wrote the *Yomiuri* correspondent, "anybody's guess who will lose."[36]

The candidate's campaign in the official campaign period has two dimensions. One is the public dimension in which the

[33] *Mainichi Shinbun*, January 18, 1967, p. 1. The same view was expressed in articles in *Nishi Nihon Shinbun*, January 19, p. 11; *Higashi Kyūshū Shinbun*, January 19; *Bunshū Gōdō*, January 19.

[34] The results of the N H K poll were provided by the editor of the news desk, Kudō Takashi.

[35] Data concerning this poll were provided by the editors of the *Ōita Gōdō Shinbun*.

[36] *Yomiuri Shinbun*, January 20, 1967, p. 14.

candidate appeals for voter support through speeches, posters, and the other limited means of publicity and exposure allowed him. There is also a private dimension in which the candidate's campaign boss and a few top-level supporters maintain communication with the members of the candidate's organization throughout the district and make vital decisions concerning campaign finances.

Campaign funds are of crucial importance in Japanese election campaigns, as they are of course in the United States and other countries. But unlike his counterpart in the United States, the Japanese candidate spends no money whatsoever for advertising in the mass media. The limited advertising allowed, as discussed above, is paid for by the government. The Election Law's provisions regarding television, radio, and newspaper advertising combined with the other articles in the Law that restrict campaign activities might lead one to expect campaigns in Japan to be rather inexpensive. On the contrary, however, campaigning is on the whole an extraordinarily expensive proposition.

The cost of campaigns for the Diet are estimated to run anywhere from ten million yen for a very strong incumbent in a safe district to one hundred million yen for a new candidate fighting a difficult battle.[37] These figures represent the extremes. It is probable that the cost of most Diet election campaigns for conservative candidates falls somewhere in the range of fifteen to thirty million yen or approximately between forty and eighty thousand dollars. What makes these figures especially formidable is that they refer to money spent between the day of dissolution of the House and election day, a maximum of forty days. They do not include the rather substantial noncampaign expenses incurred in the months preceding the official campaign.

The legal maximum campaign expenditure, it is to be re-

[37] For one L D P Diet member's account of the actual amount and uses of campaign funds, see Ikeda Masanosuke, "Seijika Ga Tsukau Bōdai Na Uragane," *Gendai,* July, 1967, pp. 54–61.

membered, averages about two-and-a-half million yen. There has never been a case of a candidate being convicted for spending more than the legal limit,[38] and accounts of expenditures submitted to the Election Management Committees by the candidates show that nationwide they spend 20 to 30 per cent less than the statutory limit.[39] Yet it is an open secret that the great majority of candidates do not stay within the legal limits.

Japanese campaign expenses fall into two broad categories. One is headquarter or administrative expenses. Included here are salaries for office workers, the costs of renting a campaign car and campaign office, printing posters and postcards, and the like. These expenses generally consume most of the money the candidate is legally allowed to spend. They account for only a fraction of the money actually spent in the election, however. The second category is what might be called organizational expenses—funds expended to mobilize the candidate's district-wide organization. In some cases 80 or 90 per cent of a candidate's total campaign expenses will go to providing campaign funds to the men who run the campaign in the district's cities, towns, and villages and in the neighborhoods and hamlets of all these areas.

It is apparently common practice for campaign funds to be distributed to campaigners in three installments. The first follows immediately upon House dissolution and is intended to set the candidate's machine in operation. It is a kind of down payment given to the leaders of the local town and village organizations in order that they get the campaign under way. The second installment is the largest and comes in the first days of the official campaign, the days immediately following *kōji,* the official notification of the election. In two or three days a campaign headquarters may be divested of ten or fifteen million yen, given out largely in 100, 500, and 1,000 yen notes. One by one the leaders of the city, town, and village organizations come to the campaign headquarters to discuss

38 *Asahi Shinbun,* December 7, 1966, p. 8.
39 *Japan Times,* January 26, 1967, p. 16.

the situation in their area with the candidate's campaign boss. Because all this activity is a violation of the Election Law, the candidate himself never takes part directly in the discussions. His campaign boss discusses with the local leader a vote quota for the area and gives him funds to be taken back and distributed to the campaigners in the local organization. The third installment of funds is distributed in the last days of the campaign. These funds are dispersed in order to strike at new targets of opportunity, to respond to demands of local supporters, and in part for no other reason than that the money is there to be spent. In a close race the fear of the candidate and his financial backers that all the sizeable resources already committed to the campaign might be lost in a narrow defeat leads them, in a spasm of fear, to divest the campaign headquarters of whatever money is remaining. A file cabinet that thirty days before had twenty million yen may be completely empty by election day.

The sources for campaign funds for an LDP candidate for the Diet fall into four groups: the party, the faction, the business community, and the candidate's own resources.

It is customary in Japan for political parties to give party-endorsed Diet candidates a set sum of money for their campaigns. In the 1920s the conservative parties are reported by one author to have contributed about 10,000 yen in terms of today's currency values to their candidates' campaign chests.[40] In the Diet campaign of 1967 the LDP gave each of its candidates three million yen in campaign funds. This alone is more than the candidate may legally spend in even the largest district in the country. The LDP maintains that the money is to help cover expenses that are legal but not included in the law-designated expenses. Despite its explanations, the party came under immediate attack in the highly "black mist" conscious mass media.[41] In spite of the temporary uproar the

---

[40] Takahashi Makoto, "Seiji to Kane no Akuen," *Asahi Jānaru,* VIII (December 11, 1966), 13.

[41] See, for instance, *Asahi Shinbun,* December 30, 1966, p. 10; *Asahi Evening News,* December 30, 1966, p. 1.

LDP Diet candidate had three million yen in his campaign chest.

The largest single source of funds is the candidate's faction leader. A faction leader's strength largely depends on his ability to financially aid Diet members and nonincumbent candidates who would join his faction upon entering the Diet. The amount of money a candidate receives from his faction leader varies in particular cases but five million yen is generally considered to be the average.[42] In some cases a Diet candidate may receive support from politicians other than his faction leader. This might be a locally powerful politician who is committed to the candidate's success or another faction leader who sees a long-term benefit to be derived from contributing to the campaign and thus strengthening his personal ties with the candidate.

A third major source of funds is the business community. Here it is almost impossible to generalize because of the tremendous variations in the nature of the support provided by businessmen to Diet candidates.[43] Perhaps one partial generalization that can be safely made is that the nonincumbent locality-oriented candidate relies on support from local businessmen rather than from large corporations in Tokyo. The candidate usually has close connections with a small number of firms in the district or prefecture that provide him with a steady income outside the official campaign period to finance his daily political activities. Such firms, having made a sizeable contribution by the time the election comes around, are anxious to protect their investment by insuring the reelection or election of the candidate they are sponsoring. They consequently contribute large sums to their candidate's campaign, the amount of their investment often being comparable to the sum given by the candidate's faction leader.

[42] This is the figure cited, for instance, in Watanuki Jōji, *Nihon No Seiji Shakai* (Tokyo, 1967), p. 62.

[43] An effort at such generalization is made by Fujiwara Hirotatsu and Tomita Nobuo, *Seijiaku E No Chōsen* (Tokyo, 1967), pp. 56–58.

In addition to large contributions from such select firms, the candidate appeals for small donations from a large number of local businesses. Contributions of from 5,000 to 50,000 yen from tens, or in some cases even hundreds, of firms[44] is a major source of funds for many candidates.

Finally, a fourth source of campaign funds is a candidate's own resources. In prewar Japan it was common to talk of "well and fence politicians" *(idobei seijika)*. What was originally the object of the phrase was the landlord who entered politics and in so doing spent so much money that he lost everything but his well and the fence surrounding his house. It is a phrase that has come to be used to refer to anyone who spends his own resources in election campaigning. It is often said that in the postwar period candidates have learned how to run for office with other people's money and that there are no *idobei seijika* left.[45] While there are perhaps fewer politicians that rely as much on personal resources for their campaign funds as did politicians in the prewar period, some degree of personal financial investment in the campaign appears to be the rule rather than the exception among LDP candidates.

The party, the candidate's faction leader, and other powerful politicians supporting his candidacy, the business community, and the candidate's own resources are the major sources of campaign funds. Within this general pattern variations are enormous, depending on the particular candidate's financial connections, his length of service and his influence in the Diet, and partly, obviously, by the amount of money he thinks is necessary to run a successful campaign.

The question of how a candidate expends campaign funds is a more difficult one to deal with than the issue of the sources of his funds. The secrecy surrounding the expenditure of funds renders most analyses elaborate cases of guesswork.

[44] *Ibid.*, p. 58.

[45] See, for example, Okano Kaoru, "Daigishi To Senkyoku," *Ushio* No. 77 (November 1966), 180.

In general, writers who have dealt with the issue have argued that most campaign expenses, over and above what is allowed in law, are for the purpose of bribing voters and buying the support of local politicians who in turn bribe the voters within their sphere of influence. There is also general agreement that there is somewhat less bribery in Diet elections than in local contests. Unlike the Town Assembly candidate, for instance, who has to deal with a relatively small number of voters, the Diet candidate must have a fairly extensive organization of supporters to reach enough voters in the district. Consequently a thousand yen note intended to buy a vote has to pass through the hands of so many people on its journey from campaign headquarters to voter that by the time it hits bottom there is hardly enough to pay the campaigner much less bribe the voter. As one study remarks, "it is usual for most of the money intended to buy votes to end up in the pockets of the big bosses, the middle bosses and the little bosses."[46] The candidate illegally distributes something like ten times the legal maximum amount of campaign funds to local bosses who pocket a large share of the money, pass the rest down to smaller bosses who keep a healthy share for themselves, and who then hand out the remaining money to the politically ignorant peasants for their votes.

Such analyses contain a modicum of truth but are at best exaggerated caricatures of campaign practices. The great bulk of a candidate's campaign funds is usually spent illegally. But the money expended is neither simply to buy votes nor to buy off local politicians. While some amount of money is certainly used for such purposes, most of the funds function to compensate the candidate's campaigners and, in part, to fulfill the demands of custom.

In the Japanese setting monetary compensation for campaigners of conservative candidates plays an extremely important role in holding a campaign organization together.

46 Yomiuri Shinbun Seijibu, *Seitō* (Tokyo, 1965), p. 21; cf. Watanuki Jōji, *Seiji Shakai,* p. 222.

Loyalties to the party, even where they exist, have little relevance to the decision to support a particular candidate because of the multimember districting system; loyalty to the candidate is not pervasive for, as has been seen, campaigners largely owe loyalties to other campaigners in the organizational hierarchy rather than to the Diet candidate himself; patronage is of little significance in the Japanese political system because of a highly developed merit civil service, and is of no meaning to the anonymous *buraku* campaigner. While the reasons for a man offering to campaign are diverse, a small "thank you" present reimburses the campaigner for any expenses incurred in his activities and makes him cognizant of the candidate's recognition and gratitude. Unlike elections in the prewar period when one powerful landlord could deliver a large number of votes, campaigns today depend on an extensive organization with supporters on all levels down to each *buraku*. Even a small monetary reward to all these campaigners represents an enormous expense.

Not only for the *buraku* campaigner but for the leaders of the village or town organizations as well, money given in the campaign is more often a recompense for support long given than a bribe to obtain support. Most of the men who organize the campaign in local areas for the Diet candidate are associated with and work for that candidate long before elections are called. While there are cases of a candidate buying the support of local bosses at the last minute, the more usual pattern is for the candidate to have obtained his elitist support well in advance of the official campaign. The politically unavoidable if legally illegitimate need to compensate these supporters for their efforts on the candidate's behalf puts the greatest demands on the candidate's financial resources during the campaign period.

This is not to argue that the element of bribery is absent from this picture. Often top-level supporters demand sums for the campaign that cannot be justified either as equitable compensation for their work or as necessary for the campaign. The candidate often has no alternative but to pay the amount requested because he is so completely dependent on the support of the local leader and his organization. He often sees his choices as one of paying an exorbitant amount for the votes the local supporter is believed capable of delivering or taking the chance of not getting anywhere near the number of votes needed. More often than not the candidate will opt for the former alternative. Even here, however, there are countervailing pressures against local leaders making exorbitant demands on the candidate. A supporter who takes too much advantage of his position of strength in demanding funds will force the candidate to seek other locally powerful people to organize his campaign. This is one reason the campaign expenses of new candidates are generally much higher than those of incumbents. It takes a few elections to find out which supporters are functioning effectively and at reasonable cost. The incumbent Diet member gradually weeds out of his organization many of those who are obviously not mobilizing votes commensurate with the monetary demands they place on the candidate. It is the new candidate who most often has to accept support proffered and at the price demanded.

On the *buraku* level the question of what is a fair recompense for a campaigner and what is a bribe for a voter is often extremely difficult to distinguish. The Japanese language itself clouds this distinction. Seldom is a voter clearly offered a bribe. When given money for his vote, the phrases used express appreciation to the voter for his support of the candidate in such a way as to make him feel like a campaigner.[47] It sometimes becomes a difficult matter to decide whether a man given 500 yen to campaign for a candidate has been simply compensated for his work or bribed when the "campaign" amounts to asking the members of his family and a neighbor to vote for a certain candidate.

[47] Translated freely, a typical approach goes something like "Look, I know this doesn't amount to very much but I'd really appreciate it if you could see what you can do to get some votes for X. We need every vote we can get, so as long as I know that I can count on yours I'm really grateful."

It is problems such as this that raise the issue of custom in determining campaign styles and in affecting the amount and uses of campaign funds. In a sense the provisions of the Election Law in what they prohibit regarding campaign practices provide a concise description of Japanese social customs. The prohibition of many activities commonly accepted as proper social behavior was predicated on the assumption that such behavior, though common, is in contradiction with democratic practices. Accordingly many campaign activities that are illegal are engaged in, particularly in local elections and in rural areas, because the candidate feels more constrained to respect cultural norms than legal rules. The prohibition of house to house calls is a case in point, and it apparently resulted from a concern with the political effects of certain "feudalistic" attitudes concerning obligation. Besides providing opportunities for outright bribery, house-to-house calls would make it difficult for a voter who was visited by a campaigner and asked for support to refuse. It would be embarrassing to say no and the voter would feel an obligation to vote as requested to do in such a face-to-face confrontation, particularly if he had in any way incurred a debt to the person making the request. Activities such as house-to-house calls were made illegal in order to prevent the input into the political system of customs that violate assumed tenets of democratic practice. In fact, however, the making of house-to-house calls is a widely employed campaign technique. All the law has done is force candidate and campaigner to be somewhat discreet in conducting this and other similarly prohibited activities. It has not eliminated the practice itself.

Another aspect of this problem is the serving of food and refreshments as part of the campaign, a practice Japanese call *kyōō*. There are clearly instances where such practices are consciously intended to buy support. One campaigner I know of brought in groups of fifteen to twenty people every evening for a period of two weeks to a certain restaurant (where he made an agreement with the owner that no records be kept that could fall into the hands of the police) in order to get the

support of an entire *buraku* for the candidate he was supporting. There was no question here but that the campaigner
was attempting to buy support for the candidate. Under some
circumstances, however, social custom makes the practice of
kyōō imperative. The candidate and campaigner must decide
between observing the law or observing social custom. The
tendency is to side with the latter as much as is strategically
possible without incurring the penalties for violating the law.[48]

Certain social practices can of course provide opportunities
for a considerable degree of corruption, and it is sometimes
impossible to distinguish between campaign styles made imperative by social custom and styles that simply take advantage of custom in order to buy support. It is apparently very
common, for instance, for voters in rural areas to receive, as a
matter of course, extremely small sums (100 yen seems a popu-

[48] The legal prohibition of the serving of food and refreshments as part
of a campaign is but one manifestation of an almost obsessive concern with
the assumed incompatibility of traditional social practices and the require-
ments of democratic practice. In the United States no one has proposed a
legal ban on campaign barbecues or picnics or on the serving of Coca-Cola
in campaign headquarters. In Japan such practices are violations of the
law. There are several dangers inherent in such severe restrictions on
campaign practices. They can, for one thing, be so unrealistic as to result
in flagrant violations and a consequent disrespect for the law. For another,
the all too apparent inconsistency between legal provisions and actual
campaign practices encourages among many Japanese a feeling that Japanese are still motivated by undemocratic, feudal values. It perpetuates the
belief that the Japanese political system is less "democratic" than the parliamentary democracies of the West and undermines public confidence and
pride in the nation's political institutions. The prohibition of the serving
of food and other activities creates the false impression that candidates for
office in Western parliamentary systems do not engage in such practices
and sets for the Japanese a standard of conduct probably impossible to
achieve and, at any rate, observed by candidates in no other country.
Finally, the greatest danger inherent in the law is the effect of its successful
application. The law so thoroughly constrains candidate and voter alike in
permissible campaign activities, that its strict enforcement would result in
an almost total lack of direct contact between the candidates and the
electorate.

lar denomination) as an advance "thank you" present *(orei)* for voting for a particular candidate. One campaigner I had the opportunity to know estimates that "almost all" of the people in his town that voted for the candidate he supported, close to 2,000 voters, received such 100-yen presents. Such a practice cannot simply be dismissed as bribery. The sum of money by itself is insufficient, even in most rural areas, to buy votes. This 100-yen *orei* is intimately related to the concept of the hard vote. The voter who is known as the supporter of a particular politician need not be bribed to vote for that politician or for the candidate supported by that politician. In rural areas, a Diet election provides such a politician not so much the chance to bribe the voter as the opportunity to express in a small but tangible way his gratitude to the voter for his continued support. In giving the voter the envelope with the 100 yen, the campaigner expresses his apologies for not being able to more fully demonstrate his appreciation for the support the voter has given him and implores the voter to take the 100-yen note as simply a token of his gratitude. Once the voter accepts, his continued support, and most importantly his vote in the imminent election, is considered assured. To argue that this is not bribery is not to assert that it may not be an insidious technique for mobilizing support. Such practices, however, find their rationale deep within the fabric of society, and many politicians, being more concerned in the short run with winning an election than with leading a revolution in social mores, spend a considerable amount of campaign funds in engaging in them.

The relationship between the hard vote and the small monetary present is in contrast to the floating vote and the outright bribe. Bribery, contrary to the popular conception of the politically apathetic farmer being the object, apparently prevails in urban areas where the voter does not feel a particular attachment to any one candidate and is therefore more likely to make his vote available to the highest bidder. In urban areas it is common to pay 500, 1,000, or even as much as 2,000 yen per vote. In a district that contains both rural and urban components, outright bribery in the final days of the campaign appears to invariably be concentrated in the urban sector.

These aspects of the campaign, because of the Election Law's restrictions, are kept the closely guarded secrets of a few top-level members of a candidate's staff. They form a current that flows beneath the surface and, though of great importance for the candidate's success or failure, are of necessity kept hidden. The public dimension of the campaign, the candidate's public campaign activities, forms a current of its own that grows more frantic and frenetic as the final days of the campaign approach.

With the last joint speech meeting in Beppu on January 26, the candidates had two final days free to campaign. Satō spent the last three days entirely in Beppu and in a paroxysm of walking. From seven in the morning until eight or nine in the evening Satō walked. Through the narrow neon-lighted streets lined on both sides by bars, coffee houses and pachinko parlors, through the former red-light districts now dominated by small inns, through the cramped backstreets of the downtown area that house many of the service trade workers whose votes would largely determine Satō's future, he walked and talked and shook hands. Shaking hands is not a common practice in Japanese campaigning, at least not outside of large metropolitan areas. Perhaps the major effect of having a foreigner staying with him was to encourage Satō to adopt two campaign techniques not used by other candidates in the district or by himself in previous elections. One was to undertake a telephone campaign. There are no restrictions in the law on campaigning by telephone. Adopting and adapting a suggestion about telephone campaigning, Satō delegated two members of his staff to use the telephone directory to make calls to unknown voters to ask for support. Interestingly, he decided that using the Japanese equivalent of the "Yellow Pages" would be more effective than the regular directory since this would increase the chances of contacting conservative party supporting voters. The other technique he adopted was shaking hands. Satō was impressed with a story he heard of how John Kennedy had shaken so many hands in his campaign for President that toward the end of the campaign he needed to have injections to lessen the pain. Satō set himself a goal of shaking 9,000 hands in Beppu in the last three days of the campaign. At six in the morning on each of those days he was at one of the three fruit and vegetable markets in Beppu shaking hands with the dealers he represents as President of the green grocers' union. By the evening of the final day of the campaign Satō was able to show somewhat proudly a raw and swollen right hand.

Satō's efforts in the last days of the campaign created a ground swell of enthusiasm. Sensing this, the largest newspaper in the prefecture, the *Ōita Gōdō*, carried an analysis of candidate strength under the headline "Satō-Top."[49] The major Kyūshū newspaper, *Nishi Nihon*, predicted in its edition on the last day of the campaign that Satō would receive 59,000 votes, highest among the candidates.[50] Several papers saw the fight for the top vote as one between Satō and Nishimura,[51] but the *Ōita Gōdō* predicted that Socialist Komatsu might take the second highest vote.[52] What was clear in all the predictions was that Ayabe Kentarō was most in danger of losing. On the last day of the campaign eighty-year-old Ayabe, the last of the prewar politicians from the prefecture still involved in national politics, dragged his legs through the main streets of Beppu in a pathetic attempt to "walk the city" like Satō. Ōita Prefecture has only had two men chosen to serve as Speaker of the Lower House. The first, Motoda Hajime, lost the election following his appointment. It seemed very likely as the campaign came to an end on the evening of January 28 that history was about to repeat itself.

49 *Ōita Gōdō Shinbun*, January 26, 1967, p. 1.
50 *Nishi Nihon Shinbun*, January 28, 1967, p. 1.
51 *Mainichi Shinbun*, January 27, 1967, p. 7; *Konnichi Shinbun*, January 28, 1967; *Yomiuri Shinbun*, January 27, 1967, p. 14.
52 *Ōita Gōdō Shinbun*, January 26, 1967, p. 1.

IX

Conclusions

⟨⟩ FOR SATŌ BUNSEI the results of January 1967 election
were all that had been hoped for. From a narrow defeat
in 1963, he succeeded four years later in not only winning
election to the Lower House but also winning with the highest
vote among all the candidates.

The results of the election are to be found in Table 15. For
purpose of comparison, the 1963 election results are included
in Table 16. Satō's vote throughout the district corresponded
very closely to the vote he had anticipated. The Beppu vote
was a little higher and the Nakatsu vote a little lower than
he had predicted, but his general performance was well within
the boundaries of his expectations. Forty-two per cent of his
total vote was received in his home city of Beppu. He was
first among the candidates in the combined vote for the four
cities of the district, receiving 63 per cent of his vote in these
areas which contain 50 per cent of the district's electorate.
He was last among the candidates in the combined vote for
the towns and villages of the district. Two-thirds of his over
15,000 vote increase from the 1963 election was accounted for
in the two cities of Beppu and Nakatsu.

The big surprises of the election were Socialist Komatsu's
extraordinary increase in votes from 46,000 in 1963 to nearly
60,000 in 1967 and Nishimura's very poor showing in taking
the third spot, 8,000 votes behind Komatsu and only 2,000
ahead of Ayabe. Ayabe Kentarō suffered the fate many had
predicted for him. He went down to defeat, receiving fewer
votes than in the previous election even though Noyori was
no longer in the race.

Various hypotheses could be forwarded in explanation of

the election results, but within the limited concerns of this study it is necessary only to note that the results were interpreted by Satō, most of his staff, and many other conservative party politicians in the district in such a manner as to leave unchallenged their basic orientations toward campaign strategy. To the professional politician, Komatsu's victory, coming within 400 votes of being first among the candidates, was seen as the consequence generally of three factors. One reason, and the one generally regarded as of least significance, was that Komatsu benefited from anti-LDP sentiment that arose with the public exposure of corruption within the party. A second factor considered by many to account largely for his success was that Komatsu's organization "overworked" itself. Because the odds seemed to be overwhelmingly against Komatsu, Socialist Party supporting unions in the district campaigned harder than ever before. Hoping to insure Komatsu's position as the third place candidate, they engaged in an unprecedented effort and consequently mobilized more support than even they had expected. The third factor professionals adduced as resulting in Komatsu's victory was that Komatsu and Satō were the two candidates best suited to succeed to the support of voters who had formerly supported conservative Independent Noyori Hideichi. An ideology far to the right of either of these candidates and particularly of Komatsu was not the important factor in Noyori's support. His was overwhelmingly a personal vote and the people who had supported him through the years could not bring themselves to support either of the men identified as Noyori's prime enemies, Ayabe and Nishimura. In the first election following his retirement, Noyori supporters, rather than vote for either of the two LDP incumbents, either abstained or voted for Satō, who was a new candidate not directly associated in the public mind with the LDP fight against Noyori, or for Komatsu, who had been most clearly uninvolved in Noyori's political career.

Table 15

Results of the 1967 Diet Election in Ōita's Second District

	Satō	Nishimura	Ayabe	Komatsu	Tsuru	No. of voters voting	Per cent	No. of eligible voters
Beppu	25,076	9,237	9,968	15,927	1,359	61,567	80.21	78,071
Nakatsu	5,912	5,714	6,158	9,685	1,136	28,599	75.95	38,263
Bungo Takada	3,564	2,906	3,009	3,144	131	12,754	84.12	15,377
Kitsuki	3,339	913	5,554	3,291	135	13,232	84.25	15,853
City Total	37,891	18,770	24,689	32,047	2,755	116,152	79.95	147,564
Kunimi	391	3,428	5,673	808	96	5,290	88.84	5,992
Himeshima	3	2,140	6	54	3	2,206	97.96	2,257
Kunisaki	1,789	5,435	2,038	2,359	157	11,778	86.61	13,746
Musashi	654	1,494	612	598	53	3,411	84.22	4,080
Aki	1,910	1,946	1,706	1,486	47	7,095	85.59	8,424
Higashi Kunisaki County Total	4,747	14,443	4,929	5,305	356	29,780	87.21	34,499
Hiji	2,191	1,049	3,139	3,993	118	10,490	83.33	12,729
Yamaga	1,749	1,242	1,322	2,391	99	6,803	84.58	8,108
Hayami County Total	3,940	2,291	4,461	6,384	217	17,293	83.82	20,837

Ōta	727	589	252	373	9	1,950	85.65	2,285
Matama	608	1,000	1,089	640	70	3,407	86.41	3,966
Kagachi	522	1,818	372	510	38	3,260	86.94	3,783
Nishi Kunisaki County Total	1,857	3,407	1,713	1,523	117	8,617	86.44	10,034
Sanko	781	855	868	993	65	3,562	89.61	4,043
Honyabakei	784	1,211	854	727	39	3,615	89.28	4,085
Yabakei	639	1,506	1,275	1,169	309	4,898	89.26	5,533
Yamaguni	1,169	635	713	851	37	3,405	86.69	4,041
Shimoge County Total	3,373	4,207	3,710	3,740	450	15,480	88.76	17,702
Innai	1,127	827	1,278	1,104	35	4,371	84.75	5,224
Ajimu	1,343	1,071	1,641	2,092	71	6,218	77.79	8,113
Ekisen	690	829	1,018	956	81	3,574	83.97	4,291
Yokkaichi	2,054	2,700	3,248	3,306	256	11,564	82.35	14,166
Nagasu	2,321	2,657	1,531	2,313	288	9,110	84.61	10,922
Usa	950	613	1,329	1,149	429	4,470	86.18	5,232
Usa County Total	8,485	8,697	10,045	10,920	1,160	39,307	82.92	47,948
Town-Village Total	22,402	33,045	24,858	27,872	2,300	110,477	85.25	131,020
District Total	60,293	51,815	49,547	59,919	5,055	226,629	82.44	278,584

Table 16

Results of the 1963 Diet Election in Ōita's Second District

	Satō	Nishimura	Ayabe	Noyori	Komatsu	Tsuru	No. of voters voting	Per cent	No. of eligible voters
Beppu	17,611	8,538	10,939	5,938	11,940	978	55,944	77.22	73,476
Nakatsu	2,948	4,176	2,973	12,261	6,318	629	29,305	80.28	36,915
Bungo Takada	2,993	3,015	3,217	996	2,912	80	13,213	81.39	16,476
Kitsuki	2,815	1,297	5,535	465	3,244	68	13,424	80.73	16,706
City Total	26,367	17,026	22,664	19,660	24,414	1,755	111,886	79.91	143,573
Kunimi	422	3,073	1,107	293	606	116	5,617	90.88	6,218
Himeshima	15	2,135	8	5	56	2	2,221	97.64	2,284
Kunisaki	1,571	5,382	2,721	843	1,784	136	12,437	86.47	14,535
Musashi	379	1,592	975	263	482	18	3,709	88.46	4,228
Aki	1,722	2,169	2,310	282	1,130	24	7,637	66.43	8,930
Higashi Kunisaki County Total	4,109	14,351	7,121	1,686	4,058	296	31,621	88.16	36,195
Hiji	2,211	1,019	3,405	316	3,403	59	10,413	81.23	12,983
Yamaga	1,589	1,122	1,785	392	2,223	37	7,148	83.48	8,646
Hayami County Total	3,800	2,141	5,190	708	5,626	96	17,561	82.13	21,629

Ōta	694	550	365	164	361	9	2,143	87.83	2,466
Matama	527	805	1,366	477	482	29	3,686	89.04	4,160
Kagachi	402	2,100	481	162	461	21	3,627	90.34	4,047
Nishi Kunisaki County Total	1,623	3,455	2,212	803	1,304	59	9,456	89.25	10,673
Sanko	435	661	454	1,651	693	28	3,922	90.80	4,358
Honyabakei	553	1,057	495	1,039	582	20	3,746	87.06	4,336
Yabakei	554	978	1,257	1,163	892	253	5,097	86.32	5,951
Yamaguni	720	627	700	993	635	21	3,696	86.67	4,322
Shimoge County Total	2,262	3,323	2,906	4,846	2,802	322	16,461	87.60	18,967
Innai	822	578	1,630	1,000	789	25	4,844	86.99	5,626
Ajimu	1,137	806	1,687	1,720	1,495	50	6,895	85.93	8,093
Ekisen	480	818	1,065	736	673	53	3,825	87.07	4,423
Yokkaichi	1,484	2,091	3,623	2,511	2,384	146	12,239	84.04	14,755
Nagasu	1,592	2,730	1,824	1,184	1,896	174	9,400	81.07	11,803
Usa	954	876	1,451	678	846	294	4,599	86.04	5,374
Usa County Total	6,469	7,399	11,280	7,829	8,083	742	41,802	84.46	50,074
Town-Village Total	18,263	30,669	28,709	15,872	21,873	1,515	116,901	86.32	137,538
District Total	44,630	47,695	51,373	35,532	46,287	3,270	228,787	82.31	281,111

For professional politicians it was more difficult, in a sense, to explain Nishimura's poor showing than Komatsu's strength. Nishimura, in their analyses, had everything necessary for an easy election victory. He was well endowed with what Japanese characterize as the "three *ban*" (*sanban*): he had sufficient financial resources (*kaban*); his position as Minister of Construction gave him an impressive title and a reputation as an influential politician (*kanban*), and he had strong organized support (*jiban*) in Kunisaki and other areas of the district. Everything would indicate that Nishimura should receive the top vote, and this indeed was the prediction of many politicians, newspaper editors, and Satō himself, at least until the very last days of the campaign. His failure to do as well as expected did not produce, however, very much questioning about the effectiveness of time-honored techniques of support mobilization. The explanation for Nishimura's poor performance at the polls given by professional politicians went something as follows. Nishimura's defeat was due to the close proximity of local elections. Elections for most local offices in the Prefecture were to be held in April. Nishimura's campaign depended heavily on the support of local politicians. Unlike Satō his strength lay in the rural areas of the district and not in Beppu, and he had not developed a large supporters' organization to stabilize his support. His strong support among local politicians would insure easy victory in most elections, but in 1967 the local politicians who supported him campaigned only halfheartedly if at all. With their own elections coming up in the very near future, there was a tendency for local politicians to keep money intended to finance the Diet campaign for their own election. Also, the black mist scandals had raised such an uproar about corruption that the police were being stricter than ever before in investigating violations of the Election Law. Because of their generally recognized role in Diet campaigns, local politicians were prime suspects for the police and they were not willing to take inordinate risks of being caught for a violation with their own election so near. Third, where local politicians might try to pressure people to vote for their candidate in Diet elections held at other times, their major concern in January was to insure support in their own election. Thus they used the Diet campaign more for building their own support than for urging support for the Diet candidate with whom they were associated. If a voter expressed preference for one of the other Diet candidates, the local politician hesitated to try to change his mind and threaten his own support in the process. The proximity of the local elections thus neutralized many local politicians who under other circumstances would have worked much harder for the Diet candidate they were supporting. Such a situation could only work to the benefit of Komatsu, who relied mainly on union strength rather than on local politicians, and of Satō, whose support among local officials was weak to begin with and whose major effort was concentrated in the cities.

Such an interpretation of the election results was generally subscribed to by professional politicians in the district. Although the results came as something of a surprise, they were not perceived as discrediting time-tried strategies of support mobilization. At the most they had a subtle effect on politicians such as Satō, pushing them in certain directions while not precipitating major re-evaluation of strategy.

The development of campaign strategy in part has been a response to the particular demands of the Japanese historical experience. The development of *kōenkai*, for example, was largely the result of the expropriation of the landlord in the early postwar years and the consequent destruction of his political power. Strategy in Japan also has had to respond to environmental factors which are more universal and which have led strategy in many parliamentary systems to develop along similar lines.

Drawn out on a historical continuum there is an identifiable progression in Japan from reliance on community leaders (the landlords in the prewar period) to the emergence of the *kōenkai* in the early postwar years, to an effort to enlist the support of voluntary associations as they multiplied later in the postwar period, and to an increasing emphasis on maximizing the possibilities for appealing directly to the electorate for votes.

Drawn out on a rural-urban continuum, a parallel pattern emerges. Reliance on local leaders is most prevalent in rural areas, while the *kōenkai* is a particularly popular technique in fairly small cities. In the large metropolitan areas, major emphasis is placed on gaining the support of already organized voluntary associations and on direct appeals to the electorate.

The direction of change appears unmistakable. Increasing reliance on utilizing the mass media is paralleled by a decreasing reliance on local politicians. Even the *kōenkai,* which a few years ago was embraced by almost every politician as the most effective means for mobilizing support, is now being downgraded in many candidates' strategies. There can be little doubt that over time campaign strategy in Japan, as in the United States and western Europe, will emphasize more and more associational rather than community interests and appeals to the electorate through wide exposure and skillful use of the media rather than through the recruiting of voters into personal support organizations.

Satō's strategy is in a meaningful sense a strategy in transition. Increasing urbanization, changing patterns of interpersonal relations, a constitutional system that is little more than twenty years old, and other factors have had an enormous effect on determining the groups that participate in politics, the styles of this participation, and, consequently, the strategies used by candidates for public office. But changes in styles of political participation and in strategies of support mobilization are at a point in time where their manifestation in actual practice covers a spectrum that reaches back into the early years of the century and the most isolated villages and moves forward into overpopulated cities and an era of instant communications. That a transition is occurring is undeniable. The main question is the speed with which the transition will be continued and resolved. In reviewing Satō's strategy, three factors stand out as particularly crucial in this regard.

One is the multimember district single entry ballot electoral system. It need hardly be stressed at this point that this system has the most far-reaching effects on campaign strategy. In a district in which several members of the same party are running for election, it forces each to rely on personal campaign organizations, makes the campaign a largely intraparty struggle, and either renders the party impotent or splits it asunder. The effect of the system is not only to inhibit certain organizational developments. Most importantly, it renders voter identification with the party largely irrelevant to individual candidate campaigns. In a single-member constituency system, the political party's position as an effective reference group for a significant portion of the electorate has the effect in most circumstances of providing a large base of votes for the party's candidates.[1] In Japan voter identification with a political party alone is not sufficient to determine which candidate will receive the vote. On the contrary, the portion of the electorate that is generally regarded as supporting the LDP is taken to mark the boundaries within which LDP candidates seek to mobilize support. Satō's basic strategic problem was to obtain the votes of as many LDP supporters as possible (at the expense of the other candidates of the party) rather than gain support of voters who might otherwise vote for an opposition party candidate.

One change in campaign strategy and general political organization that is considered essential and, indeed, the essence of modern political organization by a large number of both conservatives and progressives is the development of mass-membership parties to conduct party-oriented and party-directed campaigns. But because of the intraparty struggle generated

[1] On this point see Robert E. Lane, *Political Life* (New York, 1966), pp. 299–301.

by the electoral system, party-oriented and party-directed campaigns have remained unfulfilled desires. We have seen how attempts to incorporate individual candidate support organizations into the party in Yamanashi and Ōita Prefectures resulted in total failure. Nonetheless, Japanese politicians are committed to the development of mass parties, and this is one reason for the conservatives' long campaign to reform the law to provide for single-member constituencies.[2] The considerable frustration exhibited by the Japanese politician over the inability to effect desired change in campaign strategy and political organization because of the imperatives of the electoral system is a conspicuous and important feature of the current political scene.

A second crucial factor inhibiting change in campaign strategy is the Election Law's provisions on campaign practices. By its almost total prohibition of the use of the mass media in campaigning, the law has inhibited the development of new political techniques similar to those that have developed in the United States and western Europe. As Leon Epstein has written,

[these] new techniques involve increasing use, and increasingly skilled use, of the mass media for political and other kinds of communication. Their use is advanced by material developments, especially in television, and by behavioral research in popular responses. Moreover, increased formal education and a pervasive home-centered middle-class life style make for a large audience that is responsive to direct appeals about politics as about everything else. An organizational apparatus intervening between candidates and voters may be less necessary, or at any rate less efficient, as a vote-getting device.[3]

2 The other reason is that they expect that a single-member constituency system would destroy all minor parties and the skillful carving of districts will result in an overwhelming victory for L D P candidates. It is because they agree with such forecasts that the Socialists and other opposition parties have all strenuously opposed any change in the system.

3 Epstein, *Political Parties in Western Democracies* (New York, 1967) p. 233.

One reason Satō placed so much emphasis on organization in his campaign was his inability to use fully the techniques of communication with the electorate at which his counterparts in other countries are becoming so skillful. There is no doubt that a removal of the restrictions on the use of the mass media in election campaigning would affect campaign strategy in Japan as greatly as the media has affected strategy in other countries.[4] A third crucial factor inhibiting change in campaign strategy may be characterized as a lag in feedback. Most candidates for public office have the primary goal of being elected. In creating strategies they are likely to employ tried and proven techniques. Major changes in strategy come slowly as the environment changes and the candidate becomes aware of the new opportunities presented. While environmental circumstances in some cases demand an immediate response in strategy (a change in the law, for example, prohibiting a previously legitimate campaign practice), much of the development of campaign strategy is the consequence of a complex fugue being played between changing environmental circumstances and candidate perception of such changes. For most candidates there is almost inevitably a time lag between change in the field, individual perception of those changes, and the

---

[4] It is interesting to note the essential contradiction between the Japanese desire for mass-membership parties and the effects on political organization of a highly developed communications network. The "counter-organizational tendencies" that Epstein sees affecting party structures in the United States and Europe may well have a similar influence in Japan if the Election Law is ever changed. Even under the present law, the degree of political communication that has been facilitated by the mass media renders obsolete a major reason for mass-membership parties. In Europe parties have experienced these counter-organizational tendencies after having had developed mass-membership parties. In Japan the counter-organizational tendencies of the mass media are occurring at a time when mass party structures represent an ideal yet to be achieved. One of the interesting problems of future party development in Japan is how currently cherished models of party organization will be rationalized with an environment that makes such models already somewhat out of date.

manifestation of changed perception in strategy. This delayed reaction to an evolving structure is one reason for the coexistence in Satō's campaign of approaches, such as reliance on local elites and use of a *kōenkai,* that are rationalized by a differential perception of different parts of the electorate.

There is a dynamic tension between time-sanctioned strategies and the elements of the environment that lend support to the rationality of such strategies on the one hand, and new developments in strategy and the variables in the environment that give rise to them on the other. This study has been confined to an analysis of how this tension manifested itself in the campaign strategy of only one candidate for the Diet. However, it is expected that further research will show that, in terms of campaign strategy, Satō Bunsei is representative of the conservative Diet politician in postwar Japan. The ways in which he is responding to the demands and the opportunities presented him serve as indicators of developments in the political system itself. Indeed, the study of campaign strategy in Japan is significant and fascinating precisely because of its capacity for reflecting the tensions and the ongoing changes in Japanese political life.

Bibliography

Note: The following lists only those sources that are cited in the text. Dates are given for interviews in cases where I interviewed the person only one time. Most of the people who are cited were interviewed numerous times during the period from June, 1966, to August, 1967. In such cases only the location is noted.

I. INTERVIEWS

Aragane Keiji (Beppu).
Asada Hiroaki (Beppu), May 1967.
Baba Takashi (Beppu).
Doi Takeshi (Beppu).
Ichimaru Gohei (Beppu), May 1967.
Ikezaki Chiyo (Beppu), August 1967.
Ishikawa ? (Ōita), May 1967.
Iwasaki Mitsugu (Ōita).
Kanda Yasugi (Beppu), May 1967.
Katō Shin (Ōita), May 1967.
Kawamura Muga (Beppu).
Kiyohara Fumio (Beppu, Bungo Takada).
Kiyonari Fumito (Beppu, Kunisaki).
Koguchi Hiroshi (Beppu), May 1967.
Komatsu Kan (Tokyo), July 1967.
Kondō Takayuki (Ōita), May 1967.
Kōno Yōhei (Beppu), July 1967.
Mieno ? (Ōita), May 1967.
Mitarai Tatuo (Tokyo).
Murakami Isamu (Ōita, Tokyo).
Nakasone Yasuhiro (Tokyo).
Nakayama Makoto (Beppu, Kitsuki).
Saita Matato (Beppu).
Sakamoto Tosuke (Beppu, Honyabakei).
Satō Bunsei (Beppu).
Satō Shōzō (Ōita), May 1967.

[257]

Shutō Kenji (Beppu).
Shutō Takashi (Beppu).
Taguchi Akira (Ōita), May 1967.
Takami Takashi (Beppu, Kunisaki).
Teshima Tsugio (Ōita), May 1967.
Tomonaga Moto (Beppu).
Yoshitake Masayoshi (Ōita), May 1967.

II. PRIVATE REPORTS AND LETTERS

Asada Hiroaki. Letter Concerning High School Teachers' Union.
June 21, 1967.
Kiyonari Fumito. *Shūinsen Soshiki Taisei, Kunisaki Machi.* Report
prepared for private circulation, 1967.

III. PUBLIC OPINION POLLS

Beppu-shi Senyko Kanri Iinkai, Beppu-shi Akaruku Tadashii
Senkyo Suishin Kyōgikai. *Moderu Chiku Ni Okeru Akaruku Tadashii
Senkyo Undō No Jittai—Yoron Chōsa No Gaiyō.* Beppu, 1966.
Kōmei Senkyo Renmei. *Shūgiin Giin Sōsenkyo No Jittai—Yoron
Chōsa Kekka No Shūkei.* Tokyo, 1967.
Ōita Ken Senkyo Kanri Iinkai, Ōita Ken Akaruku Tadashii Senkyo
Suishin Kyōgikai. *Moderu Chiku Ni Okeru Akaruku Tadashii Senkyo
Undō No Jittai—Yoron Chōsa No Gaiyō.* Ōita, March 1965.
Japan Broadcasting Company (N H K). *Shūgiin Giin Sōsenkyo—
Yoron Chōsa.* Unpublished voter survey conducted during January,
1967.
Ōita Gōdō Shinbun. *Shūgiin Giin Sōsenkyo—Yoron Chōsa.* Unpublished voter survey conducted January 21–22, 1967.

IV. GOVERNMENT PUBLICATIONS, PARTY PUBLICATIONS,
ORGANIZATIONAL MANUALS AND MEMBERSHIP LISTS

Beppu-Ōita Seinenkaigisho. *Beppu-Ōita Seinenkaigisho Meibo.*
Beppu, 1967.
Beppu Shiyakusho. *Jichiin Setchi Kisoku.* Beppu, undated.
(Mimeo.)
———. *Jyūmin Gyōsei Soshiki No Chōsa.* Beppu, October 1, 1965.
(Mimeo.)
Beppu Shiyakusho Kikakushitsu. *Tōkeisho.* Beppu, 1967.
Jischishō Senkyokyoku. *Shūgiin Giin Sōsenkyo No Tebiki.* Tokyo,
1967.

———. *Shūgiin Senkyo Ni Okeru Seitō, Seiji Dantai No Katsudō No Tebeki.* Tokyo, 1967.

Jiyūminshutō. *Dare Demo Dekiru Senkyo Undō.* Tokyo, 1967.

———. *Jiyūminshutō Jyūnen No Ayumi.* Tokyo, 1966.

Jiyūminshutō Ōita Kenren. *Senkyo Soshiki Taisei No Kakuritsu.* Ōita, 1962. (Mimeo.)

———. *Katsudō Hōshin.* Ōita, 1961. (Mimeo.)

Naikaku Hōseikyoku Daisanbu. *Senkyo Jitsumu Roppō.* Tokyo, 1966.

Ōita Keizai Dōyūkai. *Ōita Keizai Dōyūkai Yōran.* Ōita, 1966.

Ōita Ken. *Chiiki Betsu Kenmin Shotoku (Seisan Shotoku).* Ōita, 1967.

———. *Kokusei Chōsa Ni Yoru Shi-chō-son Betsu Jinko No Trend.* Ōita, 1967. (Mimeo).

———. *Ōita Ken Tōkei Nenpan.* Ōita, 1966.

———. *Shōwa 40nen Kokusei Chōsa, Ōita Ken Shūkei Kekkahyō.* Ōita, 1965.

Ōita Ken Chūshō Kigyōka, Ōita Ken Shōkōkai Rengōkai. *Ōita Ken Shōkō Yōran.* Ōita, 1967.

Ōita Ken Ishikai. *Kaiin Meibo.* Ōita, 1966.

Ōita Ken Keieisha Kyōkai. *Ōita Ken Keieisha Kyōkai Yōran.* Ōita, 1966.

Ōita Ken Nōgyō Kyōdō Kumiai Chūōkai. *Ōita Ken Nōgyō Kyōdō Kumiai Tōkeihyō.* Ōita, 1965.

Ōita Ken Senkyo Kanri Iinkai. *Ōita Ken Dai Niku Shūgiin Giin Kōhosha Senkyo Kōhō.* Ōita, 1967.

———. *Senkyo No Kiroku 1946–1961.* 2 vols. Ōita, 1962.

———. *Senkyo No Kiroku, Ōita Kengikai Giin Senkyo* (April 17, 1963). *Shi-chō-son Gikai Giin Senkyo* (April 30, 1963). Ōita, 1963.

———. *Senkyo No Kiroku, Shūgiin Giin Sōsenkyo.* November 21, 1963.

———. *Senkyo No Kiroku, Shūgiin Giin Sōsenkyo.* January 29, 1967.

———. *Senkyo No Kiroku, Ōita Kengikai Giin Senkyo* (April 15, 1967). *Shi-chō-son Gikai Giin Senkyo* (April 28, 1967). Ōita, 1967.

Ōita Ken Shikaishikai. *Kaiin Meibo.* Ōita, 1966.

Ōita Ken Shōkō Rōdōbu Chūshō Kigyōka. *Ōita Ken Chūshō Kigyō Dantai Meibo.* Ōita, 1965.

Ōita Ken Shōkō Rōdōbu Rōseika. *Rōdō Kumiai Meikan.* Ōita, 1966.

BIBLIOGRAPHY

Ōita Ken Take Sangyō Rengōkai. *Kaiin Meibo.* Ōita, 1966.
Public Offices Election Law. Tokyo, 1958.
Seiji Shikin Kiseihō. Roppō Zensho. Tokyo, 1966.
Senkyohō. Roppō Zensho. Tokyo, 1966.
Sōrifu Tōkeikyoku. *Ōita Ken No Jinkō.* Tokyo, 1967.

V. NEWSPAPERS

Asahi Evening News (Tokyo).
Asahi Shinbun (Ōita edition).
Beppu Yūkan (Beppu).
Bunshū Gōdō (Nakatsu).
Fūsetsu Kaihō (Beppu).
Higashi Kyūshū (Beppu).
Japan Times (Tokyo).
Kankō Puresu (Beppu).
Konnichi (Beppu).
Mainichi Shinbun (Ōita edition).
Nishi Nihon Shinbun (Ōita edition).
Ōita Gōdō Shinbun (Ōita).
Ōita Nichinichi (Ōita).
Ōita Shinbun (Ōita).
Yomiuri News (Tokyo).
Yomiuri Shinbun (Ōita edition).

VI. BOOKS AND ARTICLES

Asahi Jānaru Hen. *Nihon No Kyodai Soshiki.* Tokyo, 1966.
Baerwald, Hans. *The Purge of Japanese Leaders Under the Occupation.* Berkeley, 1959.
Beardsley, Richard, Hall, John and Ward, Robert. *Village Japan.* Chicago, 1959.
Bennett, John W. and Ishino Iwao. *Paternalism in the Japanese Economy.* Minneapolis, 1963.
Cantril, Hadley. "Perception and Interpersonal Relations." *Current Perspectives in Social Psychology.* Ed. Edwin P. Hollander and Raymond G. Hunt. New York, 1967.
Cole, Allan B., Totten, George O. and Uyehara, Cecil H. *Socialist Parties in Postwar Japan.* New Haven, 1966.
Curtis, Gerald L. "Nihon No Kyōikumamateki Senkyo." *Bungei Shunjū,* xv (June, 1967), 174–180.

Dahl, Robert. *Who Governs? Democracy and Power in an American City.* New Haven, 1961.

Daudt, H. *Floating Voters and the Floating Vote, A Critical Analysis of American and British Election Studies.* Leiden, 1961.

Dore, Ronald P. *Land Reform in Japan.* London, 1959.

Dull, Paul S. "The Senkyoka System in Rural Japanese Communities." *Occasional Papers No. 4.* Center for Japanese Studies. Ann Arbor, 1953.

Epstein, Leon D. *Political Parties in Western Democracies.* New York, 1967.

Fujiwara Hirotatsu and Tomita Nobuo. *Seijiaku E No Chōsen.* Tokyo, 1967.

Fukutake Tadashi. *Japanese Rural Society.* Trans. Ronald Dore. Tokyo, 1967.

——. "'Jimoto Rieki' O Seiritsu Saseru Mono." Interview with Ishikawa Hideo. *Asahi Jānaru,* ix (February 26, 1967), 94–101.

——. *Nihon Nōson Shakai Ron.* Tokyo, 1966.

Fukuzawa Yukichi. *The Autobiography of Fukuzawa Yukichi.* Trans. Eiichi Kiyooka. Tokyo, 1960.

Gakuyō Shobō Henshūbu. *Senkyo Undō. Doko Kara Ihan Ka.* Tokyo, 1967.

Gouldner, Alvin W. "The Norm of Reciprocity: A Preliminary Statement." *Current Perspectives in Social Psychology.* Ed. Edwin P. Hollander and Raymond G. Hunt. New York, 1967.

Hasegawa Ryuichi, *Ōita Ken No Seijika.* Ōita, 1966.

Hayashida Kazuhiro. "Development of Election Law in Japan." *Hōsei Kenkyū,* xxxiv (July, 1967), 1–54.

——. *Senkyohō.* Vol. V of *Hōritsugaku Zenshū.* Tokyo, 1966.

Hunter, Floyd. *Community Power Structure. A Study of Decision Makers.* New York, 1963.

Ike Nobutaka. *Japanese Politics.* New York, 1957.

Ikeda Masanosuke. "Seijika Ga Tsukau Bōdai Na Uragane." *Gendai,* July, 1967, pp. 54–61.

Ishida Takeshi. *Gendai Soshiki Ron.* Tokyo, 1965.

——. *Sengo Nihon No Seiji Taisei.* Tokyo, 1961.

Jinji Kōshinsho. *Jinji Kōshinroku.* 23rd edition. Tokyo, 1966.

Jones, Charles O. "The Role of the Campaign in Congressional Politics." *The Electoral Process.* Ed. M. Kent Jennings and L. Harmon Zeigler. New Jersey, 1966.

BIBLIOGRAPHY

Kajiyama Toshiyuki. "Kane To Kōyaku No Matsuri, Sōsenkyo." *Hōseki*, February, 1967, pp. 51–67.

Kida Minoru. *Nippon Buraku*. Tokyo, 1967.

Kobayashi Naoki, Shinohara Hajime, Sōma Masao. *Senkyo*. Tokyo, 1960.

Kyōgoku Junichi and Ike Nobutaka. "Urban-Rural Differences in Voting Behavior in Postwar Japan." *Economic Development and Cultural Change*, IX, Part 2 (October 1960), 167–185.

Lane, Robert E. *Political Life*. New York, 1959.

McKenzie, R. T. *British Political Parties*. New York, 1964.

Matsushita Keiichi. *Gendai Nihon No Seijiteki Kōsei*. Tokyo, 1964.

———. *Sengo Minshu Shugi No Tenbō*. Tokyo, 1965.

Michels, Robert. *Political Parties*. New York, 1962.

Miyake, Ichiro *et al. Kotonaru Reberu No Senkyo Ni Okeru Tōhyō Kōdō No Kenkyū*. Tokyo, 1967.

Oka Yoshitake, ed. *Gendai Nihon No Seiji Katei*. Tokyo, 1966.

Okano Kaoru. "Daigishi To Senkyoku." *Ushio*, January, 1966, pp. 177–185.

Olson, Lawrence. *Dimensions of Japan*. New York, 1963.

Passin, Herbert. "Japanese Society." *International Encyclopedia of the Social Sciences*. New York, 1968.

Rose, Richard. *Politics in England*. Boston, 1964.

Royama Masamichi *et al. Sōsenkyo No Jittai*. Tokyo, 1955.

Satō Bunsei. *Ōita Ken O Kangaeru*. Beppu, 1963.

Scalapino, Robert A. and Masumi Junnosuke. *Parties and Politics in Contemporary Japan*. Berkeley, 1962.

Shigemitsu Mamoru. *Japan and Her Destiny; My Struggle for Peace*. New York, 1958.

Shinsei Dōshikai. *Shinsei*. Tokyo, August, 1967.

Sōma Masao. *Nihon No Senkyo Seiji*. Tokyo, 1963.

———. *Nihon No Senkyo*. Tokyo, 1967.

Sorauf, Frank J. *Political Parties in the American System*. Boston, 1964.

Sugimori Yasuji. "Jimintō Zengiin No Keireki Bunseki." *Jiyū*, X (May, 1968), 36–57.

Taguchi Fukuji. *Gendai Seiji To Ideorogii*. Tokyo, 1967.

———. *Nihon Seiji No Dōkō To Tenbō*. Tokyo, 1966.

Takahashi Makoto. "Seiji To Kane No Akuen." *Asahi Jānaru*, VIII (December 11, 1966), 12–19.

BIBLIOGRAPHY

Thayer, Nathaniel. *How the Conservatives Rule Japan*. Princeton University Press, 1969.

Thomsen, Harry. *The New Religions of Japan*. Tokyo, 1963.

Tsuji Kiyoaki. "Mūdo To Jitsueki No Tatakai." *Asahi Jānaru*, IX (February 12, 1967). 12–14.

——, ed. *Seiji*. Vol. I of *Shiryō Sengo Nijyūnenshi*. 5 vols. Tokyo, 1966.

Usami Shō. "Nōson No Tōshika." *Asahi Jānaru*, VIII (December 11, 1966), 20–25.

Ward, Robert. "The Commission on the Constitution and Prospects for Constitutional Change in Japan." *The Journal of Asian Studies*, XXIV (May, 1965).

Watanuki. Jōji. *Nihon No Seiji Shakai*. Tokyo, 1967.

——. "Patterns of Politics in Present Day Japan." *Party Systems and Voter Alignments, Cross-National Perspectives*. Ed. Seymour M. Lipset and Stein Rokkan. New York, 1967.

Yamada Hiroshi and Ishii Kinichirō. *Gendai Nihon No Seiji*. Tokyo, 1967.

Yomiuri Shinbun Seijibu. *Seitō, Sono Soshiki To Habatsu No Jittai*. Tokyo, 1966.

Yoshimura Tadashi. *Nihon Seiji No Shindan*. Tokyo, 1965.

Publications of the East Asian Institute

STUDIES

The Ladder of Success in Imperial China, by Ping-ti Ho. New York, Columbia University Press, 1962.

The Chinese Inflation, 1937–1949, by Shun-hsin Chou. New York: Columbia University Press, 1963.

Reformer in Modern China: Chang Chien, 1853–1926, by Samuel Chu. New York: Columbia University Press, 1965.

Research in Japanese Sources: A Guide, by Herschel Webb with the assistance of Marleigh Ryan. New York: Columbia University Press, 1965.

Society and Education in Japan, by Herbert Passin. New York: Bureau of Publications, Teachers College, Columbia University, 1965.

Agricultural Production and Economic Development in Japan, 1873–1922, by James I. Nakamura. Princeton: Princeton University Press, 1966.

Japan's First Modern Novel: Ukigumo of Futabatei Shimei, by Marleigh Ryan. New York: Columbia University Press, 1967.

The Korean Communist Movement, 1918–1948, by Dae-Sook Suh. Princeton: Princeton University Press, 1967.

The First Vietnam Crisis, by Melvin Gurtov. New York: Columbia University Press, 1967. Paperback edition, 1968.

Cadres, Bureaucracy and Political Power in Communist China, by A. Doak Barnett. New York: Columbia University Press, 1967.

The Japanese Imperial Institution in the Tokugawa Period, by Herschel Webb. New York: Columbia University Press, 1968.

Higher Education and Business Recruitment in Japan, by Koya Azumi. New York: Teachers College Press, Columbia University, 1969.

The Communists and Chinese Peasant Rebellion: A Study in the Rewriting of Chinese History, by James P. Harrison, Jr. New York: Atheneum Publishers, 1969.

[265]

PUBLICATIONS OF THE EAST ASIAN INSTITUTE

How the Conservatives Rule Japan, by Nathaniel B. Thayer. Princeton: Princeton University Press, 1969.

Aspects of Chinese Education, edited by C. T. Hu. New York: Teachers College Press, Columbia University, 1969.

Economic Development and the Labor Market in Japan, by Koji Taira. New York: Columbia University Press, 1970.

The Japanese Oligarchy and the Russo-Japanese War, by Shumpei Okamoto. New York: Columbia University Press, 1970.

Japanese Education: A Bibliography of Materials in the English Language, by Herbert Passin. New York: Teachers College Press, Columbia University, 1970.

Documents of Korean Communism, 1918–1948, by Dae-Sook Suh. Princeton: Princeton University Press, 1970.

Japan's Postwar Defense Policy, 1947–1968, by Martin E. Weinstein. New York: Columbia University Press, 1971.

Election Campaigning: Japanese Style, by Gerald L. Curtis. New York: Columbia University Press, 1971.

China and Russia: The "Great Game," by O. Edmund Clubb. New York: Columbia University Press, 1971.

Imperial Restoration in Medieval Japan, by H. Paul Varley. New York: Columbia University Press, 1971.

Li Tsung-jen: A Memoir, edited by T. K. Tong. Berkeley: University of California Press, forthcoming.

Money and Monetary Policy in Communist China During the First Five Year Plan, by Katharine H. Hsiao. New York: Columbia University Press, 1971.

Law and Policy in China's Foreign Relations, by James C. Hsiung. New York: Columbia University Press, forthcoming.

OCCASIONAL PAPERS PUBLISHED BY COLUMBIA UNIVERSITY PRESS

Taiwan: Studies in Chinese Local History, edited by Leonard H. D. Gordon. New York: Columbia University Press, 1970.

The Introduction of Socialism into China, by Li Yu-ning. New York: Columbia University Press, 1971.

The Early Chiang Kai-shek: A Study of His Personality and Politics, 1887–1924, by Pichon P. Y. Loh. New York: Columbia University Press, 1971.

Index